PHOTO BY DEFORD DECHERT

PETER L. BERGER was born in Vienna
and came to this country in his late teens.
He has a Master's and a Doctor's degree in
Sociology from the New School for Social
Research in New York. After two years in
the United States Army, he taught at the
University of Georgia and the University
of North Carolina. He is now an Assistant
Professor in Social Ethics at the Hartford
Seminary Foundation. Mr. Berger writes
regularly for professional journals in the
fields of the social sciences and religion,
and is the author of THE NOISE OF
SOLEMN ASSEMBLIES.

The Precarious Vision

PETER L. BERGER

The Precarious Vision

A Sociologist Looks at Social
Fictions and Christian Faith

DOUBLEDAY & COMPANY, INC., GARDEN CITY, NEW YORK

All of the characters in Chapters 2 and 7 of this book are fictitious, and any resemblance to actual persons, living or dead, is purely coincidental.

Library of Congress Catalog Card Number 61–12493
Copyright © 1961 by Peter L. Berger
All Rights Reserved
Printed in the United States of America

CONTENTS

PART III—EXODUS

PART ONE
Burden of Egypt

INTRODUCTION

1. The Experience of Alternation

SOCIETY APPEARS TO MOST PEOPLE AS GIVEN. THERE ARE IN-
DIVIDUAL AND GROUP EXPERIENCES IN WHICH THIS GIVENNESS
SHOWS ITSELF TO BE SPURIOUS. THIS RECOGNITION OF THE
PRECARIOUSNESS OF SOCIETY IS THE NECESSARY STARTING POINT
FOR AUTHENTIC EXISTENCE IN SOCIETY.

Can a truly contemporary person be a Christian?—
In America, where religion is still an integral part of the
social order, this question may strike many as an odd one.
They are likely to answer with the words "Of course!" very
much in the sense in which the Lynds analyzed "of course"
statements in the famous *Middletown* studies—statements
which reflect the common, taken-for-granted convictions of a
society, statements which one doubts only at the risk of questioning the very foundations of the social order. In Europe,
where the disintegration of religion and society has gone much
further, the question will seem odd to far fewer people. Both
religious and nonreligious people have been moved to ask this
question, though different answers may be given to it. There
are even wide segments of the population, such as the working
classes and the intelligentsia of some European countries, in
which the question is likely to be answered with the words
"Of course *not!*" Leaving aside the way in which this question
appears to the vast world on the other side of the Iron Curtain,
it is very likely that even in the so-called uncommitted societies only few thinking people would respond with a positive
and axiomatic "Of course." At the very least, the question
will be regarded as pointing to a real problem.

This essay is written in the conviction that a positive
answer to the question is possible, though certainly *not* an

answer that could be prefaced with the words "Of course." Furthermore, the writer feels that such a positive answer can only be given with intellectual integrity when the full weight of the problem behind the question is perceived.

The reader of this essay is being invited to follow an argument that may seem bizarre in places and the outcome of which may only appear clearly at its conclusion. For this reason it may be well to begin with a brief preview of the entire argument and with a few comments on its character.

This essay is not a scientific work, although in places (especially in Chapters 3 and 6) reference will be made to materials from the social sciences. At the same time, the fact that the writer is a sociologist will be apparent in many places in the argument. Nor is this just a matter of personal bias. If the social sciences in general and sociology in particular have any value at all to the general reader, it lies in the extent to which they are able to illuminate the contemporary situation and his existence within it. Two chapters of the essay (Chapters 2 and 7) are in the nature of *belles-lettres*. They fit into the argument as "exercises," to serve as illustrations and to make an appeal to the imagination, especially to the latter's ironic dimensions. The reader who dislikes irony may skip them without losing the thread of the argument, though we would contend that the ironic perspective often makes the truth stand out more sharply than the unruffled operations of intellectual analysis.

The first part of the essay will seek to outline a certain perspective on society which the writer feels to be especially characteristic of the social-scientific enterprise, although other avenues of experience and thought can lead to it. What characterizes this perspective more than anything else is the manner in which it transforms a world which we are taught to take for granted into one that is very questionable indeed. It is this perspective which we refer to in the title of the essay as "the precarious vision." At the conclusion of the first part we shall ask what the ethical implications of this perspective are. The second part of the essay will try to show the way in which the religious phenomenon appears in this perspective. Both first and second parts together constitute the description of the problem that lies concealed behind our opening question—"Can a truly contemporary person be a Christian?" In the third part of the essay we shall try to show how a positive answer to the question may be given from the viewpoint of the Christian faith and without brushing aside the problem as Christians often do. It goes without saying that such an argument cannot be convincing in the way a scientific hypothesis is verified. It must contain both *cogito* and *credo*. It cannot be validated step by step, or given the weight of authority by footnotes. It will be necessary in places to indicate and allude, to send out signals in the hope that there are those ready to understand them. If such an enterprise carries an element of risk in a way that no purely scientific (or, for that matter, purely theological) argumentation does, it is a risk that the writer is willing to take. At least in part such risk is inherent in any attempt to communicate in matters of faith.

Now that the reader has an idea of where this argument will take him, it may be in order to take a closer look at its beginning point, a point from which the argument starts and to which it will have to return a number of times. This point lies in the experience in which a new perspective on society is acquired. Needless to say, such an experience need not be a unique or instantaneous one. It may stretch over a long period of time, although for some it may come in a sudden flash of recognition. We call this experience that of alternation. It is an experience that leads to a very specific form of consciousness, particularly a certain consciousness of existence in society. Perhaps the most characteristic feature of this consciousness is an overwhelming sense of the precariousness of social existence. This sense is achieved in most cases by an experience or a series of experiences revealing society to be something radically different from what had previously been taken for granted. For most of us, as we grow up and learn to live in society, its forms take on the appearance of structures as self-evident and as solid as those of the natural cosmos. Very likely society could not exist otherwise. Nor is it likely that socialization could take place if this were not the case. Yet this consciousness of what Alfred Schuetz has called the "world taken for granted" is not of such solidity that it cannot be breached. When such a breach occurs the world is transformed, takes on new dimensions and colors. If the breach occurs suddenly it marks the day after which life will never be the same again.

For those who have experienced wartime bombings a picture suggests itself here. A street. The street is familiar. We have walked through it often. We know each house. Then one night the street radically changes its appearance. The house which we knew so well from the outside, whose balconies and portico we had often admired, is suddenly cut in two. For the first time we can look inside. We see the rooms and corridors that had previously been hidden from our eyes. The façade is gone. The secrets of bedrooms, cabinets, and backstage staircases disgorge themselves into public view. This street will never be the same for us. Even if the rubble is removed, the ruins rebuilt, we remain conscious that the façades which now meet our eyes again are just that. We know of the hidden reality behind the façades. The breach in the taken-for-granted consciousness of society is very much like this picture. What we had previously taken for structures of steel now appears as the façade of a paper house. Life being what it is, we may continue to act as if the façade were all of reality. Our minds being what they are, we may even forget what happened, shut it away in those dark corners where catastrophes and terrors are stored. All the same, our innocence will have been lost. The memory of what we have understood will remain to haunt us and, given certain circumstances, will burst forth once more and transform our world.

There is an entire generation in Europe whose awareness of society is marked by this experience. It separates them from both their elders, who have more easily slipped back into older ways of looking at the world, and from the new generation again growing up in a society which seems intact. The

generation of young Germans who fought in World War II is
a good example of this. The rapid economic recovery of western Germany has led to a strange isolation of the consciousness which marked the formative years of this generation.
To their elders (not considering those who were committed
Nazis themselves) the period of totalitarianism, war, and
hunger often appears now as an interlude to be remembered,
if at all, as an interruption in the normal functioning of
society as it ought to be. The new generation growing up amid
the glittering reconstruction of the German "economic miracle" finds it difficult even to imagine this period, let alone to
consider its insights significant for their own view of the
world. There remains the consciousness of those for whom
the world of ruins (both physical and cultural) opened up a
new understanding of the precariousness of all social existence.
It is possible that similar forms of consciousness are to be
found in those who are living through their formative years in
countries of rapid social change, of revolutionary political and
economic transformations.

In America, where the façades of society have never been
subjected to a comparable shock, there are different avenues
leading to this consciousness. We can locate this consciousness
without much difficulty in contemporary American literature,
especially those tendencies within it that express a deliberate
disaffiliation from American society. As was probably the case
in different periods of history, this consciousness of the
precariousness of social reality is to be found especially among
underprivileged and ostracized groups of the population. In
the American case one might point to the perspective of the
Negro, to the worlds of prostitution or homosexuality, or to
that peculiarly American ethos of the hobo that for one
historic moment reached political articulateness in the violent
episode of the I.W.W. In all such cases we are confronted
by perspectives which challenge the taken-for-granted view
of society, which point up the contradictions and artificialities
of what those who "belong" regard as normalcy.

In the experience of the writer this consciousness has frequently been detected among those engaged in the social sciences. In speaking of what he calls "the sociological imagination," C. Wright Mills has described this consciousness as follows:

"The first fruit of this imagination—and the first lesson of the social science that embodies it—is the idea that the individual can understand his own experience and gauge his own fate only by locating himself within his period, that he can know his own chances in life only by becoming aware of those of all individuals in his circumstances. In many ways it is a terrible lesson; in many ways a magnificent one. We do not know the limits of man's capacities for supreme effort or willing degradation, for agony or glee, for pleasurable brutality or the sweetness of reason. But in our time we have come to know that the limits of 'human nature' are frighteningly broad."[1]

It is significant that the chapter from which this quotation is taken has the heading "The Promise" and that the bulk of Mills's book is a sharp criticism of contemporary American sociology. It is certainly not contended here that all American social scientists share the sense of precariousness being discussed. Indeed, the social sciences have become so much part of the intellectual scene taken for granted that sometimes the sociological enterprise itself can become for an individual an excellent method of avoiding any existential encounter with the social reality within which he is located. He may then segregate his insights into that reality very carefully within the confines of his professional role and live the rest of his life fairly much like the other organization men on his block—a bizarre and instructive form of bad faith, indeed! Nevertheless, within a society that continues to appear intact the "sociological imagination" provides Americans with a perspective which in Europe has been the outcome of massive social disintegration. It is the excitement of this which repeatedly breaks through the institutionalized dreariness of professional social science and, incidentally, is capable of capturing the imagination of students as an invitation to intellectual adventure.

Anthropologists use the term "culture shock" to describe the violent surprise occasioned by coming into contact with a drastically alien way of life. The shock is not merely because of what one sees in the alien culture. More importantly, the shock comes from suddenly seeing oneself in a new way in the mirror of the other culture. As Albert Salomon has pointed out in discussing Montesquieu's *Persian Letters*, the startled question of the Parisians looking at the strangers in their midst—"How can one be a Persian?"—is really another question—"How can one be oneself?" The missionary who goes to a foreign land and then finds his own convictions tottering against the solid consensus of negation confronting him experiences this question in its most searching dimensions. But even the casual tourist, who finds to his surprise and perhaps his delight that things can really be done in a way very different from what he is accustomed to, experiences a milder variety of the same shock. The degree to which this experience has become diffused, and possibly diluted, as a result of modern means of travel and communication is an interesting sociological question that need not concern us here. It is also possible that institutionalized travel, taken for granted in wide circles, manages to neutralize the shock of perceiving an alien culture in a very similar manner to the way in which institutionalized social science neutralizes the shock of perceiving one's own. What is of interest here is that the pursuit of the "sociological imagination," especially as it leads to a fresh encounter with the insights of the social sciences, can lead to an experience very similar to the "culture shock" of the anthropologists. The person who perceives another culture in depth realizes that things can be very different from what they are at home, which naturally leads him to the insight that even at home they are not what they seem. The person who perceives his own culture in depth reverses the sequence. He sees that things are not what they seem, which naturally leads to the conclusion that they might very well be different. In both cases what previously seemed to be iron necessity now appears as the most precarious of conventions.[2]

As was pointed out above, this sense of precariousness easily becomes routinized and segregated in the consciousness of the professional social scientist. To a degree this is probably inevitable. After all, one cannot live all the time with one's mouth open. This is why teaching, and especially the occasional teaching of introductory courses, is a salutary activity for the professional social scientist. In the reactions of students to what he presents he can re-experience the freshness of the "sociological imagination," sometimes even its liberating quality. The experiences of beginning students (needless to say, it is the brighter students who are at issue here!) afford a good illustration of the nature of the shock which the social sciences are capable of administering.

There are, of course, a variety of shocks connected with the recognition that social reality is not what one's high-school civics classes led one to believe. There are specific shocks as one looks into the phenomena of class, of power, of the relativity of customs and morals. But perhaps the greatest shock comes when one suddenly locates oneself within the more or less disagreeable objectivities being studied. It is not only the shock of being located in a certain place in society ("I come from a lower-middle-class background!") but the shock of being located at all! One's own perspective on the world, and that of one's family, which previously had been unquestionably normative, are now seen as being located in a specific way among innumerable perspectives, each one normative within a certain group of people. One's chances in life are seen to be overshadowed by forces over which one has no control and never will have much. One's very private life and convictions (say, one's sexual attitudes and behavior) are seen to be crucially connected with this social location. Such shock can be found quite easily among students in any well-taught introductory course in sociology or anthropology. How these students then deal with the shock (such as neutralizing it effectively as being part of the game of acquiring three elective credits in Soc. 100!) is another matter. Nor is it necessary at the moment to go into the more complicated forms which this shock may take as the student goes on into more advanced work in the social sciences, dealing with such subjects as the internalization of society in the formation of personality, or the relationship of social structure and ideas as elaborated in the sociology of knowledge, or the functional analysis of belief systems. Even in a very elementary encounter with a social-scientific perspective there may occur, even if only in flashes, the kind of transformation of consciousness discussed above.

If the attempt is made to elucidate further the character of this consciousness, one may find a rather paradoxical phenomenon. On the one hand, the social-scientific perspective leads to an oppressive sense of bondage. On the other hand, it leads to the liberating feeling that the social world is far more tenuous than had previously seemed to be the case. This paradox is only a superficial one. The liberating feeling comes from the valid insight that the social world is an artificial universe, whose laws are conventions, rules of the game that have been agreed upon but that can also be broken and against which one can cheat. The sense of bondage comes from the equally valid insight that society not only encompasses us about but penetrates within us, that we are ourselves products and playthings of society, irrevocably social in our innermost being. The one insight uncovers the fictitiousness of society, the other its oppression. The fact that our bonds are frequently spun from illusions only rarely lessens our bondage. The knowledge of the Negro that race does not exist in the meaning of his oppressors does not free him from their oppression. The knowledge of the ugly girl that standards of beauty are culturally relative does not brighten the loneliness of Saturday night. Taking together the insights into the fictitiousness and into the oppression of society, we arrive at a very specific sense of precariousness. Which is the point of these remarks.

It should be obvious that such a sense of precariousness must also extend to the inner convictions, as these convictions are perceived to be related to social situations and their relativity. It is not necessary at the moment to go into the psychological uncertainty that underlies statements beginning with the remark "I may be rationalizing, but . . ." It is quite sufficient to consider the uncertainty about the social location of one's convictions that marks a statement opening with a disclaimer like "I may be a Southern Baptist, but . . ." What is involved here is not just uncertainty and doubt about the legitimacy of one views, but the curious ability to look around the corners of one's own *Weltanschauung*, the ability to imagine oneself holding quite a different position. One knows that one thinks as a Southerner and as a Baptist. By implication one can then imagine oneself as an emancipated cosmopolitan and as a Catholic. What is more, it then becomes possible to change oneself into the imagined figure. Very logically, then, the sense of precariousness makes for a proneness to conversion, meaning by this generally the intellectual and existential jump from one *Weltanschauung* to another. Thus the Southern Baptist may go North and become a leftwing radical, and the radical may become a Catholic, and the Catholic gets himself psychoanalyzed and loses his faith. What is involved here is a more general, perhaps more diluted version of what Kierkegaard meant by the "leap," that one great jump from unbelief into faith. This general proneness to be uncertain of one's position and to be ready to change it may be called alternation. It goes without saying that the very awareness of alternation in this sense may well lead to a great hesitancy to jump anywhere at all, that determined skepticism which in postwar Germany has been well caught in the phrase "*ohne mich.*"

Arthur Koestler, in this instance discussing the alternation between political commitment and the psychological awareness of one's motives for this commitment, has provided us with a vivid picture of this phenomenon:

"To-day I am going to fly off at a tangent from the twisted path. I have not many illusions about the reasons why I am doing it, nor about the cause which I serve. As children we used to be given a curious kind of puzzle to play with. It was a paper with a tangle of very thin blue and red lines. If you just looked at it you couldn't make out anything. But if you covered it with a piece of transparent red tissue-paper, the red lines of the drawing disappeared and the blue lines formed a picture—it was a clown in a circus holding a hoop and a little dog jumping through it. And if you covered the same drawing with a blue tissue-paper, a roaring lion appeared chasing the clown across the ring. You can do the same thing with every mortal, living or dead. You can look at him through Sonia's tissue-paper and write a biography of Napoleon in terms of his pituitary gland as has been done: the fact that he incidentally conquered Europe will appear as a mere symptom of the activities of those two tiny lobes, the size of a pea. You can explain the message of the Prophets as epileptical foam and the Sistine Madonna as the projection of an incestuous dream. The method is correct and the picture in itself complete. But beware of the arrogant error of believing that it is the only one. The picture you get through the blue tissue-paper will be no less true and complete. The clown and the lion are both there, interwoven in the same pattern."[3]

Instead of Koestler's tissue-paper another picture could be taken, that of a stage with differently colored lights. A switch is pulled and the entire stage is flooded with yellow light. Another switch is pulled and the stage becomes purple, so much so that it seems inconceivable that it could ever have been anything else. Yet one pull of the switch will bring back the yellowness in all of its self-evident permanence. Moreover, the apparatus of switches does not stand outside this alternation of different perspectives but is itself basked in the particular color that has been chosen. Each perspective seems not only to include all of reality but to include within itself all other possible perspectives and the passages from one to the other. To put this in different terms, Catholicism has a theory of psychoanalysis and a theory concerning what happens when a Catholic becomes converted to psychoanalysis. But psychoanalysis returns the compliment. There is a psychoanalytic theory of Catholicism and of conversion to Catholicism. And then there is a Marxist theory of both Catholicism and psychoanalysis. And so on *ad infinitum*—and *ad nauseam*.

The awareness of alternation and its existential possibilities now becomes a sensation of vertigo. In the consciousness delineated here this vertigo need not, of course, be constantly present in actuality. But it always lurks in the background as a possibility. Once the apparatus of switches has been perceived, the stage never quite loses its precarious character. Somewhere, even if just under the threshold of everyday thinking, remains the memory of metamorphosis, of masks and cloaks, of the artistry behind the settings of the stage.

We have been concerned in the last few pages with delineating a specific form of consciousness of social reality. We would like to leave aside the question, however fascinating, as to the constituency of the group that may share it in our own society or in other parts of the world. Also, we would avoid becoming entangled in the equally intriguing question as to whether such consciousness is a peculiar characteristic of modern man. In other words, this essay in no way purports to offer a "theory of modern man." This disclaimer is especially important in terms of relating this consciousness of society to the religious phenomenon. We might then delve into very interesting questions indeed. Does modern man have a consciousness that sharply separates him from the mentality of earlier times—such as those out of which the Biblical literature comes to us? Does this modern consciousness involve a new and radical secularization of the world? Are we confronted with a general secular mentality? Is it likely to mark the future, at least of Western civilization? An affirmative answer to these questions has led some people to maintain that religion is a matter of the past, at least in its traditional forms, or that we are now living at the beginning of the "post-Christian era." Such questions, of course, are of vital importance to the sociological interpretation of contemporary religion and contemporary culture in general. However, we shall avoid burdening this essay with them. The argument we intend to follow will be significant for those ready to enter into its premises. The question as to how general this significance is in terms of the modern world is beyond our scope.

We would only contend its strong significance for those to whom the experience of alternation, in any of its forms, is a central reality with which their existence (including their religious commitments) must come to terms.

To possess (or, as one might almost be tempted to say, to be afflicted with) this precarious vision of society does not in itself lead to specific moral positions. The experience of alternation can stand at the beginning of very different moral paths—rebellion or resignation, collaboration with the *status quo* or resistance against it, the sad wisdom of the conservative or the absolute aspirations of the revolutionary. However, we would argue that the precarious vision enters decisively into certain moral choices. This point will concern us particularly in Chapter 5 of this essay. Suffice it to say at this moment that the moral texture of a situation will vary as does one's perception of it. The man who has perceived the precariousness of racial categories may still choose to be a racist, but it will be more difficult for him now to cloak his oppression by reference to the nature of things. The man who realizes the precarious character of sexual identities can continue to persecute the homosexual, but it will be harder for him to do so than for one who believes that the Boy Scout ideal of virility is grounded in the ontology of human existence. Or to take an example to which we shall have occasion to return a number of times, the man who has perceived the artificiality and fictitiousness of social institutions will be less likely to be in favor of capital punishment than one who believes naïvely in the official morality. The issue of capital punishment is paradigmatic in terms of the moral significance of the precarious vision. Many facets of this consciousness come together in the spectacle of an execution—the fictitious character of social reality, the hypocrisy of those who identify with the fictions, the bad faith of what is taken for granted by the official morality, and the human agony which suffers torture and death as part of the stage management. Society is fiction. The fictions murder. In these two statements we may find a paradigm of the precarious vision. It is no wonder then that this issue repeatedly finds those drawing together whose experience of alternation leads them to say that capital punishment is beyond the limits of the morally possible. That this point of view is not a peculiar eccentricity of the writer may be seen by looking at just a few of its spokesmen—Nicholas Berdyaev, Albert Camus, Arthur Koestler—not to mention all those who saw in the execution of Caryl Chessman a terrifying symbol of the nature of American society.

If we have now given, as it were, a preview of the precarious vision and its moral significance, we may also indicate in a preliminary way how the religious phenomenon relates to our problem. It is not by chance that religious people are more likely to believe in society as it is taken for granted than those who have emancipated themselves from religion. As far as the American situation is concerned, there would seem to be little doubt about this assertion. Why should this be so? We would contend that in its social function religion appears over and over again as that which validates the carnival of masks. Most importantly, religion tends always to deny the phenomenon of alternation. It will give the illusion of absoluteness to one particular coloration of the social stage, thus reassuring and ratifying the individual illusions of the actors. The most solemn rituals and superstitions of society receive their ultimate sanction from religion. The precarious identities of actors, clutching their respective masks, are pronounced by religion to be the truth. Religion provides the legitimation of power and the explanation of suffering. Religion is thus capable of providing the mystic link which unites the hangman and the victim in the act of execution. At this point religion becomes subject to an ethical judgment. It is an indecency. Perhaps these considerations may already make intelligible that there are situations in which the opening question of our introduction may become an even sharper question—"Can a decent person be a Christian?" We shall have occasion later on to discuss various aspects of this question and various possibilities of answering it. First it is important to grasp the import of the question.

For the individual religion can thus become the refuge from the frightening vertigo of alternation. It gives him the semblance of a face. It gives his world structure and purpose. It makes demands upon him, even threatens and punishes him, but even in the possibility of damnation it allows him to live in an ordered cosmos. Hell is also part of the religious universe. What is more important for our argument, religion provides the common frame of reference within which the actors on the stage can coordinate their little parts. In a very real sense, religion provides both script and *dramatis personae* for the social play. It may even add the reassurance that the play is written and directed by the master impresario himself. The bleeding bodies and the chopped-off heads become part of this stage management.

If we now seem to be on the verge of an atheist manifesto, this is neither an accident nor a mistake. It will be our task later on to show why the atheist critique of religion is important and what it means to the perspective on society here described. We shall now come to a close of this introduction by pointing to the only Christian resolution of our argument that we can find—a confrontation of our perception of society with the figure of Jesus Christ. It is this figure of the crucified one which continues to haunt both the oppressors and the oppressed, casting its shadow over the religious celebrations and at the same time intruding its disturbing light into the corners where one escapes the sacred drums. Our task thus begins where it seemed to end. We now find that it is not enough to perceive society and religion, but we are compelled to relate this perception to a demand that transcends both society and religion—the demand to follow this figure of the crucified one. This demand calls us to an exodus, not only out of the Egypt of social mythology but also out of the Zion of religious security. The exodus takes us out of the holy city, out past the scene of cross and resurrection, and beyond into the desert in which God is waiting. In this desert all horizons are open.

2. Exercises in Alternation

In this chapter we shall try to clarify our concept of alternation with the use of the imagination. The chapter consists of four fictitious cases. The first two cases, that of Susie Q. and that of Gustav, illustrate alternation as it operates in the actual biographies of individuals. The case of Susie Q. is intended to illustrate the matter in a low key, as it were. It presents a story which could happen any day, anywhere in America. Between the plain narration of what happened to Susie and various "alternating" interpretations of these events is inserted a brief passage providing a sociological conceptual apparatus which can be used to analyze not only the events but also the various interpretations. The sociological point of view expressed here will be developed further in Chapter 3, but an indication of it is introduced here to facilitate our "exercises." Coming then to the case of Gustav, alternation here presents itself *fortissimo*, with the clash of cymbals and the blare of trumpets. Each step in the story presents us with the spectacle of *Weltanschauungen* engaged in a titanic competition for our character's allegiance. The last two cases are frankly surrealistic. One might even ask whether such fantasies have a place in our argument. We would contend that they do. They serve to illustrate alternation at the point of vertigo, where all our assumptions concerning the nature of the universe appear as questionable. What is more, they may entertain those on whom it has dawned that the ploy may be a cosmic principle.

(i) THE CASE OF SUSIE Q.

(a) *Record of the Case* (Needless to add, the story here told is imaginary—suppose that this record is being read by a flat-chested social worker, in a voice from which all affect has been sucessfully purged.)

Susie Q. is twenty-one years old, a senior in a college in the northeastern section of the United States. Both parents are living. Susie is the oldest of three children, the only daughter. Both parents are white, native-born Americans, active members of the Episcopal church. They are in their middle forties. The two boys are aged fifteen and twelve. Susie's father is employed as a salesman for a vacuum-cleaner firm. The family lives in their own house in a medium-rent residential area of a city with a population of about 100,000.

In an intelligence test taken in her freshman year Suise's I.Q. was found to be 120. She is in excellent health. Susie is considered an attractive girl in the various groups she has associated with.

The Q.'s are regarded as a "fine family" by their neighbors and associates. Family decisions are normally taken on the initiative of Susie's mother. Before coming to the city in which they now reside, the Q.'s were Methodists. Susie's mother joined the Episcopal church, her husband following her some years later.

During her sophomore year Susie began to associate with a group of fellow students known as the "beatnik crowd" on her campus. For several months she dated a young man belonging to this group. After a time of increasingly intimate sexual play the couple spent a night in a motel and engaged in coitus. This episode was Susie's first sexual experience. She did not experience orgasm. Immediately after the motel escapade Susie broke off all relations with the young man and the group to which he belonged. She became very active in the campus Canterbury Club, of which she had been a very passive member before, and was elected its president at the end of the academic year. She told her pastor that she had gone through a profound religious experience and discussed with him the possibility of going into graduate work in religious education. During the summer vacation between her sophomore and junior years she worked in an inner-city missionary project of her denomination.

During her junior year Susie began dating a young man, eight years her senior, employed in a minor executive position in an advertising agency in a nearby city. This young man, regarded as an "egghead" by his associates, introduced Susie into a group of young people, most of them engaged in various aspects of mass communications, sociable mostly with each other, and given to what they themselves considered "sophisticated" activities. Susie refused sexual relations with her new young man, and when alone the couple mainly engaged in conversation, in the course of which Susie discussed at length her family background and the "beatnik" episode of the previous year. Her interest in religious activities diminished again and she resigned from the presidency of the Canterbury Club, pleading overwork. The couple announced their engagement in the spring. After the engagement had been announced Susie consented to sexual relations. Again she found herself unable to reach orgasm, despite earnest attempts and supplementary reading. In the beginning of her senior year, upon the advice of her fiancé, Susie began seeing a psychotherapist.

(b) Sociological Propositions

Social interaction is organized in roles (of this more later).

Individual roles are organized in clusters within which consistency is functionally desirable. Such consistency is both external and internal. External consistency means that the individual's actions present a cohesive whole to the outside world. Internal consistency means that his actions present such a whole to himself, in terms of his ideas, emotionality and picture of himself. If such consistency cannot be maintained, chances are that the individual will experience anxiety and become psychologically disturbed.

Each cluster of roles is related to a specific reference group; that is, the individual in his actions refers himself to certain distinctive groups of people.

Each of these reference groups exists in a specific world-taken-for-granted. Putting this into different words, human groups differ in their meaning systems, in the beliefs and perceptions of the world through which they give order and consistency to their actions. Such meaning systems vary greatly in intellectual elaboration and in degree of comprehensiveness. A highly comprehensive meaning system will seek to include all other available meaning

systems within itself, interpreting them in its own terms. A less
comprehensive meaning system will simply exclude, reject or even
fail to perceive other meaning systems. In the case of Susie Q.
meaning systems of both high and low comprehensiveness are
involved. In the case of Gustav, following it, the interaction of
three highly comprehensive meaning systems may be observed.

Choice between reference groups will involve choice between
their respective meaning systems. That is, social affiliation or disaffiliation involves specific ways of looking at the world and of
conceiving it intellectually.[1]

(c) The Worlds of Susie Q.

THE HOME WORLD: The horizon is South Elm Street; beyond
it is the Cathedral. The world is safe, essentially in order, grouped
in concentric circles around the Q. home. This is America—white,
middle-class, Protestant—but there really is no counter-world.
Those outside this America are themselves suffused in benign
light. They may even be objects of benevolent concern. They
cannot seriously threaten or disrupt. Other worlds are hard to
imagine, if at all then in a romantic conception. Susie moves
through this world as the bright, young, all-American Thing. She
is father's little girl, mother's little helper, and big sister. She is
cheerful, sweetly sloppy, makes practical jokes, wears any old
clothes. One talks easily, gossips, and kids one another, only drops
into a serious hush in the shadow of the Cathedral. From within
its charmed circle this world looks at Susie and interprets what
has happened to her:

"Susie has always been a volatile, breathless girl. Maybe she didn't
get enough discipline when she was a child, but she was always
so sweet that it was hard to interfere with her. Usually she got
her way, sooner or later. Even so one certainly couldn't say that
she wasn't properly raised. She would never do anything wrong
knowingly. So it was quite a surprise when she started going
around with that mixed-up crowd in college. As it turned out it
didn't do her much harm. She never talked much about this
time at home, but we can be sure of one thing—she would never
do anything that her parents would have to be ashamed about.
Perhaps the whole thing even did her some good. It made her
see the other side, so to speak, and gave her an appreciation of

the way she was raised. She snapped out of it in no way at all. Her fiancé is a fine fellow. Polite, well brought up. He's going to be very successful in his chosen field. He'll give Susie a decent home. There's no reason why they shouldn't be very happy together. Well, from what Susie now tells, they move around with a crowd a little faster than her Dad or Mom would feel comfortable with. But then they are still young. They'll settle down. And one has to be reasonable and make allowances for changing times."

ALTERNATION: In the world of the "beatnik crowd" (the adjective would meet with derision in San Francisco) Susie is a female novice. This world transforms America from cosmos to dungeon. On the horizon is Madison Avenue, the counter-world of the enemy, but within the group there is refuge and liberation. As its counter-world, this world does not grasp or penetrate intellectually alternate ways of life. It excludes them, though its exclusion is more hostile than that of either Madison Avenue or South Elm Street. Here Susie is rather quiet, trying to pick up cues, eager to learn the expectations of the group but trying not to show her eagerness, for it is important not only to be cool but always to have been so. Within the limitations of her budget and equipment, Susie's outward appearance begins to come up to the standards of the group. This allows the rest of the campus to identify her as a member of the group, an identification she anxiously seeks and then haughtily looks down upon. It is by no means easy to be a sophomore. But Susie's residence in this world is only a transitory one:

"Susie's a good kid—or could be, if she let herself. She's got looks, brains. If she wanted to she could really swing. But you got to make allowances for her background. The worst. Hick town. Hick folks. The living room a nightmare of Americana. Still-life prints on the walls. Antee-cues underneath them. A complete set of the *Encyclopaedia Britannica* next to the TV. Church programs all over the place. The old man sells vacuum cleaners and the old lady runs missionary bazaars. What can you expect? She tried, poor kid. For a few months she tried and for one miserable night in a miserable motel room, with a Gideon Bible on the table and a coin radio on the dresser. It was too much for her. Now she's gone back to her very own. She's engaged to a station wagon

and a mortgage, 3.2 kids on the runway, suburbia here I come! It
was good while it lasted. So long, Susie, and good luck to you!"

ALTERNATION: The world of Susie's religious conversion is not
quite that of the Cathedral, because the Cathedral doesn't quite
have the right point of view as yet. It's rather the little Anglo-
Catholic chapel down the street, where Father Schleissbauer lisps
through High Mass and a visiting Anglican Benedictine lectures
on English plainsong to the ex-Baptist wives of successful insurance
salesmen. Susie is a young Christian woman, in the process of
deepening her faith. She is not too far away here from South Elm
Street, but the sloppy teen-ager is now suffused by Sunday-morning
earnestness. This world prides itself on the all-embracing quality
of its perspective and a considerable intellectual machinery is set
in motion to interpret (and thus reinterpret in one's own terms)
alternate ways of life. As to Father Schleissbauer, he sees himself
in sacerdotal images (which occasionally frighten himself) and his
words as caught up in the sweep of centuries—which means that
his interpretations are brought forth with great assurance:
"The true story of any human being is the story of faith. This is
why the decisive point in Susie's story is the point of her conversion. Looking at her story in any other way will distort the picture,
because only at this point, where a human life touches upon the
divine, is truth to be found. Certainly there were elements of
immaturity in this experience. However, faith can never be understood in terms of the conditions of its inception. Susie knew what
she was doing. With full deliberation she confessed the Catholic
faith and was willing to take the consequences in her life. But
Susie's main sin has always been vanity, the desire to please and to
be flattered. Perhaps her parents, good Christians though they are,
have contributed to this through the lax way in which she was
raised. Susie wanted to please her college friends. Now she wants to
please the sophisticated crowd to which her fiancé belongs. Since
pleasing now involves her in sin (and not only the mortal sin of
the flesh), she wants to find a way by which her change of life can
be excused. She has found this excuse in psychotherapy. It is surely
no accident that she chose a Freudian as her therapist, so that the
so-called libido becomes the final criterion of her actions. After all,
it was sexual sin which started her on her course of apostasy. Her
present therapy is nothing but a giant rationalization to cover up

the betrayal of her faith. Neither her parents nor her fiancé can understand this. But deep down in her heart Susie understands. She will find out (hopefully before it is too late) that one cannot escape the 'hound of heaven.' "

ALTERNATION: The world of Susie's fiancé also has Madison Avenue on its horizon, but here it serves as a positive image. Its less positive aspects are reconciled in amusement. This world is neither home nor enemy. It is a world to be made. You're in the know, you're with it, and America is good to you. You're sophisticated, you live in the twentieth century, which means that you understand everything, so you can be quite tolerant of other angles on life. Susie now begins to live up to the images of the billboards. She is becoming smooth, knowing, calculates within the arithmetic taken for granted by this group. This is expressed in her dress, manners, language. In fact, she is on the way to becoming a mature American woman:

"To understand Susie one must understand her background. Only then can you see how far she has come on the way to becoming a mature person. Maybe class is one of the most important things to understand. Susie's parents are respectable, lower-middle-class people, living in a typical medium-sized town, trying hard to become upper-middle-class. They furnish their home in what they think is good taste. They send their kids to college. They subscribe to the *Encyclopaedia Britannica*. They join the Episcopal church. Sure, they mean well. They are basically fine people, once you abstract from their prejudices. But no wonder Susie wanted a little taste of gutter once she got beyond the range of South Elm Street gossip. No wonder, either, that she felt guilty as hell after the very first taste of it. It'll take a little time for Susie to stand on her own two feet and to make her way in the world. But she'll make it. Religion was a crutch. Right now psychotherapy is another, though, of course, a much better one. But she'll get so she doesn't need any crutches at all. When that happens she'll make the finest little wife anyone ever had in any of the fifteen regional offices of Apex, Inc.!"

ALTERNATION: The world of Susie's psychotherapist is a world unto itself, but of all her other worlds it is most closely related to that of her fiancé. Over the incestuous puddles and the dark

swamps of homicide rises the vision of the happy life, understood
in terms not too different from those of Susie's fiancé. Psychotherapy is part of the pursuit of happiness. The world is darker
than it seemed at first, but it is still to be made. This world seeks to
include all others within itself and for this purpose has at its disposal an impressive array of intellectual tools. Susie is as impressed
as they come. And she likes it. She is a young American woman,
growing up though troubled. But her troubles are interesting.
Curled up within herself in the posture dictated by the psycho-
therapeutic gymnastics, she perceives herself in a new way:

"In the case of Susie Q. we can see in operation an almost
classical combination of forces. A strong, aggressive mother. A
weak, pliant father. Siblings do not appear until well into Susie's
genital stage. Her sexuality well fixated on her father, it is threatened powerfully by the mother. At the same time, the mother is
the moral and religious direction-giver of the family. Susie's morality and religiosity, then, can be seen as appeasement of the mater-
nal rival, essentially a mechanism of guilt abreaction. Since sexuality involves the constant resurgence of the incestuous impulse,
with the accompanying guilt and anxiety, it is strongly repressed.
But not wholly so. The 'beatnik' episode, occurring during Susie's
first physical separation from her parents, was the first onslaught of
Susie's libido against the maternally oriented superego. It may be
indicative of Susie's appeasement syndrome that she chose a 'beatnik' group for her first steps into sexuality—there are decidedly
feminine, if not masochistic, traits to the sexuality of this group.
Not surprisingly, the first step of sexual liberation is followed by a
headlong flight into guilt. Now the appeasement of the mother is
almost explicit. Susie undergoes a religious conversion. It is surely
no accident that she chose the Anglo-Catholic group as the milieu
of her conversion. The peculiarly feminine character of Anglo-
Catholic religiosity is patently obvious. In the sacramental-liturgical
universe, between incense and soft words, the guilt is atoned. Yet
Susie's repressions have been relatively benign and her libido continues to press against her defenses. In her fiancé she has met
the first strong father-surrogate of her young life—an older man,
but not weak or pliant, rather an aggressive, virile individual. As
she begins to feel secure in this relationship the repressions weaken.
Through her present psychotherapy, helped by the understanding
attitude of her fiancé, Susie is beginning to understand herself.
She is well on the way to sexual and social adjustment."

(ii) THE CASE OF GUSTAV

(a) Record of the Case

Gustav was born in the late 1920's in a medium-sized industrial town in the Middle West, the only child of Scandinavian immigrants. Gustav's father, a small businessman of moderate but comfortable means, had married Gustav's mother a week after her engagement to a rival suitor and left with her for America the next day. Gustav led a very protected childhood in a bilingual home, had few friends until the age of adolescence, early developed an avid interest in reading. He was a regular Sunday-school pupil and altar boy at the local Scandinavian Lutheran church, always very serious in the performance of his religious duties. Gustav's father died in an accident when Gustav was twelve years old, leaving behind him a business that could adequately support the widow and her child. Two years later, while Gustav was going through instruction for confirmation, he showed signs of great emotional disturbance over a period of several months. During this period he attached himself even more closely to his church, became active in its youth program. Considered a very precocious child by those around him, Gustav read a large number of religious books. His pastor, who took a kindly interest in the boy, let him make free use of his library, and Gustav became highly conversant in Lutheran theological writings, also took a great interest in the works of Kierkegaard.

Gustav was drafted into the service just before the end of World War II, spent only about one year in uniform, all of it in the South. Upon his release he began studying at the University of Chicago, majoring in philosophy. During his junior year in college he came into contact with a group of Communist students, among whom he formed some warm personal friendships. Among these new friends were Jack, a very intelligent young Negro holding office in the campus Communist organization, and Ilona, an exchange student from Hungary. Gustav began a passionate affair with Ilona, the first of his life—his sexual experiences so far had been fleeting relationships with pickups much below him in social status and a few visits to brothels while in the service. Gustav made a serious study of Marxism and wrote several articles on what he called "the Christian alternative to Communism." He initiated a plan to start an interracial Lutheran church in a section of Chicago increasingly invaded by Negro residents. This plan failed as a result of strong opposition from conservative churchmen in Gustav's denomination. At this point Gustav broke off all his church connections and involved himself wholeheartedly in the Communist organization run by his friend Jack.

In the summer after his graduation from the University of Chicago, Gustav received an invitation to attend a Communist-sponsored youth conference in Budapest. Ilona and he traveled to Europe together, arrived in Budapest after a few weeks of tourism in various European countries. One week after their arrival there, Ilona was arrested by the political police on suspicion of espionage. She was formally expelled from the Young Communist League and disappeared in a penal labor camp. Gustav attempted to intervene on her behalf with police and party agencies, was himself arrested and turned over to American authorities at the Austrian border.

Gustav suffered a nervous breakdown. After some weeks in an Austrian sanatorium he returned to America, took a job with a publishing firm in New York. Two months after his establishment in New York he entered psychoanalysis. He lived in New York for a year, then decided to resume studying. He received a scholarship to a Swiss university and began graduate work in philosophy. During his stay in Switzerland he became very friendly with Armin, an older student with special interests in the study of mysticism.

(b) Documents in the Case

JOURNEYS OF GUSTAV: The following are extracts from Gustav's diary, which he began to keep shortly after he started college. The extracts are marked to show the period during which they were written. The first extract is from the early pages of the diary, written shortly after Gustav's establishment at the University of Chicago:

"Men need faith. The Christian faith is not the only one that offers to satisfy this need. There is, as it were, a market of faiths. What are we going to buy? Many of the faiths offering themselves on this market are most seductive to our intellect, while others promise us profound revelations into the meaning of life and peace of mind. Sometimes the Gospel may seem poor by comparison with this array of worldly proclamations. Yet Christian faith knows that ultimately it is the only alternative to despair. All other faiths ultimately lead to one or another form of desperation (quiet or otherwise). What remains for ever is the Christian proclamation that at the very center of the universe is infinite love. . . .

"Christian faith is never like the false securities offered by the faiths of this world. One can never put one's hands on the object of faith and say, 'Ah, now I have it!' Christian faith is always insecure, always trust and surrender in Him whom we cannot see. As Kierkegaard put it, Christian faith is venturing far, far out onto the sea, swimming over 70,000 fathoms of deep, out where there is nothing but emptiness—and God. Because Christian faith has this character, the Christian life is one of adventure, the adventure of daring to follow Jesus Christ. Recently I came across a modern version of Pascal's famous 'betting argument' in the writings of Kaj Munk, the Danish pastor murdered by the Nazis because of his courageous opposition to the persecution of the Jews. This is (in so many words) what Kaj Munk says: Yes, perhaps it is all a mistake, this business about Christianity. Sometimes it really looks to me like that. Perhaps all this talk about God and Jesus Christ and the salvation of man is just a collection of fairy tales. And I am a minister. I am in the employment of Jesus Christ and for this work the Danish government pays me 40,000 crowns as a salary. Perhaps this is a mistake too. Perhaps it is a mistake to preach love and forgiveness in a hate-torn world, to rescue those who are in need, to teach the children, to comfort the lonely and the dying. But if it is a mistake, then it is a beautiful mistake. If Christianity should turn out to be true after all, then unbelief will have been a very ugly mistake. . . ."

The next extract is from the period just before Gustav broke off his relations with the church and began to consider himself a Marxist:

"Above all, I have the feeling with Marxism as if, for the first time in my life, I have come to grips with reality. It is a terrifying experience, yet full of the freshness of a breeze coming in from the lake. It seems to me now that all the words I have written on these pages before (so many words!) were nothing but a smoke screen preventing me from looking at the world with honesty. Especially it seems to me that, with all my words about love and humanity, I have never really seen people before. For example, I never really *saw* those stupid board secretaries who squelched our interracial project. I looked at them as representatives of the church, members of the invisible body of Christ. Nor did I really *see* the people on the South Side that our project was to serve. Between my eyes and social reality stood some sort of a silly picture—maybe the castle church in Wittenberg and good old Luther hammering his theses on the wall—as if this had anything to do with my life or theirs! . . .

"I have asked myself whether my feelings about Ilona are coming in the way of my judgment. After analyzing my feelings as sharply as I can, I come to the conclusion that this is not so. If I were as certain about Christianity as I was a year ago, I would go on my way even if it meant losing Ilona, no matter how painful that might be. Yet I think that there is a social element in my present thinking, though it is not concerned exclusively with Ilona. It is a question of whom one wants to belong to. I think of the bloated, embarrassed faces of the Lutheran board secretaries to whom I presented our interracial project, or the benevolent face of my pastor, when he advised me (with so much kind understanding!) of my youth and inexperience in matters of the church. And then I think of the faces of my Marxist friends—no, not just Ilona—but all of them, arguing heatedly in Tony's smoke-filled back room—that pock-marked old Spanish anarchist who got into such a fight with Jack the other day—and always Jack, with his face lighting up under a new thought, with that cigarette perpetually dangling from the corner of his mouth. And then I know where I want to belong! . . .

"I have had the curious experience that I begin a day as a Christian and end it as a Marxist, or vice versa, with moods of insight (that's a poor term, but the best I can think of right now) changing back and forth within me. Yesterday, for instance, I got up with a headache (as so often these days), decided to cut my morning classes, instead sat in Grant Park reading Lenin. Page by page I bit my way through his analysis of the Bolsheviks' differences with Kautsky and Plekhanov in the years before the October Revolution, was taken up by the argument, swept away into the world from which these thoughts came to me. In the afternoon I went to hear an address by a visiting theology professor from Germany who talked about the reinterpretation of Reformation theology in recent years. I suddenly found myself shaking with the fear of losing my Christian faith, left the meeting with the thought that I ought not to give up quite yet, that I ought to hold on to the one great certainty I ever had. In the evening I met Ilona, Jack, and some of the others. We sat at Tony's until two in the morning, drinking beer and talking, talking, talking. I kissed Ilona good night, much later, and on the long El ride home Christianity seemed as far away as last year's snow. In this way I am literally shaken by every 'wind of doctrine.' I tried to combat this helplessness by the means which Christian faith enjoins. I prayed, read the Bible, went to services, partook of the Sacrament. My state did not change and these practices seemed increasingly dishonest. The voices from my own past, all the things that I had said and that had been said to me about Christianity, keep coming back to my mind, holding me back from the step I am considering. To quote St. Augustine in reverse, as it were, all these things keep holding me back, whispering in my ear, 'Are you sending us away? . . . From this moment shall we not be with you, now or forever?' Yet the persistence of my 'Marxist voices' remains and these latter voices are beginning to drown out the voices of my past. I feel that I am moving toward a decision. It will not be long now, I think. As Lenin wrote in the spring of 1917, 'it is time to cast off the dirty shirt, it is time to put on a clean one.' "

The last extracts from Gustav's diary that we want to submit here were written in Austria, after the events in Budapest and as he was recovering from his nervous breakdown. The pages from this period are very disorganized and only fragments of the material make cohesive sense:

"I still cannot conceive how this could have happened, how it did happen. The morning in Stalin Stadium. The thousands of banners, flags, marching youth, the warm sunlight. The night in the police headquarters, the many impassive faces, the explanations in the language I could not understand, the laborsome translations. Ilona gone, gone! Oh my God! . . . The night before they arrested me I walked for hours, it must have been miles, from one end of the city to the other, over countless bridges, again and again the dark stream of the Danube under me, the rattling of dilapidated streetcars, rubble, empty construction lots, a chilly wind I hardly felt. There was no God, no future, not even a present, just the screaming-silent memory of what had happened. Her smiles, the smell of her body, the way she raises her eyebrows, her indestructible accent. . . . The illusion has gone like smoke, all of it. The mask has been torn from the face of God and behind it is a fat little man in a grayish uniform, with three stars on his collar, fingering a typed sheet of paper and quietly speaking in Hungarian. I hate. I hate. I never thought I could hate so completely. . . . For a few moments it seemed to me as if again I could see the hand of God, that old God of my Christian faith, the judgment calling me back to faith. Fragments of the litany kept drifting through my mind. 'In all time of our tribulation; in all time of our prosperity; in the hour of death . . .' 'To beat down Satan under our feet . . .' Obscenities all. Nothing but obscenities. There is nothing 'beyond' anywhere. There is nothing but this insane, tormented world of men. I thought of killing myself, but I didn't. Why do I live? What keeps me alive is fear and hate. Nothing else. Not a shred of a shred of faith. . . ."

THE WORLD OF DR. VLADIMIR HLOBUNKA: Dr. Hlobunka practices his art in a rather gloomy office in the East Sixties of Manhattan. Peering through his thick glasses, he explained to Gustav in his *Mittel*-European accents that the payment of an adequate fee was essential to a successful analysis ("This may seem a little funny to you now, especially with your Marxist past"—a benevolent smile through the glasses—"but at a later stage of the analysis you will understand fully"). Gustav didn't have any particularly Marxist thoughts. He reflected briefly how it could be that people so often looked like their caricatures, as if reality was trying to keep up with the cartoonist, rather than the other way around. But he was in no mood to argue or to have amused thoughts. The following are extracts from Dr. Hlobunka's notes on the case of Gustav, kept in near-illegible longhand and stored in the near-magnificent disorder of a battered filing cabinet (Dr. Hlobunka to his friends, "I possess a most remarkably anal character"):

"The evidence indicates almost complete failure to resolve the Oedipal conflict as a child. Faced with a strong, domineering father and a mother always sickly, meek, submissive, the conflict must have been very sharp in Gustav's early years. The number of his childhood diseases may indicate this too. Then the conflict was evidently repressed very deeply. Gustav became a 'good child.' He obediently submitted himself to his father's castration. He was a good student in school, 'well behaved,' attached to his home, faithful in his religious duties. Then, at a crucial age, came the trauma of the father's sudden death. The patricidal wish, acting magically out of the unconscious, was suddenly fulfilled. The father was (literally) killed and victory in the Oedipal conflict seemed to be in Gustav's hands. Now, of course, terrible guilt set in. The Oedipal wish had to be repressed even more deeply. With the oncome of puberty the conflict became unbearable. Gustav's 'conversion' to an active Christianity was his attempted solution.

"Gustav's religious 'conversion' constituted an attempt to solve the Oedipal conflict by a deeper submission to his father, becoming reconciled with him, only that now the father took on the cosmic proportions of the Christian God. The Lutheran theology, which Gustav now avidly absorbed, offered a perfect pattern for such an attempt. The father is accepted by the child as an overwhelming castrating figure—God is holy and can only be approached in acute terror. Facing this father, the child is utterly impotent—man is sinful by nature and cannot redeem himself out of his own strength. In acknowledging this impotence and submitting to the father completely, the child can still be saved from the threat of castration and death, which threat is accepted as the just reward for the child's patricidal sin—the confession of sins, 'We are by nature sinful and unclean,' and so on in the Lutheran liturgy. The father's answer to this act of complete submission is forgiveness—the Lutheran experience of grace. Moreover, there now begins a new life with the father, whose forgiveness enables the child to live, in spite of his impotence, out of the father's potency—the paradox of the Christian life as expressed in Luther's *simul iustus et peccator*. In this way Gustav became a Christian. His compulsion is now to convert all other rebels against the father. The missionary syndrome —each conversion is an assurance that the forces of rebellion within oneself are successfully quelled. It is indicative that Gustav's missionary zeal picked on Negroes as an object—the Negro, of course, being a primary phallic symbol—the black penis offered sacrificially to the avenging father![2]

"It is important to see in what way Gustav's intellectual conflicts are rationalizations of his unconscious conflicts onto a conceptual plane. With his Marxist friends in Chicago Gustav encountered a group of seemingly successful rebels, free and apparently unshaken by guilt. When Gustav became a member of this group (one is reminded here of the American adage of 'When you can't lick 'em, join 'em!'), Marxism again provided him with a

pattern highly suitable to resolve his inner conflicts, as Lutheranism
had been before. Here he found rebellion against the father (now
symbolized by all constituted authority in society as it exists)
openly espoused—a creed of total revolution. The father is proudly
killed—Marxist atheism. All guilt about this is dismissed as an illusion—religion is the opium of the people. The rewards to Gustav
were immediate. In his sexual relationship with Ilona he appeared,
finally, to have achieved victory in the Oedipal conflict. At the
same time, his act of rebellion was not an isolated one, but he
found himself sheltered in the horde of fellow patricides—the
brotherhood of the world-wide Communist movement. It might
have happened that Gustav could have maintained a precarious
adjustment with the help of his Marxist pattern, constituting, as it
did, a neurotic adjustment socially acceptable within a certain
group. The events in Budapest, however, brought on a new trauma,
shattering this precarious structure within which Gustav's virility
could operate and bringing up again the old conflict with renewed
violence. It now seemed to Gustav that his rebellion had only
brought him a temporary victory. The hand of the father had
struck again—God is not mocked! For was it not the father who
had taken Ilona away, turned the brothers into enemies, and
threatened Gustav himself with terrible death? This was the moment of Gustav's most complete impotence. He might easily have
regressed to the infantile masochism of his old Lutheran pattern.
It is indicative of the amount of libidinous liberation that had
actually taken place during Gustav's Marxist (*sic*) period, despite
its obvious neurotic dimensions, that he did not take this course.
Instead, after his return to America, Gustav began to understand
the unconscious dynamics at work and found his way into analysis.
Prognosis: excellent!"

JACK'S WORLD: Some time after his return to America Gustav
wrote to Jack. The following is from Jack's reply:
"Your letter is full of subjectivities and abstractions to which an
answer is impossible. Let us speak concretely. What really happened
to you has nothing whatever to do with the mystifications you
mouth in your letter—'human dignity' and 'basic decency' and
'deception by false Messianism'—to mention but a few of the
glittering phrases you throw at me. What really happened is that
Ilona, a girl you slept with for some time, has been arrested as a

spy. This is *all* that happened. The rest is nothing but a movement within your own mind. You maintain that Ilona has been 'innocently' arrested. You write that, all the time you knew her, Ilona was evidently a convinced Communist and that it is beyond imagination that you could have been deceived. I could certainly say a few things here about the rather patent limitations of your imagination, about the obvious fact that imperialist agents sent into our camp will not advertise themselves as such, and about the long experience of our party organs in tracking down such scum. The party, my dear Gustav, does not make mistakes very easily! But I think that, from your own point of view (assuming that you still retain the capacity to think clearly) it might be more profitable if you asked yourself what the word 'innocent' means. Even if we assume that subjectively Ilona had no antiparty thoughts when (in your company, incidentally) she rubbed shoulders with American intelligence agents in London, Paris, and even after the beginning of the Budapest congress—this changes nothing in the case. The party is not interested in Ilona's so-called 'inner life.' The party is interested in the objective character of her actions. Speaking concretely, and pushing away the abstractions which becloud the issue, Ilona is as guilty of treason as the worst Trotzkyite in the textbooks—and you know it!

"But now let us come to you, my little ex-Communist. *Your* treason does not even have the courage of conviction. It is the sickly, cowardly reaction of the petty-bourgeois that, at heart, you always were—even when you were strutting around with a red banner waving over you—or rather hanging from your petty-bourgeois penis, for it is right there that the matter really rests! It was some bourgeois French painter who made the statement, 'I paint with my penis'—you were a Communist with your penis! Yes, Gustav, don't shrink away from yourself—look at yourself honestly! Why did you come to us in the first place? For one reason and one reason only—to get over your Midwestern lily-white inhibitions and shack up with the first girl who'd given you more than a passing glance. The most disgusting thing about your opportunism is its erotic character. As I look back now on those days in Chicago, the vilest fascist seems cleaner by comparison!

"I predict a great future for you in America. Perhaps you can write some articles for the newspapers—'My Years as a Communist Dupe' or 'Red Terror in Hungary'—and be nominated Ex-

Communist of the Year by the American Legion. Or, of course, you might return into the bosom of religion—provided, of course, that your Lutheran ecclesiastics can forget your shocking suggestion that the inferior races be welcomed into the congregation of the saints. For the moment, I gather from your letter that you have decided to 'get at the roots' of your troubles and submit yourself to psychoanalysis. An excellent idea, Gustav! At least you'll be able to deal at your heart's content with the sexual dirt which seems to be the natural habitat of your Christian soul.

"I would not bother to write you at all were it not for the fact that the American party needs men—even such dubious men as you. I am writing you in the dim hope that you still retain a vestige of Marxist consciousness, that you can remember at least something of what you learned with us. But don't misunderstand me—I'm not wooing you and I cannot promise you that the party would take you back, even if you came crawling on your knees. Let me only say that it would be your last act of manhood if you tried."

ALTERNATION—BACK TO DR. HLOBUNKA'S WORLD: Brief entry from Dr. Hlobunka's notebook:

"It is interesting that, in the Gersthoff Dream-Sequence Test, Gustav associates 'Ilona' with ANOLI—a striking illustration of the pregenital character of this relationship. Also note: 'Jack' (a Negro, to boot)—frequently found American idiom for penis (along with 'Dick,' 'Peter,' et alia). Also in the Gersthoff Test, Gustav associates 'Hungary' with its German form 'Ungarn,' adds 'ungern' (German adjective for displeasure), then speaks of a 'dark stream,' 'many bridges.' Look up 'scrotum complex' in Meyer & Hlobunka (the 1931 edition)."

ARMIN'S WORLD: It is perhaps not fair to Armin to mention that he comes from a long line of Swiss chocolate manufacturers, that he wears impeccable clothes and speaks a fastidious Hoch-deutsch which, on occasion and for special effect, he uses contrapuntally with the thickest Bernese dialect. It might be mentioned quite fairly that Armin is an avid and careful letter-writer. Although Gustav and Armin lived about four blocks apart in the Swiss university town where they studied, they frequently wrote each other long letters. It is not necessary here to go into Armin's rationale concerning this, involving, as it does, a very complicated philosophy of language and the written word quite beyond our immediate interests. The following is from one of Armin's letters:

"Your basic problem is with time. Because you cannot bear to remain silent and waiting, even for a moment, you 'leap' (to use your own Kierkegaardian term) from one position to another —into Christianity and out of it, into Marxism and out of that too, and into that peculiarly massive mythology of your psychoanalysis. To put this in somewhat different terms, all your religious and quasi-religious positions have been of the nature of nervous desperation. This is what I mean when I say that your basic problem is with time. What you must come to understand is that truth is not a matter of decision. This goes for religious truth too. And here I would suggest that your Lutheran starting point may have a lot to do with what happened to you subsequently. In Lutheranism (and, I suppose, in Protestantism generally) religion tends to become a matter of subjective choice. This gives, indeed, a very one-sided approach to religion. May I suggest to you that there are other religious possibilities? And may I suggest further that you might find more insights into your problems by turning to the great mystic teachers (to what Aldous Huxley has referred to as 'the perennial philosophy') than by continuing to fight in the void of religious illiteracy with various Protestant prophets (and their all-too-Protestant Marxist and Freudian imitators)?

"You will only begin to understand your life, I think, when you see it as a journey toward yourself—into yourself. So far you have only scraped the surface of your own reality. Your journeys on the seas of *Weltanschauung* have been only intellectual, did not really involve your being. You have recently complained to me about this series of 'crises of faith' that you have gone through, then added with a wry smile that you now find yourself 'in the unenviable position of a man who believes absolutely nothing.' Well, I would say that if this were true (unfortunately it is not—you still believe far too much!) there is no more promising condition that you could be in! Stop 'believing' altogether! Try to *know!* Abandon 'faith'! Try *knowledge!* Those old heretics (whom the proto-Lutherans of the early church did their best to liquidate) had a good terminology for this alternative—stop being a 'pistic,' a believer—become a 'gnostic,' a knower! Unlike the violent decisions of 'faith,' however, such a path requires immense patience, painstaking searching, infinite self-discipline. This is why the world is full of believers and very short of searchers after knowledge.

"I would venture one further interpretation to you. Your past may have a deeper relationship to such a possible future than you think. What has happened in your past is that all the 'faiths' you have tried have crumbled before your eyes. This is very important. Only when all 'faith' crumbles is the way opened to enter onto the path of knowledge. This crumbling of 'faith' is what mystics have called the 'negative way' (or, to be more accurate, it is involved in what is called this). When you have gone through the deepest negation you will suddenly see one tiny opening into affirmation. At that point the 'positive way' will begin.

"Let me make one final suggestion for tonight. Stop worrying your head about interpreting and reinterpreting your past. None of it is interesting enough for such cerebration. At best it is a prologue. And never think again in psychological terms of asking what your 'motives' were for this, or that, or the other thing. What men like your Hlobunka call 'depth-psychological' relates to the ocean of your self like a speck of sand relates to the total mass of the earth! You haven't even dreamed yet what 'depth' really means! Take instead the little book I gave you last week. Sit down in a quiet place and start reading, very quietly, very slowly. Don't bring to the book your own interpretations. Let the author be your guide. And give yourself very, very much time!"

(iii) THE CASE OF THE INCONVENIENT SCROLL

> ". . . the discovery of the Dead Sea Scrolls, which —in spite of much sensationalism in the publicity given to it—has opened the eyes of many people to the problem of biblical research but *which has not changed the theological situation at all.*"
>
> *Paul Tillich*[3]

Archaeological Institute of St. James the Less,
Old City of Jerusalem

June 5, 1985

The Most Reverend Father
Monsignor Luigi Respirelli
Director of the Apologetic Section
ROME

Most Reverend Father,

I am sending you by special messenger the enclosed document,
one glance at which will convince you of the urgency of this matter.
Besides myself, only two of the Fathers here know about this. The
original scroll, of which the enclosed is a translation, is numbered
V 5778 and belongs to the group of the Qumran fragments on
which our Institute has been working for the last decade. There
can be no reasonable question about the authenticity and date of
the scroll.

We pray and await your reply in the greatest anxiety. It is perhaps
not saying too much, Most Reverend Father, if I add that the fate
of the Catholic world lies between these lines.

signed P. Jean Bartou, S.J.

Translated from the Aramaic by PP. Girard, Schwertfeger, Bartou:

Peace salutation (be) unto you forever.
This greeting (to the) master (of the) congregation.
Greetings (to) all brothers in (the) congregation (of) righteousness. (The) bonds (of) death (have) not held me. Delivery came
(by the) power (of the) Name (from the) wickedness (of the)
Roman and (the) malice (of the) children (of) darkness in Israel.
Death (did) not come on (the) Roman's cross. My body (was)
lain in (an) empty tomb (to be) rescued by Shimon and Yocha-
nan on whom (be) peace. (I) rest in (the) house (of) Miriam
(the) sinner. (I) give thanks (to) YY for my deliverance. (The)
cup (of) bitterness (has) passed.

My great desire (is) to return (to the) peace (of the) congregation. Too much rumor (has) troubled Judea (of) new Messiahs
and (of) mighty events. Now men say foolishly (that) my body

(has) risen from (the) realm (of) death. YY alone lives forever.
(I) seek peace. (I) bow (to) you master. (I) hold unto (the)
congregation and wait (for the) coming (of the) teacher (of)
righteousness on (the) clouds (of) light. Yeshua bar Yosef whom
(the) people call (the) Nazarene.

(iv) THE CASE OF THE INCONVENIENT MARTIANS

> "The possibility of life on other planets is not
> seen, therefore, as a threat to the Christian view
> of the drama of redemption."
>
> *Martin J. Heinecken*[4]

The *Esquire* calendar tacked onto the door of the pilot cabin
showed June 1995. The small jet craft was two hours out of New
Hoboken, Mars, on a routine scouting mission. Its crew of three
was gathered up front drinking what passed for coffee on Mars.
There was little else to do. Underneath, the flat desolate landscape
stretched on mile after mile. It was as uninspiring as the coffee.

The three men were wearing the dark blue uniform of the UN
Space Authority. Two of them, Brady the pilot and Hirabashi the
ecologist, had worn that uniform when they were with the first
space ship that landed on Mars three years previously. The tremendous excitement of those first days had paled somewhat. Life on
Mars had become to these men a routine almost like any other.
Most of their life took place within the small bubble domes that
marked the scattered human outposts on the alien planet. The rest
consisted of endless flights over empty continents, ocasionally landing, taking samples and photographs, plotting coordinates on the
meager maps already available, and preparing new maps for the as
yet uncharted areas. And, once every six months, Earth—a few
weeks of recovering the threads with one's past, with one's mind
and senses, recovering the feeling of matter-of-fact humanity.

The third crew member, Bartou, was on his first hitch to Mars.
Nothing on his uniform indicated that, in addition to being a
commissioned archaeologist with UNSA, he was a Jesuit father.
Since his arrival he had had little to do. No signs of intelligent life
had been found on Mars. Yet there had been the interesting palaeo-

logical findings, not far from New Hoboken, which several authorities felt sure were implements of some sort. All the same, the small, rotund French priest had ample time to work on his doctor's thesis, or rather his second doctor's thesis—he had begun some ten years before a work on the Dead Sea Scrolls, but had then switched to a very interesting problem in Central-American archaeology.

"I suppose, Padre, you must be quite relieved that no Martians have turned up here after all," said Brady, scratching his stubbled chin. "Wouldn't that have been quite embarrassing? I mean, after all, what would you do with those little bastards? Make them all Catholics? And what if they thought so differently from us that we couldn't communicate with them at all? What if they were terribly superior?"

"I don't see," replied Bartou, "how any of this would have changed the basic religious questions. The God whom the church worships is the God of Mars too. What the church teaches about Him on Earth would be just as valid on Mars."

"But what about the little bastards?" pressed Brady.

"Your attitude is revealed rather well in the way you speak about these hypothetical creatures," said Bartou. "Even so, the question is not without theological interest. It may interest you to know that the question was already debated in the 1950s. A Catholic theologian (a Jesuit, by the way, if I may point this out) then made the point that the church would have to rule concerning the state in which these creatures would be in. If the church finds that they are in a state of sin (that is, that in some way they participated in the fall of Adam—or had a fall of their own) then, of course, the church would seek to convert and baptize them, just as it did with the Indians that the discoverers encountered in America. If, on the other hand, it is found that these creatures are in a state of innocence, then, obviously, they would be in no need of the means of grace at the disposal of the church—just as little as the angels would be. No, there is no great problem here at all."

"But even so," commented Hirabashi, "even if you can maintain this position, wouldn't it bother you that these creatures were totally unaware of what your religion regards as an event of cosmic significance? After all, your whole religion is based on one little bit of human history. This looks like a pretty precarious basis even if you look at it from, say, a Japanese point of view. Would the basis

not seem even more precarious if you were staring some Martians
in the face (assuming they'd have faces!)? Would this not raise any
doubts in your mind about the claims of Christianity?"

Bartou thought quietly for several minutes. Then he answered:
"I have had, in my life, a number of experiences where the claims
of Christianity seemed very precarious indeed. By holding onto
the church and its infallible authority none of these experiences
succeeded in alienating me from my religion. I cannot see that the
Martian encounter that we're imagining here would bring about a
completely new situation in matters of faith." After a pause Bartou
smiled. "Just imagine the opposite, though! Suppose that we had
found intelligent life on Mars, beings that we could communicate
with. And suppose that they *had* heard about Jesus Christ, about
the Christian religion—perhaps even believed in it! How about
that? Would that settle the question?"

Hirabashi smiled politely. "Yes, I must grant you that—it would,
indeed, settle the question."

Brady had let his attention shift back to the controls the last few
minutes. Suddenly his body tensed. "Look!" he whispered.

Beneath them, lying snugly between two little hills, was a settlement. Maybe fifty buildings, some with small domes over the roofs.
In the center, a little tower. A village, without any doubt. And
they were flying over uncharted areas, hundreds of miles from the
nearest human outpost.

It was perhaps twenty minutes later that the three men in their
space suits walked slowly toward the settlement. The sun was
sinking toward the close-seeming Martian horizon in the west. Its
rays were caught beautifully on the domes of the houses. The men
had come no more than some two hundred feet from the tower
when they noticed the creature standing on top of it. They could
see it clearly now. It was perhaps three feet tall. It did not seem to
wear clothes. Its skin was of a pale, bluish color. And now it raised
what looked like three thin feelers, slowly lifting them toward the
sky, and a surprisingly powerful voice issued from the large opening
in the center of the creature's head:

*"LA ILLAH AL ALLAH, MUHAMMAD RASSUHL
ALLAH!"*

"What the devil is *that?*" gasped Brady.

There was a long, long silence among the three men as the creature in the tower repeated its call. Then Bartou answered very quietly: "It is Arabic. It means, there is no god but Allah and Muhammad is his prophet. It is from the Moslem call to prayer."

3. Society as Stage (Scholarly Remarks)

THE SOCIAL SCIENCES PRESENT A PICTURE OF SOCIETY AS A STRUC-
TURE OF DRAMATIC FICTIONS. THESE FICTIONS DETERMINE HUMAN
ACTIONS, BUT THEY ALSO CONTAIN THE POSSIBILITY OF HUMAN
FREEDOM.

The idea that society is a stage upon which men act out
their lives is certainly not new. It is at least as old as Erasmus'
famous question, in *The Praise of Folly*, "What else is the
whole life of mortals but a sort of comedy, in which the
various actors, disguised by various costumes and masks, walk
on and play each one his part, until the manager waves them
off the stage?"[1] Yet the results of the past sixty years or so in
the social sciences have given very strong impetus to what may
well be called a dramatic conception of social existence. It
is also of considerable interest that the crucial contributions
to this conception were made in America. It is often pointed
out that, despite its great achievements in the accumulation
of empirical data, American social science (especially sociology) has been forced to lean constantly on European
theoretical formulations, being apparently unable to produce
anything comparable to these itself. While this is probably
less true today than it was, say, fifteen years ago, there is still
considerable validity to this statement. All the same, the
development that interests us here is almost exclusively an
American one. It may well be that future historians of ideas
will regard this development as one of the most important
American contributions to our thinking about man and
society.

This dramatic conception comes to a mature articulation
in what is now called role theory in sociology and social

psychology (although, as we shall point out below, the general picture of man involved here extends beyond the limits of role theory proper). There can be little question as to where we must look for the intellectual ancestry of this development. There are probably few short pieces of writing that have exerted as much influence as the short passage entitled "A Man's Social Self" in William James's *The Principles of Psychology*. Here follows the key paragraph from this passage:

"Properly speaking, *a man has as many social selves as there are individuals who recognize him* and carry an image of him in their mind. To wound any one of these his images is to wound him. But as the individuals who carry the images fall naturally into classes, we may practically say that he has as many different social selves as there are distinct *groups* of persons about whose opinion he cares. He generally shows a different side of himself to each of these different groups. Many a youth who is demure enough before his parents and teachers, swears and swaggers like a pirate among his 'tough' young friends. We do not show ourselves to our children as to our club-companions, to our customers as to the laborers we employ, to our own masters and employers as to our intimate friends. From this there results what practically is a division of the man into several selves; and this may be a discordant splitting, as where one is afraid to let one set of his acquaintances know him as he is elsewhere; or it may be a perfectly harmonious division of labor, as where one tender to his children is stern to the soldiers or prisoners under his command."[2]

After which James goes on to say that the most peculiar social self is that related to the image of those we love. In this brief passage we have *in nucleo* the basic features of not only role theory but so-called reference-group theory as well. Much of American social psychology since James has been concerned with the systematic elaboration of this germinal insight.

It would be quite beyond our scope in this essay (even if this chapter is to be a scholarly interlude!) to trace the development of this conception in American social science.[3] All we can do here is sketch this dramatic conception as it developed in a number of parallel efforts, after which we can relate it to the main concerns of this essay.

If William James is the ancestor of the conception, its fathers are certainly Charles Horton Cooley and George Herbert Mead. It was Cooley who developed the famous concept of the "reflected" or "looking-glass self," greatly sharpening James's original formulation, and then took the crucial step of relating this concept of the self to the problem of socialization—that is, to the process of training by which the child becomes a full participant in society.[4] With Mead the conception reached the dignity of fully elaborated theory and at the same time its most radical formulation.[5] In the cases of James and Cooley the development of the "social self" was still seen in some relationship to other aspects of the self not considered to be "social." With Mead this distinction disappears. The "social self" is the only self that is empirically available. The self is seen as originating in a social process. To put this somewhat differently, socialization is now seen not just as the process by which the self becomes integrated into society but rather as the process in which the self is actually produced. This process is carefully traced in the development of the child, related to a social-psychological theory of language. With his concept of the "generalized other," finally, Mead provided a precise theoretical formulation as to the way in which society becomes internalized psychologically. The place of Mead in the development of the conception under discussion here is crucial. With Mead the drama of society becomes identified with the drama of the self. Thus a new perspective is given to the old insight that man is a social being—irrevocably and essentially so.

The concept of role is central to Mead's theory and this concept continued to be the focal point for the further elaborations of the theory. Mead saw as the essential process of socialization the child's capacity to "take the role of the other" —that is, the child's capacity to react to himself as an object in the way in which others (to begin with, his mother) act toward him. In this act of "reflection" (to use Cooley's term) the image of the self appears. This reaction of the child will vary with different situations and with the "others" involved in these situations. That is, the child learns how to play different roles. As long, however, as these roles are not organized into a cohesive whole, no cohesive image of the self can emerge. When the expectations of society toward the child are organized into a larger unity, the concept of the "generalized other" appears—that is, the child now reacts not only to specific "others" but to a more highly abstract notion of what society ("all the others") expects. At this point it really becomes possible to speak of "self" in any empirically meaningful sense.

Different approaches to social psychology will have varying interpretations of the precise way in which this process occurs. It can be said without exaggeration, however, that the basic pattern as sketched by Mead is today generally accepted by both social psychologists and sociologists.[6] It might be pointed out that this appropriation of Mead's basic approach and concepts can be and has been done effectively by many who would in no way identify themselves as "behaviorists," in Mead's sense of that term.[7] For the social psychologists Mead's basic approach actually provides the rationale of their discipline. For the sociologists this approach has been a much-used nexus with the work of the psychologists. Moreover, sociologists have found the concept of role highly useful in understanding the way in which institutions operate and manage to integrate individuals into them.[8] In one of the most elaborate attempts at system-building in contemporary American sociology, that of Talcott Parsons, the concept of role occupies, again, a central place within the theoretical system.[9] This sociological use of the concept is a logical extension of Mead's original use as applied to the individual. The role is an organization of the individual's multifold reactions into a consistent whole. The individual's total social behavior is thus seen as a cluster (or repertoire!) of roles. But each role relates the individual to the roles of many other individuals meeting in specific situations. Social institutions thus appear also as clusters of roles. In different words, each individual plays different roles (say, husband, employer, citizen). But all

these roles are not in the same play. Different roles thus relate
the individual to different larger dramatic contexts (say, the
family, the economy, the state). These larger contexts are
the social institutions the analysis of which is the sociologist's
principal concern. With this enlarged perspective, role theory
can now make clear the relationship not only between individuals and society in general, but between individuals and
specific societies or sectors of society. The roles of military
man and clergyman are greatly different. *Ipso facto*, the
personalities to be found in the military and in the church
will also tend to be different. In fact, each "person" is the
product of a very specific social process.

Needless to say, this extended use of the concept of role has
been especially useful for comparative studies of personality in
different cultures. In this way the concept and the theory of
socialization going with it have been widely used by anthropologists. Role theory in American anthropology has been
most closely associated with Ralph Linton, though others
have taken very similar approaches.[10] Thus, for example, the
concept of "enculturation," as used by Melville Herskovits
to describe the individual's integration into a culture, alludes
in different terms to very much the same process that role
theory concerns itself with.[11] What is perhaps even more
interesting is that such an approach has become increasingly
used to give a sociological dimension to the psychoanalytic
tradition, originally most hostile to this sort of interpretation. The work of Harry Stack Sullivan is perhaps the best
illustration of a rapprochement between psychoanalysis and a
theory of personality based on Mead.[12]

Again, it cannot be our task here to integrate this enormous
amount of material into a consistent theory. This attempt has
been made most ambitiously by Parsons. However, we can
ask, in quite simple language, what this confluence of interpretations means for our picture of man in society. It would
then seem that the picture of society as stage, what above we
called the dramatic conception, becomes a compelling one. It
is certainly no accident that the key concepts of "role" and

"person" are both of theatrical origin—the latter (from the Latin persona=mask, as used in classical drama) evoking most suggestively the picture of a "sort of comedy," as Erasmus put it. But while Erasmus may well have thought of only certain aspects of man's life under this category, the picture invoked here suggests that *all* of man's life is encompassed by this stage. It is on this stage that man becomes an individual in the first place—by learning to play parts, then by integrating these parts into a consistent over-all part which defines his place in the *dramatis personae*, all of this occurring on stage and in interaction with other players. As long as man is alive he cannot escape the stage. He cannot even think of himself apart from the stage, because his image of himself depends upon the images others hold of him. His most intimate ideas about himself are still related to that same stage, because even and especially these ideas depend upon their recognition by others who are particularly close to him (what role theory calls the "significant others"). If this recognition is suddenly withdrawn the whole personality system is threatened with collapse. We have here a vast new perspective on the old idea that man is a "contingent" being—that is, that (unlike God) his existence depends upon others. To come back to Cooley's picture, society holds up its mirrors to us—and only as these mirrors are available to us can we recognize ourselves as anything at all. This is true even when we are alone, because even then we cannot do anything else than continue the roles we have learned on the stage, playing them now to an invisible audience within our own thoughts. Thus even the madman remains on stage. As our parts, and our selves, depend upon others in the rapidly changing situations of the social drama, our existence in society is not only contingent but infinitely precarious.[13] All of us are balancing our acts like acrobats precariously standing one on top of the other. One false move and the whole human edifice comes crashing down. Thus society is comedy indeed—but tragedy at the same time, for as the acrobats come crashing down, there is real pain and real terror.

If one was asked in what way the social sciences have contributed most to our understanding of the human condition,
the developments in social psychology just described might
come to mind first. However, there is another important
development that is needed to round out the picture, namely
the perspective on our stage provided by the sociology of
knowledge. While the latter discipline is hardly concerned
directly with what has here been called the dramatic conception of society, its insights give an added dimension to this as
to any other systematic picture of social reality. Only with
this addition can we become aware of the full implications of
our drama.

Unlike role theory and the developments coming from it,
the sociology of knowledge is of European origin.[14] With an
intellectual ancestry including German historical thought in
the nineteenth century on the one hand,[15] and heavily influenced by Marx and Nietzsche on the other,[16] the problematic of the sociology of knowledge was first defined by the
German philosopher Max Scheler in the 1920s.[17] It was
Scheler who coined the name of the new discipline. The introduction of the sociology of knowledge into the English-
speaking world was largely the achievement of Karl Mannheim,[18] who spent the closing years of his life in Britain.

The sociology of knowledge concerns itself with the social
location of ideas, values, beliefs. It seeks to demonstrate that
specific ideas are related to specific types of social structure. At
the simplest level of explanation this may explain, for instance, why societies that are strongly dependent on rainfall
may develop religions in which rain gods occupy a central
position. While this may be a truism, the analysis of the
relationship of class structure to, say, the moral notions preva-
lent among different classes can be a very complicated matter.
It ought to be emphasized that analysis along sociology-
of-knowledge lines does not necessarily base itself on the assumption that ideas simply emanate from, or reflect, social
structure. Even if this assumption may be made in certain
situations, the sociology of knowledge (unlike most versions of

Marxism) does not assume that such a relationship exists in *all* cases. Rather does it attempt to illuminate the manifold interactions between social structure and the world of ideas through careful empirical study.[19] Perhaps one of the most important values of the discipline is that it provides a highly fruitful sociological avenue to approach problems of history. The artificial division between political-social history and the history of ideas disappears. Even if sociologists will not accept Marx's view that life *produces* thought, they will attempt to relate the way people think to the way they live. Confronted with ideas of any sort, their instinctive question will be "Says who?" The answer to this question then involves the analysis of the social location of the one who voices the ideas.

It goes without saying that the sociology of knowledge raises quite disturbing problems for anyone personally committed to ideas thus analyzed. A person holding certain moral convictions does not take kindly to the suggestion that they can be accounted for, or even very much related to, the fact that he comes from a lower-middle-class background. But there are serious problems beyond this level of personal irritation. These problems relate directly to the whole question of the relativity of values and perspectives on the world indicated in the first chapter. When we take the example just given of moral ideas and class background, the fact of social mobility (people moving from one class level to another) by itself raises the specter of what we have called alternation. Again, the ground seems to shake under one's feet. These problems, however, need not concern us at the moment. What is very interesting for our purposes is to relate the insights of the sociology of knowledge to the social-psychological dynamics discussed above. It is rather remarkable that, so far, those writers identified with the sociology of knowledge have taken little if any interest in doing this. This may be explained by the fact that their attention has been focused on broad historical and structural interpretations, rather than upon the way in which socially located ideas are internalized and organized in the life of individuals. On the one hand, the sociologists of knowledge have only very limited interest in psychological processes, while, on the other hand, the social psychologists usually even fail to notice the historical dimension of their data. While there may be good biographical reasons for this state of affairs, and while there is here a considerable task of theoretical formulation, it is not really very difficult to bridge this gap. The perspectives are not contradictory. Far from it—they are complementary. For our purposes a nexus is wanted between role theory and the sociology of knowledge. It cannot be our task here to elaborate this nexus theoretically, but we can look at its implications for our picture of social reality.

If no such possible nexus existed we would have to invent it. We would contend that such a nexus, however, exists at least *in nucleo* in what has been called reference-group theory in recent American social psychology. It should be added quickly that, at any rate for most people using this approach, there is no explicit intention along these lines. Nevertheless, the kind of problems dealt with and the approach used are very conducive to establishing this nexus. In other words, we would contend that reference-group theory provides a useful link between the understanding of the social location of ideas on the one hand and the individual's organization of roles on the other—that is, a link between the sociology of knowledge and role theory.

The term "reference group" was first used by H. H. Hyman in 1942 and rapidly became popular after that among social psychologists and sociologists.[20] The concept of the reference group was used for a few years with a variety of meanings, until the situation was clarified by an article by T. Shibutani, who proposed to limit the concept to one sharply defined meaning.[21] Shibutani suggests that the concept be used only to describe "that group whose perspective constitutes the frame of reference of the actor."[22] The application of the concept is quite simple. For example, a person involved in climbing up the social ladder will feel relatively rich or relatively poor depending upon, respectively, his looking down to where he came from or up to where he wants to go. That is, if the person's reference group remains the circle of his family and friends which constitutes his background, this will give him a perspective on his situation different from the one he would get if his reference group has become the circle of successful people toward which he aspires and by whom he hopes to be accepted. The example of social mobility is instructive because it shows that the individual changes reference groups in the course of his biography and (what is even more important) that he may have different reference groups at any stage of his biography. It should be clear now that there can be considerable conflict between the perspectives of such different reference groups.

If one uses the concept of reference group in Shibutani's sense, one can certainly admit that one is not dealing here with hitherto undiscovered facts. It has been for quite some time a commonplace of social psychology that not only behavior and emotions but cognitive processes as well are subject to group influence.[23] There have been some very interesting experiments demonstrating how individuals will modify their judgments and accept even palpably absurd interpretations of events under the pressure of group suggestion.[24] It is presumably a root fact of social existence that most men tend to think as their fellows do. This tendency acts as a powerful psychological instrument of social control, bringing back into line the individual whose thinking deviates from the norms set by the group. How far this tendency can go has been shown by the evidence concerning Communist "brain-washing" techniques in recent years.[25] What reference-group theory does, however, is to relate these psychological findings directly to the analysis of social structure. Thus, for example, in the case of American prisoners of war brainwashed by the Chinese Communists, it now becomes possible not only to analyze the psychological processes inducing some remarkable conversions to the captors' points of view, but to show how these processes relate the individuals in question to specific social worlds. In this particular example the sociology-of-knowledge implications are particularly obvious, since the conversion now involves a totally different perspective on the political scene. To return to the terminology previously used in this essay, our understanding of the phenomenon of alternation becomes rounded out intellectually by a combination of role theory, reference-group theory, and the sociology of knowledge. Which rounding out is, of course, the aim of this chapter.

The sociological propositions attached to "the case of Susie Q." in the second chapter may now be seen against the background of a specific development in social-scientific theory.[26] Role conflict is seen as related to conflict in the choice between reference groups; these, in turn, can now be related to the ideological conflicts between distinctive social worlds, as understood by the sociology of knowledge. Our concept of alternation may, then, be integrated into the intellectual enterprise of the social scientist. As has already been said, it would be ludicrous to attempt a full integration of these strands of theory within the confines of this essay. The reason for indicating some directions here is mainly to bear out our previous contention that, especially in America, the social sciences afford an access to the experience of alternation which we consider to be basic to the perspective on social existence under scrutiny.

Let us now return to the dramatic conception of society evoked by role theory. Our consideration of sociology of knowledge and reference-group theory has (hopefully) added another dimension to this conception. We now see our actors once more upon the stage, playing their various roles. But now we see a *Weltanschauung* dangling from the end of each role. Thus the world of ideas too is drawn into our picture of the social theater. The stage involves not only action and emotion. It involves thought as well. To put this a little differently, each role provides a particular perspective on the entire stage, not only illuminating the present moment in the play but providing an interpretation of the past and constructing projects for the future. Not only do we think within our social roles, but we reminisce and we hope within the perspectives of these roles. It may even be said that the various *Weltanschauungen* available on the stage provide the script for the action. The actors move and speak and think within the confines of the libretto. Where the theater of society differs from that on Broadway is in the often inconvenient fact that it has not one single script but many. The problems of stage management and dramatic unity occasioned by this fact are illuminated by the findings of the social sciences.

The relationship of role, reference group, and *Weltanschauung* is particularly observable in the area of the sociology of occupations. A somewhat neglected field of sociology, the systematic study of occupations, including that of the ideologies of occupations, has been for a number of years centered at the University of Chicago. Everett C. Hughes and his students have, without doubt, made the principal contributions to this field.[27] Nor is this fact incidental. Of all the activities of life that shape the human being after initial socialization has occurred, preparing for and carrying on one's occupation is probably the most potent. This is true not only of people in the so-called professions but also (perhaps in some ways even more so) of people in occupations with inferior social status. Occupation gives the readiest index for social identification—and, therefore, for self-identification, as should be clear from the preceding. "Who are you?"—"I am a palaeontologist." "Who are you?"—"I'm the janitor from downstairs." In this social game of being asked and giving names is located not only a man's self-esteem but also his self-image (or at least an important part of it), and beyond that the angle he has on the world. In other words, occupation involves not only roles but also ideology.

If one understands this point, quite a new perspective is given on occupational training. This is now seen as far more than the teaching of certain information and skills necessary for the carrying on of the occupation. It is also a novitiate, in which the new recruit to the ranks of the occupation has his person molded into the recognized image of that occupation and is made to absorb a point of view which justifies the

occupation's place in the world. In other words, it involves
"brain-washing" in the double sense of psychological formation and ideological indoctrination. Needless to say, there
can be no mechanical result of this process. Human beings
are plastic, but not totally so. Also, there are, of course,
differences in the intensity of this novitiate. An Academy of
Hairdressing is not quite like Annapolis. But it has obvious
and important similarities. Coiffeurs and admirals both have
to play very specific roles in society and both may on occasion
have haunting doubts about the legitimacy of their activities.
In both cases, then, ideologies have to be provided which
justify the occupational enterprise. The raw barber and the
raw ensign are provided with the rudiments of a conceptual
system that will allow them to function in their roles effectively. Since the occupation of the ensign involves a much
more elaborate act of stage management (with homicide
included in the bargain, at least as a possibility), it is obvious
that his ideology must be a more comprehensive and more
deeply embedded one than that of the barber. Consequently
it is easier to stop being a coiffeur than to stop being a Navy
man.

As an individual goes through his basic occupational training it is not only the formal educational process which
leads him to identify with a certain image (after all, some
occupations do not have such a process—even in this time of
professionalization!) but the informal processes of associating
with fellow trainees, those more advanced in their training
and the masters of the trade do this in a much more powerful
way.[28] That this self-glorification does not necessarily involve
a developed intellectual system is well illustrated by the following passage from a study concerning the development of
the professional boxer:

"The boxer is involved in a scheme of relationships and traditions
which focus upon building confidence. The boxing tradition is full
of legends of feats of exceptional fighters. Most gymnasiums have
pictures of past and present outstanding boxers on the wall, and
identification with them comes easy for the incoming fighters.

Past fights are revived in tales. Exceptional fighters of the past and present are compared and appraised. Second, the individual boxer is continually assured and reassured that he is 'great' and that he is 'coming up.' As a result, many fighters seem to overrate their ability and to feel that all they need are 'lucky breaks' to become champions or leading contenders. Many get self-important and carry scrapbooks of their newspaper write-ups and pictures."[29]

This passage, with minor alterations, can be applied to the training of gangsters or funeral directors, insurance salesmen or Presbyterian clergymen. One important difference is that boxers, on the whole, live in a less delusional world than Presbyterian clergymen, so that the latter require much thicker ideology.

As Hughes has pointed out, medicine is perhaps the prototype of the professions.[30] The training of a physician thus involves in particularly strong measure the absorption of a large mass of personality traits, attitudes and behavior patterns, and, finally, ideological viewpoints. Hughes is quite right in using the term "medical culture" (anthropologists might say "subculture") in referring to this complex. Becoming a physician thus involves an "enculturation" process basically analogous to that of the little animal-infant who grows up to be an Englishman. Thus the physician must learn not only to detect an appendicitis but the right visage to exhibit to patient and onlookers as this detection is undertaken. In other words, he must not only learn medicine but how *to be* a medical man. The ideology which this will involve has been neatly illustrated by the reactions of the medical profession to the various proposals for national health programs in recent years.

Or take a student preparing for the ministry. No matter what motives originally propelled him into theological study, the performances of the ministerial role will at first evoke in most students a sense of embarrassment and uneasiness. The minister walks around in outlandish costume, and his principal activities are carried on in buildings carefully constructed to be outlandishly different from normal human habitations. Many of the minister's operations invite a comic reaction from himself and others. He uses archaic language, has to pretend ignorance of commonly known facts of life, is forced into ritual acts on occasions when others enjoy conviviality. He must perform sacramental ceremonies that may seem bizarre to his audience if not to himself—throwing water at screaming infants, feeding wafers into mouths opened wide under the brim of stylish hats, asking triumphant young American brides whether they will obey their husbands, burning mortgages, and blessing patriotic displays. There are few students of this occupation who will not feel at times that they are engaged in a circus of preposterous nonsense. It is at this point that the occupation provides the psychological and ideological means by which such thoughts can be banished. For one thing, there is habit. After some years one even gets used to oneself staring out of the mirror over a Roman collar. But, more important, there are the others. Surely not *all* fellow seminarians can be engaged in a meaningless enterprise! "If *they* don't feel ridiculous, why should *I?*" But there are not only other trainees to reassure one. There are the professors, the bishops and elders and superintendents, the visiting hierarchs, theologians and teachers of the church— all engaged in one great conspiracy against one's own sense of humor; all proclaiming with one voice that what one is preparing for is legitimate, important, nay, sacred. Against this array of witnesses one's little doubts and amusements disintegrate. The cloak of Elijah can now be put on with the increasingly absolute conviction that not only is it there but that it firmly belongs on one's own shoulders.

The sociology of occupations gives one a magnificent panorama of the systematic delusions which people will adhere to in defense of their roles in society. Thus ministers will stoutly maintain, in the face of all evidence, that what they preach on Sunday has a real influence on the business decisions made by their parishioners on Monday. And insurance salesmen will tell one with probably genuine sincerity that their business is akin to the ministry in its humanitarian outlook. Morticians believe sincerely that respect for the dead can only be expressed by an elaborate (and, incidentally, costly) funeral. Advertising men believe that motivational research is nothing but the building of a bridge between manufacturer and consumer—the most democratic of enterprises. Psychoanalysts believe that charging a high fee is conducive to therapeutic results. All kinds of physicians believe that defending their right to charge what the traffic will bear is equivalent to defending the achievements of medicine itself. Farmers believe simultaneously that the government is a dangerous octopus devouring our liberties and that it ought to give them foolproof guarantees against possible economic loss. And government officials believe simultaneously that the budget must be curtailed and that their staff must be expanded. All such occupational ideologies afford excellent exercises for the sociology of knowledge. And in each case we can observe the development of a particular point of view following logically out of the identification with a certain role and a certain group of people sharing that role. Occupational ideologies vary both in terms of intellectual comprehensiveness and in the degree of distortion they inflict upon social reality. What they have in common is their basic function of justifying the occupational enterprise, giving the members of an occupation a particular picture of themselves and of the world in which they live.

It might be mentioned in passing (to round out the picture of this comedy) that the occupations whose avowed mission is the scientific study of society are in no way immune from this ideological tendency. Thus sociologists whose theoretical system places great emphasis on functionality will tend to disregard phenomena of *dis*function in society.[31] Economists will tend to raise to the dignity of natural law their particular preferences in the field of economic action.[32] Political scientists, fascinated by the intricacies of constitutional analysis, will frequently verify in their pronouncements the observation of the German comic poet Christian Morgenstern that "what *may* not be, *can* not be." We might also mention social workers, who will firmly state that the purpose of their undertaking is to help deviant individuals to adjust to society, and

who are then deeply outraged when one points out to them
that they are thereby functioning as the kinder arm of the
police forces. If one would go on now and discuss in detail
the factional disputes between different schools of the same
academic discipline, and the surrealistic distortions of reality
to which such vested interests drive their adherents, the
comedy would take on the character of a savage farce. Suffice
it to say that the scholarly cloak of the social scientist is anything but a safe protection against the hazards of ideological
befuddlement.

Nevertheless, as this chapter may have shown, the social
sciences (especially as developed in America) provide some
intellectual tools with the help of which a fairly viable observation tower on society *may* be constructed. The unfortunate
fact that instead these tools are frequently used to construct
underground shelters for systematic fanatics, whose last wish
would be to look at the social scene in the light of day, does
not change this. It might also be possible to speculate as to
why this possibility arose in America, of all places, despite the
fact that American society has been preserved from many of
the jolts and shocks that other societies have gone through.
The reason might well lie in the pioneer background (still a
very recent one) of this society. Take the academic carnival,
as an example. When a group of academicians get together in
some brand-new Midwestern college, built on the ill-gotten
gains of some philanthropic railroad tycoon, teaching in imitation Tudor buildings to bored sons of ranch owners aspiring
to become grain speculators—when these academicians then
assemble in medieval robes and hand out diplomas in Latin—
under such circumstances it is a little easier to see society as
a bag of tricks than amid the time-ingrained fetishism of, say,
Oxford or Cambridge. This does *not* mean that Oxford is the
real goods, while Iowa can only pretend. Far from it. It just
means that the Iowa instructor has a better chance of seeing
the whole thing in the perspective of a county fair than the
Oxford don. Again, it is another story that with greater

maturity as a society America is progressively losing this refreshing slant on reality.

It is sometimes remarked that the social sciences produce a melancholy picture of determinism. For just this reason sociology is possibly in the best position to take over the title of "the dismal science" once applied to economics. Certainly there are areas in the social sciences in which a sense of determinism is almost unavoidable. The area of social stratification is one such—the gloomy recognition that class and caste determine not only one's economic chances in life, one's style of life, and the things one may expect to achieve, but also one's tastes and morals (even to the point of one's sexual preferences, which one had liked to think of as the most private of eccentricities), and even one's chances of health and (literally) one's life expectancy. Other areas of the social sciences, such as social psychology, constitute a formidable threat to any highly voluntaristic doctrine of man. Yet we would contend that, taking the total output of the social sciences as a background to our thinking, it is not so much determination as fictitiousness which is the main impression. In other words, it is the dramatic conception of social existence which we tried to outline in this chapter. The social sciences present us not so much with man the slave as with man the clown. The precariousness of personal identity in society is to be seen the result not so much of iron bondage but of the dramatic necessities of the stage. It is true that, like the physical man, social man is a most sensitive creature. Just a little more heat, or a little more cold, and man dies on the spot. Just a little social rebuff, a couple of picayune failures, and the precious construction of self-esteem and self-respect falls to pieces. But most of the bonds that bind us are invisible, myths, conventions, fictions agreed upon as rules of the game. It is not so much these fictions themselves that bind us as our own social natures. We *want* to be part of the game and thus we accept, assimilate, and fervently believe its regulations. The result of a serious immersion in the social sciences is that this fictitious universe is breached, if only to the extent of a little finger stuck through a colossal zeppelin. This is why the serious pursuit of the social sciences is a dangerous undertaking and well deserves the suspicious attention of all guardians of public order.

Erasmus describes very well what will happen to a man who shows up on the stage, tears the masks off the actors' faces, and reveals the comedy for what it is.[33] He will end up being thrown out on his ear. If this does not happen inevitably on the stage of society, the reason very often is a general lack of good police organization. But, quite apart from this, the debunker in the social sciences might occasionally ask himself what right he has to even try to disturb the play, to open eyes, and to point to the Potemkin villages. If one is fairly pessimistic about social progress (as social scientists will naturally tend to be), the only plausible answer is a belief in the possibility of human freedom. And freedom begins with consciousness.

We may conclude with a picture. If we combine the notion of determination with that of drama we arrive at a provocative vision—that of the puppet theater. And thus we perceive men running about to and fro on the stage, going through the motions of the play—all the time with keys turning slowly and predictably in their backs. But there is one decisive difference between the puppet theater and the social stage. We may, indeed, be puppets of society, but with a strange, almost sinister capacity. For we can stop in our tracks, turn around and look over our shoulders—and perceive the keys turning in our backs. This act of consciousness is the first step into freedom. That this act is a possibility is the decisive justification of the social-scientific enterprise.

4. The Stage Is Made of Cardboard Paper (Nonscholarly Remarks)

THE PERCEPTION OF SOCIETY AS DRAMATIC FICTION MAY BE SHOCK-
ING AT FIRST. FURTHER REFLECTION ABOUT IT REVEALS THE
DEEPLY COMIC ASPECT OF SOCIAL EXISTENCE. THERE IS A LIBERAT-
ING QUALITY TO THIS REVELATION.

Any task in scientific understanding is necessarily serious in its mood. The social sciences are no exception to this. However, we would contend that this need not mean at all that social-scientific insights can only be used within a grimly humorless perspective on the world. We would even go further than that and argue that the terrible seriousness of much sociological writing presents not only a literary problem but also an analytic one. It is not just that such writing is very boring, but it is quite possible that the total absence of any sense of humor actually interferes with the attempt to give an intellectually adequate picture of society. The preceding chapter has given us a picture of society as a dramatic stage. To grasp fully the existential import of this picture it may be necessary to look at its comic aspects in a quite nonscholarly way. Our perspective on social reality then undergoes a change of mood. We may now see society as a costume party and its actors not too far removed from children playing with awesome titles. We would argue that an understanding of society which does not, somewhere and in some form, contain this perspective is liable to distort the social reality. It should not be difficult to see why this is so. Society has, indeed, the character of a costume party. To take the costume party too seriously means *ipso facto* missing an essential aspect of social reality. Sometimes we must laugh in order to perceive.

It is hardly a coincidence that some of the best jokes are

Jewish jokes. The margins of society have been the Jewish habitat for many centuries. From a marginal position one sees things more clearly—and therefore more comically! It may well be that the same social forces which have produced such a great number of Jewish analysts and interpreters of society also underlie the phenomenon of Jewish humor.[1] The humorous capacity to put oneself in the other's position, to look at oneself doubtfully and self-critically, to take all serious matters with a grain of salt—these classically Jewish characteristics may all be seen as the fruits of marginality. We would argue that a measure of these is necessary for an adequate perception of the social stage.

Within American social science the best example of the intellectual possibilities of satire and the comic perspective in general is afforded by the work of Thorstein Veblen. However, we would turn for a moment to the work of a European sociologist. Georg Simmel has called sociability the autonomous or play form of sociation.[2] It is certainly true that at a party, an occasion of pure sociability, all interaction between people takes on the character of a game. Like all games, the game of sociability sets up an artificial universe with artificial rules. Behavior within this charmed circle is different from what it is outside. Simmel points out how eroticism becomes coquetry, communication becomes conversation, ethics becomes tact—in all these cases sociability creates a play form of what outside would be an earnest activity. Under the aspect of sociability, society can be enjoyed as a fascinating pastime, a "human comedy," in which one is involved but which one need not take with ultimate seriousness. To quote Simmel:

"The connection between sociability and play explains why sociability should cover all phenomena that already by themselves may be considered sociological play-forms. This refers above all to games proper, which in the sociability of all times have played a conspicuous role. The expression 'social game' is significant in the deeper sense to which I have already called attention. All the forms of interaction or sociation among men—the wish to outdo, exchange, the formation of parties, the desire to wrest something from the other, the hazards of accidental meetings and separations, the change between enmity and cooperation, all overpowering by ruse and revenge—in the seriousness of reality, all of these are inbued with purposive contents. In the game, they lead their own lives; they are propelled exclusively by their own attraction. For even where the game involves a monetary stake, it is not the money (after all, it could be acquired in many ways other than gambling) that is the specific characteristic of the game. To the person who really enjoys it, its attraction rather lies in the dynamics and hazards of the sociologically significant forms of activity themselves. *The more profound, double sense of 'social game' is that not only the game is played in a society (as its external medium) but that, with its help, people actually 'play society.'*"[3]

It is clear that the comic perspective on human existence is particulary close at hand in this play world of sociability—despite the fact that "comedy" and "play" are categories that are not synonymous, albeit closely related.[4] This is why parties afford such a delightful occasion for observing and participating in the comedy of human foibles, vanities, deceits, and imagination. While etiquette establishes the ground rules for the game (and these are obviously different in different social contexts—say, between a cocktail party on Park Avenue and a church bazaar in Tennessee), there is near-infinite variation in the combinations and permutations that the participants at the party may construct. While this chapter is labeled as nonscholarly, it might be permissible to remark that an excellent commentary on Simmel's conception of sociability is to be found in the writings of Stephen Potter.[5] The world of sociability is an intricate work of art. As such it is very precarious indeed. What Potter calls "ploying" is the subtle destruction of the web of understandings that holds this world together. Etiquette provides the glittering façade of this social edifice. The "ploy" is the gentle but deliberate touch that makes the façade fall in—revealing that it was made of cardboard paper in the first place.

Take the world of a New York cocktail party. However sophisticated this world takes itself to be, it has an etiquette of its own, in which some things are taken for granted and

some are not. To appear at such a party in the role of a
Southern fundamentalist may quickly cause sufficient embarrassment and lack of ease to threaten the whole edifice with
collapse. We might call this an American adaptation of what
Potter calls "religionship." Incidentally, "religionship" is an
excellent method in almost any American gathering to disrupt
the flow of interaction. Almost any social demand can be
effectively countered by saying, "I'm sorry, but this is against
my religious principles"—no matter whether this involves
having a drink, telling a bit of gossip, or participating in a
parlor game, people will almost never ask *what* those religious
principles are. The writer has had occasion a number of times
of falling back upon this gambit and can guarantee a very
high probability of success. Switching the scene to Tennessee,
"religionship" in a different key can be used to destroy sociable
occasions there as effectively. The writer once had the opportunity of visiting a large educational establishment operated
by a fundamentalist sect in the South. The young lady who
served as a guide was patently eager to enter on a religious
argument and to start selling the particular message of salvation which her group was offering. It was also clear that
her approach would be tailored according to a system of
categories into which people might be fitted—somewhere along
a continuum of the sanctified, the saved, the lukewarm, and
the scoffers. When she finally brought herself to ask what the
writer's church affiliation was, she received the casual reply
that he was a Shi'ite Moslem. This, of course, prevented the
evangelistic machine from even getting into first gear.

Let it be said quickly that there is no intention here of
advocating this kind of drawing-room Machiavellianism. It is
simply suggested that a little Potterite experimentation will
readily offer an object lesson of what Simmel is talking about
when he calls the world of sociability a precarious artifact.
We would argue, however, that Simmel's conception can be
legitimately extended to a wider field. If Simmel speaks of
sociability and its games as "playing society," we find here a
startling resemblance with G. H. Mead and the role theory

coming from his work. Simmel is quite correct in viewing sociability in this light, as Mead is in understanding in the same way the playing of children. If we bring together Simmel's and Mead's perspectives, it would seem that this possibility of "playing society" would not exist at all unless society (that is, the "serious" society outside the charmed circle of the game) had in itself the character of a play. Seen in this wider perspective, the artificiality of the cocktail party is only of a special kind, not essentially different from the artificiality of the allegedly more "serious" forms of sociation. The social skills of the drawing room are actually (*mutatis mutandis*, of course) applicable to the "serious" arenas of life. In this fact lies the essential rightness of finishing schools and the validity of using the word "social" as it will be used by its headmistress. All of us learn "to be in society" as part of a game and by virtue of this training become capable of "going out into society." The character of society as game, play, drama is what explains this simple fact. Obviously the game will be different depending upon the sector of the great stage onto which we go. But everywhere we shall find the artifacts which define what the "social" means, everywhere there are certain very precarious rules of the game, which must be learned—and which can be skillfully broken. And this revelation of the precariousness of social structure is a comic revelation. It is of one stuff with the comedy of sociability. It is sociology under the aspect of laughter—not a bitter laughter but a redeeming one, as we shall have occasion to argue later on.

Society is a stage—the stage is made of cardboard paper. It is these twin proclamations of the comic revelation which underlie the peculiar fascination which the great swindler exercises on our imagination. For in the figure of the swindler is symbolized the liberating message that the walls of society are full of holes—for, lo and behold, the swindler comes and goes through the walls at will. The figure referred to is not, of course, the little embezzler or the cautious thief but the great artist of deception, the social gambler, the Napoleon of

impersonation, flattery, and fraudulence. One might think
here of such literary figures as Balzac's Rastignac, Gogol's
Inspector-General, Gide's Lacfadio and Protos, or Thomas
Mann's Felix Krull. But this figure is also very much part of
the American scene, and not only in literature. There is a
peculiarly American fascination with the really great gambler,
the fixer, the quick-talking sharpie, the confidence man in
his various incarnations—and a peculiarly American humor of
surrealistic braggadocio in which these figures are at home.
The salesman who sells a farmer ten elephants at cost, the
revivalist who comes into town and clears out in a brand-new
Cadillac, the bland-faced clerk-typist who bamboozles the
colonel and actually runs the regiment—all of them beckoning
that the ominous Goliath of society is afflicted with myopia,
trench mouth, and athlete's foot, and that there are other ways
of getting around him than by walking up bravely with a
slingshot. We can call this figure the great anti-Puritan dem-
iurge of the *other* America, the counter-hero of Horatio
Alger, about whom most Americans learn sooner or later in a
very *un*authorized civics course (which, if it needed a text-
book, might use selected works of H. L. Mencken). The
Puritan world was an unusally serious one. Its mores and
morals were protected against laughter with walls as thick as
men have ever devised. It is understandable that its counter-
world was bound to be an unusually picaresque one, with
laughter strong enough to pierce through this dungeon of
earnestness.

The great swindler is a very different figure from the rebel
or from the one who withdraws from society. Unlike these,
the swindler is fully in society. He understands it, operates
fully within it, and has all the skills needed to do so successfully. It is not only his morals which separate the swindler
from the average citizen but his perspective on social structure.
Unlike the average citizen, he sees through the pretense,
the "as-if-ness" of society. Consequently he has a better
understanding of what really goes on. Thus what to the

average citizen is *destiny* is for him a *possibility*. What to the average citizen is *law* is for him a *technique*. All men, as we have seen, have repertoires of roles which they play on the social stage. The difference between the swindler and the average citizen is that the former has a greater control over his repertoire. There is also a difference in the consciousness of one's roles. Both swindler and citizen may engage in morally reprehensible conduct. What is more, both may engage in propaganda campaigns to demonstrate that what they have done is really quite ethical. The swindler will typically know that his propaganda is for the consumption of a gullible audience. The citizen will believe his own propaganda. It might be added (shelving for the moment the question of ethics) that the swindler is typically the better sociologist. Which, incidentally, may be another reason why sociologists studying so-called "social pathology" can often be of fairly magnificent naïveté—after all, they normally follow the propaganda line of the cops.

The world of the erotic would be an excellent field to serve by way of illustration of the comic perspective. From time immemorial the erotic has revealed the fantastic fictions under which we live and thus given us a profound glimpse of the human condition under the aspect of the comic. One may, for instance, read Montaigne and then wonder how it is possible for anyone to even approach this subject in a mood other than the comic:

"And when I think, as I have done many a time, of the ridiculous titillation of this pleasure, the absurd, giddy, crackbrained emotions which it stirs up in Zeno and Cratippus, of that unreasonable rage, that countenance inflamed with fury and cruelty at the most delightful moment of love, and then that solemn, stern, ecstatic mien in so extravagant an action; when I consider besides that our joys and excrements are lodged together pell-mell, and that sensual pleasure at its height is attended, like pain, with faintness and moaning, I believe it is true what Plato says, that man is the plaything of the gods. . . . and that Nature was in a mocking mood when she left us that most common and most disturbing of our actions to make us all alike and put us on the same level, wise men and fools, men and beasts. The most contemplative and wisest of men, when I picture him in that attitude, appears to me a humbug with his wise and contemplative airs."[6]

The essence of the comic is always some sort of discrepancy. There are few discrepancies as comic as that between spirit and sexuality. A university professor bent on seduction may illustrate this discrepancy very well. Driven by forces that defy any spiritual interpretation, the libidinized scholar finds himself in strange and unaccustomed places, suddenly sees himself acting in ways that would have seemed unthinkable a few hours before. Yet we are not dealing here with pure biology without any relationship to the palace of the spirit. On the contrary. The tremendous intellectual energy, which perhaps was thrust for years against some mighty mystery of the cosmos, is now employed with full force to captivate some female whose mental capacity (in sober moments) our scholar would have regarded as barely anthropoid. The maneuvers of seduction now begin, an intricate pattern of ploy and counter-ploy, of flattery, deception, and self-deception, all geared to that one instant in which the spirit fades away into oblivion. Roles are put on and discarded instantaneously. He is now Don Giovanni, laughing out of a deep throat. But she is Messalina, who devours Don Giovannis as others eat breakfast cereals. Quick change. He is now very serious, the consoler, the one who understands, knows better and more deeply, would like to help. Quick change on her part. She is still Messalina, but a tormented one, in anguish, misunderstood, driven by things deep within her that she cannot understand, asking for kindness and help. *He* has a choice now. There are, after all, different ways of consoling. Whatever the outcome, be it bed or altar, it has been the result of an amazing sequence of gambits—which on the Broadway stage would probably be called quite unrealistic by the critics!

Our so-called sexual and marital mores are built out of *this* kind of material. Imagine, then, a totally earnest student studying the field of marriage and the family! He may read, for example, that the American family appears to be passing from a patriarchal through an equalitarian to a matriarchal pattern. These are still, no doubt, useful categories—though they will usually leave out the picturesque process of ploying and counter-ploying involved in this. But then he may be told very seriously that our courtship and marriage system is of the romantic type. He may then find a very detailed analysis of the romantic beliefs and norms in question, and perhaps even a mild suggestion that romanticism is not necessarily the best basis for a lasting marriage. Since all of this is quite true, in a way, and since the evidence has been carefully collected and documented, the student may actually end up with the conviction that he now seriously understands the subject. The reality, of course, is that the romantic experience normally functions as a ratification of decisions already undertaken for very different reasons, such as wanting to be respectable, exhaustion from the insecurities of bachelorhood, sexual frustration, boredom, or a possibility of economic gain. We are not suggesting here that people don't fall in love or that this experience cannot sometimes be the primary reason why they get married. We are just saying that, at any rate for most people, the experience is rather carefully engineered, consciously or unconsciously. Since women rationally have more to gain from marriage in our society, the engineering is more likely to be conscious in their case. That is, the men are more sincere in their emotional entrapments—in other words, they are more likely to believe their own propaganda. Now the real irony of the earnest study of this subject is that what began as an investigation of behavior ends up as a guidepost for it. After reading about the romantic pattern, even those who did not previously feel the need of this emotional ratification will now have to produce it, if not to convince themselves at least to convince their public.

Take the case of a girl in her middle twenties employed in some white-collar capacity in the provinces and beginning to

panic. She decides to go to graduate school. Upon arrival
there she expresses the overwhelming conviction that she
must enter the particular profession for which her course
is designed to equip her. Within three months she is going
steady—in fact, she is falling in love. Love being a volcano
that explodes where it will, it is obviously a coincidence that
this particular explosion is taking place in just the right
grooves of race, class, income bracket, and (last, not least)
marital status of the object. But after four months, on a most
romantic occasion, it comes out that there had been some
misapprehension about the last condition of the intoxication.
It turns out that the man is still legally married, though his
wife (let us assume) is confined to an insane asylum. Under
an administration of tender condolence and sharp questioning
it becomes clear that (let us assume further) he cannot think
of a divorce because of some particularly involved legal circumstances. At this point, or immediately thereafter, our
young lady realizes (she tells us) that she had not really fallen
in love at all. It had been a mistake. A few months later we
find her engaged. The same torrid experience, of course, but
this time only occurring after every possible aspect of *l'état
civil* has been prudently explored. She is radiant, she is happy,
she is madly in love. The madness stops short of real sex,
though. This is postponed either until the happiness has
been formally guaranteed by church and state or at least
until the engagement has been announced and it is clear that
its dissolution would be a most embarrassing matter to all
concerned. At that point the romantic pattern culminates in
apotheosis. Now this little story is a boring vignette that
anybody could construct by glancing at the society page any
day of the week. That is exactly the point. We are dealing with
a common American phenomenon. The earnest analysis of
all this is most likely to miss the crucial point—that the
romanticism operates as a mode of one-upmanship (or, if you
prefer, as an ideology). Whether the young lady does or
does not believe in the validity of her emotional experiences
is of minor interest here. That question has nothing to do

with romanticism but with the psychology of deception and self-deception. It might just be added that the girl will be operating more effectively (indeed, be one-up!) if her tactics are conscious.

The comic world is one of magic. The clown waves his wand and the walls disappear, the laws of gravity cease to apply, the gorilla turns out to be a fairy prince. The comic perspective on social structure makes the same magic leap into view (while the earnest perspective is frequently taken in by the magician). We can accompany our girl just one step further, to the foot of the altar. It is "five in the afternoon" on a sunny Sunday. It is a rather nervous bull that is being led here to his moment of truth. Let us assume that the key words are pronounced by the ecclesiastical functionary at 5:15 P.M. This is the magic moment. What would have been fornication at 5:10 P.M. is smiled upon by all at 5:20 P.M. The one magic moment changes all. The girl who now leaves the sanctuary is a different one from the girl who entered it a few minutes before. Everyone present believes it and everyone is quite touched. If we can imagine that the discarded lover of a few months ago is present in the audience, there is a good chance that he is deeply touched himself. For a moment he has a thick feeling in his throat, but then he too succumbs to the conjury of the occasion. Here she comes, a radiant young matron—and he had the audacity to think of her as a little bitch! Perhaps he catches her eye. In his look there is recognition, apology, and admiration. The magic has reconciled all.

It is not only the premarital phase of the erotic which can be seen as a Potterite process of ploying and one-up-manship. The process continues into the marital life itself, of course. It also is very much in evidence in the way in which the married couple presents itself to the outside world in what Erving Goffman has called "impression management."[7] Take the example of a young man, a bachelor, who frequently associates with a married couple. In this association there can be a very interesting process of one-upmanship. One

evening, say, the bachelor arrives just after a particularly
venomous exchange between the spouses. Now, naturally,
marital "impression management" demands that such domestic discords be kept out of sight of the general public.
Whatever has happened in bedroom, bathroom, or kitchen,
the couple emerges into the living room radiating matrimonial
bliss. But on this particular, evening the bachelor's arrival
takes place just too soon after the eruption for all the traces
to be removed from the stage. The husband still has a red
face and is angrily puffing on his tenth cigarette—the other
nine, half smoked and brutally squashed, are crowding one
tiny ash tray. The wife cannot quite switch yet from her
recent shrillness to the suave voice of polite conversation.
What is more, her hand is still trembling and her face is
white, lipstick smudged and hair come loose. Well, on this
evening there can be no doubt about the bachelor being
one-up. Into this scene of squalid domesticity he steps as
the hero of wild and reckless freedom. He brings with him
the aroma of a wider world in which sophisticated men and
women live mature, modern lives. This is how it seems to
him and this is also how he looks to the distraught couple
trying hard to gather about them their social wits. But now
let us take another evening, a few weeks hence. This time there
has been no quarrel. As a matter of fact, a sort of uneasy,
almost comfortable armistice has reigned for several days.
Our bachelor, on the other hand, has just had his third
sexual rebuff in one week. He is thoroughly frustrated and
has been thinking about his age. For dinner he has had to eat
a badly burned steak, and the reason he burned it in the first
place is that he lost track of time standing in front of the
mirror and meditating on his visibly expanding bald spot.
Tonight the roles are reversed. Our bachelor is the poor
traveler on roads of loneliness who is being permitted for one
brief moment to warm himself at this happy hearth. The
one-upness of the couple is clearly recognized by all three
parties. Indeed, so much is the wife one-up that she finds
herself asking solicitously about the bachelor's love life and

mentioning, after his hollow laugh, that there is a new girl working in her office, not quite young, and hardly a beauty, but . . .

In the example of nuptial sorcery above we touched upon what is possibly the element of social life in which fictitiousness may be obvious more readily than anywhere else—namely, the world of law. A person working in a printing press once remarked that it was a continuing marvel to him how he could keep on reading books and taking all these words seriously once he started putting them together on his job. The writer has had parallel wonderings about lawyers, but since even gynecologists marry it is perhaps not surprising that lawyers exist who take the law very seriously. While there are many human activities in which magic plays an important part, in the legal enterprise it is the essence of the matter. Any piece of litigation presents us with the spectacle of competing wizards struggling to imprison and then magically transform reality by this or the other formula of incantation. It is not surprising that the litigants have great difficulty recognizing themselves and what happened between them in either of the formulae. It is also a great pity that American jurisprudence has done away with much of the mummery of its British heritage. One *should* wear a wig when pronouncing incantations! Sit in any court, criminal or civil, and you can see the fictitiousness of society being just about thrown in your face within a span of a few hours. People are transformed magically before your eyes. The married are pronounced single. Bastards are pronounced adopted. The citizen becomes a criminal in one instant and a convict in the next. Corporate persons are created *ex nihilo* and dissolved again into the nothingness out of which they came. What before was individual knavery is now corporate finance. What was a lighthearted misdemeanor becomes a felony. And the felony may fail to be pronounced because somebody mumbled, or failed to mumble, some words at a crucial moment. This witchcraft goes on day in and day out. Some of it is benign, even necessary; much of it, all the same, operating very much as voodoo maledictions do. Both the law and the maledictions can operate only because most people believe in their fictions. The relatively few cops who can enforce the law are just about adequate to deal with those who insist on contempt of court. The voodoo man, for the same purpose, has a limited supply of poison soups.[8]

As soon as we get beyond the strictly technological aspects of society, there are few of its aspects that cannot be sharply illuminated in this comic perspective of fictitiousness. Whether one looks at the world of learning, or the world of power, or the world of religion—everywhere one will find actors carefully masked and costumed to put over some magnificent fakery on the rest of the cast. A good case in point is the progress of a young scholar from the status of graduate-student nonentity to that of academic oracle. What is especially interesting is that, in many cases, this progress has nothing whatsoever to do with intellectual prowess or learned achievement yet may outwardly look exactly like the progress of a genuine giant of the spirit. Take a young scholar of moderate intelligence and mediocre imagination but with some abilities in the art of erudite one-upmanship. Let us call him Smith. It is his good fortune that he is studying at the school which houses the brilliant professor Tatarescu. Let us emphasize again that he is studying at Tatarescu's *school* —whether Smith ever studied with Tatarescu himself is of little significance. While a graduate student, Smith had little use for Tatarescu, indeed belonged to a little circle of bright young men who condescendingly told funny stories about the old man and were all agreed that he was far behind the times in the field. Let us also assume, for the sake of the argument, that Tatarescu is one of those scholars (rapidly becoming extinct in the United States) who have little interest in publication and whose influence is therefore confined to a rather limited circle. Well, let us allow Smith to graduate, by the skin of his teeth, and start looking for a job. Through a friend he receives an interview at an obscure denominational college in the remoter hinterlands. By a freak of fate it happens that the dean who interviews Smith has heard of Tatarescu, expresses his interest in any scholar in Tatarescu's field actually coming from Tatarescu's school, and how is the old man, and so forth. Within the thirty minutes of the interview Smith has transformed himself into an avid Tatarescan. He reserves his right, of course, to differ with the master on some minor points of interpretation—but all, mind you, within the Tatarescan system. Unfortunately Smith knows very little about this system, is not even sure there really is one. But there are several months left before the beginning of Smith's activities at his provincial seat of learning—time enough to Tatarescanize oneself. A little rummaging in old journals, some casual borrowing of other people's notebooks on Tatarescu's courses, perhaps even a little visit of loyal homage to the master himself, and the task is accomplished. Smith begins his teaching career. Since he is a young bachelor and 40 per cent of his students are girls, and since (not knowing how else to fill fifty minutes of class time) he is more entertaining than educational, he is a great success at the college.

In response to his popularity with the students, his grading becomes progressively more lenient, which in turn increases his popularity. His first articles are written—very modest, rigidly circumscribed intellectual exercises, mentioning loyally the author's profound indebtedness to Tatarescu. What with the printing of these articles and the fact that his students believe everything he says, Smith is beginning to think that perhaps there is more to his own scholarship than he suspected. His new assurance is noticed and, since he is popular with students and since bright young men have a way of leaving the hinterland, he is rather quickly promoted. With each national convention of his learned society Smith makes his appearance with a firmer tread. True enough, it is not too long before he receives and accepts a call to a not-too-obscure college in what is definitely *not* the hinterland. By the time he has been there a couple of years he has taken on the demeanor of an academic nabob. Within the limits of

his capacities he has developed the rudimentary Tatarescan
system with which he began, but the name of Tatarescu is
now rarely mentioned in his teaching or in his increasingly
frequent publications. In fact, he is rather anxious (if the
subject comes up) to dissociate himself from his former
master. Indeed, it is not long before another young man
(younger than Smith and currently teaching in the very re-
mote hinterland indeed) presents a paper at one of the conventions and actually speaks of the "Smithian approach."
From now on Smith has arrived. The journals are open to
him. At the conventions he moves strictly in buyer circles
(he has now become department head). He writes recommendations, endorses research proposals, reviews important
books, and receives lavish grants. From now on he can say or
write whatever he pleases—or, for that matter, say or write
nothing at all. It is well-nigh impossible for him to be dis-
lodged from the status he now occupies. So much for
academic careers.

Another very interesting area of fictions is the world of
power. It goes without saying, of course, that power is an
important fact in any society. It is a fact that some men
always command while others obey. But it is also a fact that
only very rarely is power based on tangible superiority in the
means to impose one's will. Sometimes a man becomes chief
by having a bigger stick. More commonly he just succeeds
in convincing the rest of the tribe that his stick is bigger (or
that he has a stick at all). This is as true of "civilized" societies
as it is of "primitive" ones. An illuminating example is the
attempts of various categories of social scientists to determine
exactly what groups hold power in a society. The writer
recently had an experience with one such attempt that
illustrates the point. An American sociologist recently made
another study of the organization of power in our society.[9]
Among other findings the study listed a number of groups
thought to be high up in the power structure. The writer
mentioned this finding to a fairly important functionary of
one of the groups thus listed. The functionary had not heard

of the study, was greatly excited and pleased by the report, and was going to tell other people in the organization. Or, as a Jewish joke recounts the landing of Columbus in America, the Indians said: "Thank God, we are discovered!"

It might be pointed out here that this incident does not necessarily throw doubt on the findings of the study. It is very probably one of the key characteristics of power structure in our society that many of the people in it are nervously uncertain of their position. Viewed from the outside (say, from the lower reaches in which sociologists have their social being), the organization of power may appear as a monumental monolith. Seen from the inside, it may be the most confusing of arrangements. For example, it is highly unlikely that any one individual can have an intelligible overview of power in a society as complex as ours. As long as he cannot achieve such an overview, he cannot be quite sure of his own position. Putting this in another way, the effective exercise of power depends upon accurate information. When an organization of power has to depend on information upon an immensely complex bureaucracy handling its channels of information, nobody can really be sure that the communications that land on his desk are not an accidental or deliberate distortion. The result of this is not only that one arm of the organization may be in total ignorance of what another arm is doing. The final result of this situation may well be that top-level Washington reads the Washington newspapers to find out what goes on in top-level Washington. "*May* well be?" We can only hope that the use of the subjunctive is justified!

The suspicion that the world of power is not what we thought is not only disturbing because we live in an age in which wrong information can easily lead to global disaster. There is a more ancient origin to our disturbance. There remains something in all of us of the childish belief that there is a world of grownups *who know*. There *must* be—because we, evidently, *don't know*. It is very shocking then to suspect that the knowers do not exist at all. Everyone is groping around in the dark, just as we are.[10] In the political area this is, perhaps, the most subversive of thoughts—the dawning realization that the great policy-makers may be as uncertain as we are as to what their next move is going to be!

Perhaps it is this suspicion—that the knowers do not exist—which can sum up the general state of mind that results from the comic revelation that society is fiction, magic, precariousness. The expertise of all the experts is painfully synthetic, whether they specialize in love or learning, power or (as we shall still have occasion to see) faith. Again we would contend that this attitude is not a one-sidedly oppressive one. It also has a liberating side. For while it is rather bad news to hear that the oracles are ghostwritten by nervous little men who copy from each other, there is also some comfort in this news. While it may undermine our civic confidence it may at the same time restore our trust in our own stature. If there are no oracles, there may be something to our own knowledge!

It would certainly be a misunderstanding of this chapter if it were interpreted as a polemic against the serious study of society. Far from it. But if, as we tried to show in the last chapter, the serious study of society presents us with a picture of society as a dramatic stage, the notion of fictitiousness which this picture brings with it calls for the comic perspective. The revelation of the comic character of society is important not only for understanding it intellectually but also for seeking a path of moral action within society. This will be the problem of the next chapter. As for this one, we might refer to the German satirist Kurt Tucholsky. This was the insight which Tucholsky enjoined upon his reader, a simple one, almost a truism, yet the beginning point of any understanding of the world of men: Things are not what they seem. They are different. Quite, quite different.

5. Fiction and Alibi

TO TAKE THE FICTIONS AS REALITY CAN BECOME A MORAL ALIBI.
IT THEN BECOMES POSSIBLE TO AVOID RESPONSIBILITY FOR ONE'S
ACTIONS. TO LIVE IN UNPERCEIVED FICTIONS IS MORALLY DANGEROUS
BECAUSE IT LEADS TO INAUTHENTICITY.

There is a certain tension between a perception of society as
it has been described in the last few chapters and having
any sort of moral hopes about society. If we look at society
with the expectation, however timid, of finding in it some
possibility of moral engagement, we are always prone to the
temptation of taking some particularly attractive fiction seriously after all. When the drums begin to roll many a social
skeptic begins to look at the flag with a newly throbbing
heart. When one's children begin to grow up and ask questions, one begins to answer them with consideration for their
childish tenderness, then later one begins to believe the
answers one gave—if only because one would like one's children to live in a world that has moral validity. Or to take
another example, if one has any commitment at all to the
Christian faith, the temptation to find hope in the empirical
church when there is none is almost irresistible. This is why
total cynicism often makes for good social perception (even
though sometimes the total cynic misses precisely those moral
factors in a situation which do not fit into his frame of
reference and which, since man does have moral aspirations,
are often important elements of social reality). One is reminded here of the comment made somewhere by H. L.
Mencken to the effect that he had a constitutional incapacity
for outrage. This incapacity may be of help if one wants to
see clearly. Like any passion, outrage tends to cloud our vision.

There are people who share the insight into the precariousness of society but not the moral reaction to the crimes committed in the name of that society. There are occasions
when the consciousness we have tried to delineate may find
itself in alliance with the cynical consciousness. Situations
in the military may be a good example of this, where a
common "them" can be found in the tyranny which seeks
to impose itself on one's dignity and which one resists in
various ways. The cynic may not only see but act in a way
very similar to "ours." But there are other situations in
which the ways would part sharply. The cynic may see very
clearly what the racial situation is, but it is very unlikely
that his actions will somehow seek to change that situation.
Racial beliefs and racial oppression are for him but another
instance of the pervasive stupidity of society. In other words,
we can often share with the cynic our contempt—our moral
outrage divides us.[1] Consequently it is impossible to arrest
ourselves at the stage which our argument has reached in the
last chapter. We cannot limit ourselves to the perception of
the fictitiousness of society, but we must go on and raise
the question of its moral significance. We can only hope
that our perception does not dissolve in this process.

It may be in order here to return to the case of capital
punishment. When a man is processed toward his execution
in our society, great care is taken to make it clear at each
step that nobody involved is carrying out a personal act—that
is, an act for which he is personally accountable. Of course
he is supposed to be accountable in his particular social role
—that is, he is supposed to be a good judge, a good prosecutor,
a good hangman—but it is maintained that his accountability
is limited to this role, that he is accountable *qua* judge but
not *qua* the one, individual, unique human being that he is
personally. Thus a prosecutor may say that, irrespective of his
personal feelings, *qua* prosecutor he has no option but to
prosecute a defendant to the limits of the law—which may
include asking for the death penalty. The jury in the case
may be most carefully instructed to dismiss completely from

their minds the issue of punishment; in the drama of the courtroom their part is strictly limited to determining the defendant's guilt or innocence—his fate after the verdict is none of their business. The judge, when he pronounces the death sentence, is again supposed to act in a strictly non-personal way; he may, like the prosecutor, say that he had no option whatever once the verdict was given—and, of course, in the world of legal fiction he may be quite right. Whoever else may later be involved in the matter—other judges, boards of pardon, the governor of the state, and the warden of the prison—will all act or fail to act within the same magic circle of personal nonaccountability. Even the person who eventually springs the trap, releases the electricity or the poison gas is supposed to act in a strictly nonpersonal way. This final fiction is perhaps best illustrated by the practice in some American prisons of having several electric switches pulled by several individuals—only one switch releases the current into the body of the man in the electric chair and nobody is supposed to know which switch it is. The same idea is behind the practice at military executions of including blanks among the bullets issued to the firing squad—nobody will know whether his shot contributed to the killing. We can put the matter quite simply. Nobody did any killing at all. It was the law itself that killed. But the law, as we know very well, is incapable of killing. Only men kill. And a man is dead. There must, then, be something radically wrong with the whole argument.

We would contend that the process is one of bad faith from beginning to end. It is a lie that prosecutor and judge have no option. At the very least they have the option of resigning from their positions. They also have the option of defying the law. It is a lie that the jury can dismiss from their minds the question of punishment. At each moment of the trial the matter of the life or death of a man lies in their hands—and they know it. It is a lie that their positions dictate to the governor or the members of the pardons board what course of action they must take. These positions are defined arbitrarily by men and men are capable of redefining them. No matter what method of deceit is finally used in the execution itself, it is a lie that nobody is doing any killing. A man is dead and his killers are known. They are Mr. Smith, the district attorney; Mr. Brown, the judge; Mr. Jones, the warden—and so on, by name and most personally indeed, to the executioner. This is the reality. The rest is fiction, mythology, alibi.

It is interesting that many people who would be shocked by this interpretation would have wholeheartedly endorsed the verdicts of the trials of Nazi war criminals. The position taken at these trials was that the Nazi legal system could not be used as an alibi for carrying out Nazi criminal orders. It is important to point out here that, strictly speaking, whatever the Nazis did was within the law—their law, that is. Thus the jurisdiction of the SS was carefully defined legally as against the jurisdiction of the German courts; at a certain point, the Jews were carefully removed from the jurisdiction of the German courts into that of the SS; within the SS organization there were carefully worked-out regulations and competences. Of course, at some stage of the game somebody's competence included certain gas chambers—but it would obviously be ludicrous, under the law, to hold him personally accountable for this bureaucratic exigency. Let it be emphasized most strongly that the differences between an SS colonel and our warden in an American penitentiary, many though they may be, do not touch upon the point at issue here. *Men who kill are responsible for their actions.* If there is justification of the actions, they as men must provide the justification. They cannot fall back upon a social alibi. Those denying this interpretation might point out that this imposes a terrible burden on individuals—that, perhaps, we might find nobody to do certain unpleasant jobs if this point of view was generally adopted. This is quite true—and that is exactly why these fictions were concocted. But our concern at the moment is not with the recruitment of judges and prison guards. The burden of personal responsibility is not imposed by a certain interpretation but by the reality of human existence. The question is not whether such a burden is pleasant but whether it can be safely denied. Finally, it might be argued more broadly that legal fictions are probably a necessity of society. This, again, may be quite true. All of us are involved in this great game of social make-believe. All of us will have the chance of playing certain parts with relish. We become grown-up men, husbands, admirals, archbishops, boxing champions, and judges of the supreme court of errors. Much of this game can be harmless. The moral dimension becomes relevant when the game begins to involve murder. The task of conscience at that instance is to tell the children to stop playing.

Insofar as the writer of this essay understands Sartre, it is intended that the term "bad faith" be understood in a sense analogous to Sartre's.[2] The writer hopes that Sartre's meaning is not distorted too far if the term is used here, within the context of our argument, as indicating the use of social fictions for the providing of moral alibis. In other words, we understand a man to be in bad faith who excuses himself by pointing to his social role and to the ideologies in which the role is enveloped. Still very much conscious of his philosophical incompetency, the writer also feels that Heidegger's concept of social generality as expressed in his term "*das Man*" is also very relevant to our argument.[3] It is now in order to develop this within our argument.

The possibility of bad faith means that the fictitiousness of society is morally significant. Bad faith means that society assists us in hiding our own actions from our awareness. The role becomes a moral alibi. It goes without saying that this possibility is inherent in the most basic way in our social existence. Indeed, if this possibility did not exist the process of socialization could not take place. Already a very little boy will put on his cowboy uniform and inform his mother that he is now speaking to her not as little Johnny but as Davy Crockett. As our little boy grows up he only continues the same operation in a more serious vein—that is, while he

knew very well that he was putting on an act when he
addressed his mother as Davy Crockett, he now seriously
believes himself that a magical change occurs when he speaks
to her not as her son but as a patriot, a priest, or a representative of other broader interests. The reason why it is difficult
to be a prophet in one's home town is that most mothers
are struck by the similarity between the old and the new
masquerade—there goes Johnny with a new hat! But others,
who cannot remember little Johnny playing at being an
important person in the big world, are ordinarily quite ready
to be impressed. Take, for example, a man who is the perfect
figure of a judge. Each gesture, each word, is in perfect
harmony with the role upon the bench. In fact, one is tempted
to say that this man *is* truly his role. If we later find out
that our man liked nothing better as a child than to enact
the most sinister occasions of a judge's work, we may see
things differently. This illustration, by the way, is taken from
life. In 1952 a British newspaper contained the following delightful episode from the boyhood of Lord Goddard, then
Lord Chief Justice and one of the staunchest defenders of
capital punishment:

"When he first went to Marlborough, it was apparently a school
custom to make every new boy sing or recite in his dormitory.
Called upon to sing, the future Lord Chief Justice is said to have
surprised the other boys by chanting in a piping voice: 'You will
be taken from here to a place of execution and hanged by the
neck until you be dead. And may the Lord have mercy on your
soul.'"[4]

As we know, this little boy had excellent opportunity later on
to carry out his fantasy. If such biographical information does
anything it sharply illuminates the bad faith of the role being
used as a moral alibi. It makes clear that, after all, it is the
man who chooses, accepts, or at least assents to the role. He
cannot escape the responsibility of his own choice. When he
tries to escape he is forced to lie.

The astonishing thing is that commonly not only is it the

oppressor who envelops his actions in the fictions of his role, but the victim is seriously expected to do the same. What is even more astonishing is that sometimes he fulfills this expectation. This can again be illustrated by certain cases involving the death penalty, cases in which the intended victim succeeds in keeping himself alive for a number of years by using every legal trick available to him or his lawyers. There are many people, especially in the legal profession, who are morally annoyed by such behavior and whose attitude toward the prisoner is stiffened because he carried on these evasive tactics. Recently, in refusing another appeal from one such prisoner, a state supreme court blamed him for playing a cat-and-mouse game with the courts and thus making a mockery of the legal process. It may be worthwhile to imagine how the prisoner ought to have behaved in order to have the respect of these august gentlemen. He might perhaps have written a letter to the court, saying that he very much wanted to live or even that he was innocent of the crime, but that he had a very high regard for due procedures of law and, knowing very well the overcrowded condition of our courts and the difficult existence of judges, he now preferred to be executed quickly and respectably, without further ado. Put in these terms, such a reaction might seem absurd, but even such instances occur in real life. Preceding the execution of a prisoner convicted of having been a Russian spy by a German military tribunal during World War I, the man spent the major part of the time left to him preparing himself for the execution as one would for a parade. He even read the German military manual containing the instructions for executions. When the day came he was ready. He died not only bravely but correctly—literally by the book. We may take it for granted that he had the full respect of the young officer who fired the last bullet into his neck. Here bad faith is not an alibi from guilt but rather an alibi from terror. Both torturer and victim are in bad faith. The torturer says, "I am not killing—a military execution is taking place." The victim says, "I am not dying—a military execution is taking place."

The bad faith of the victim is one of those merciful veils which nature often lets fall over the consciousness of animals in torment. The bad faith of the torturer is one of the few convincing arguments for a doctrine of hell.

The following episode might serve to illustrate that such collusion in deceit is not inevitable. During the French collapse of 1940 the story has been told of an anti-Nazi refugee trying to get away from the advancing German troops and being stopped by a French gendarme. The latter examined the refugee's papers and found that he had no police permit to be in that department, thereupon told the refugee to accompany him to his station. The refugee tried to argue with him, pointing out that the Germans might arrive any moment, that if they caught him it would mean his certain death, then added: "And you are a Frenchman too. What is achieved if you help the Germans to kill me?" To which the gendarme replied: "We shall both have the satisfaction of knowing that you died in accordance with the laws of the French Republic." He then looked at his watch, advanced it several hours, and added: "I note officially that it is now 5:05 P.M. I go off duty at 5:00. I am now off duty. I shall now tell you the best way to get out of here."

Modern bureaucratic procedures provide an excellent occasion for the denial of personal responsibility. However, it would be an error to put all the blame on bureaucracy or to regard bad faith as a peculiar modern invention. This is quite fashionable today, in line with the painting of horror frescos depicting "mass society," but it is hardly accurate. Bad faith, in the sense here described, must have been an accompaniment of the earliest human societies. While the modern hangman has, as it were, a more streamlined model of the old thing, the most savage chieftain chopping off a head in the name of a demon of revenge possessing his body is practicing bad faith in just the same sense. We are dealing here with original sin indeed—that is, sin presumably dating from the origins of the human adventure. It is most difficult to imagine any society not containing the possibility of bad faith. Perhaps bad faith is one of the essential ingredients of being human. Which is another way of putting what was once expressed by someone who defined man as the animal that can hide.

It is not necessary to go to the extreme situations of human life in society to see in operation this mechanism of evading the moral questions. For example, the ideologies of occupations provide very much the kind of alibi in economic life that national and military creeds do in wartime, or that the law does in the administration of what is commonly called justice. "Business is business" sums this up fairly well. It means that little Johnny is putting on one of his magic hats and announcing: "I'm not speaking to you now as John Smith. I'm not speaking to you either as your friend, your neighbor, and your prospective brother-in-law. I'm speaking to you as chairman of the board of this company. As such, I have no option but to say to you what I just said." At which point the knife falls. The interesting problem, once more, is contained in the words "no option." Now it is perfectly true that there are economic necessities over which our man has no control. It may, for example, be true that he can only stay in business by dumping inferior products under threat of some kind of economic blackmail. That's the way this business is, there's nothing to be done about it, and the alternative is bankruptcy. True enough. This does not change the fact that the man has first of all chosen to go into this kind of business, probably knowing what its economic realities are. What is more important, it is he who accepts and assents to the so-called economic necessities. If the alternative to blackmail is really bankruptcy, then it is he who chooses not to go bankrupt. Now it may quickly be said that the man could never make the other choice, that he has a family to support, stockholders to face, and so on. Again, true enough. But then let him say honestly that he is performing blackmail for the sake of his family and his stockholders. In other words, between the possibilities of blackmail and bankruptcy, he is opting for the former. It need not be our concern at the

moment what the moral implications of this choice are. It is
enough to point out that the alibi "no option" will not with-
stand even a cursory examination.

To put this in a different way, all our actions have a price.
It is we who decide at what point we agree to be bought. As
in the story of a conversation between a very sophisticated
gentleman and a very respectable lady at a party. They are
talking about prostitution. "Well," says the gentleman, "just
for the sake of our argument, suppose I offered you $1000—
would you spend the night with me?" The lady, smiling
coquettishly: "Who knows—I might very well!" The gentleman: "Now suppose I offer you $10 for the night?" The
lady: "But what do you think I am?" The gentleman: "We've
already established what you are. Now we're just haggling
over the price."

Bad faith is so important because it is the other side of
freedom. Bad faith is the denial of freedom, because it deludes men into thinking that they have no choice in a
situation. In reality there are very few situations indeed
where the words "no option" are literally true. At the very
least, as the Stoics knew, there is the choice of death. If
a man chooses not to die he is *ipso facto* opting to continue
living under the particular circumstances of the situation.
But again it is not necessary to demonstrate the point by
going to the extreme case in which suicide is the only
free option. Most of the situations in which men speak of
necessity are actually cases of choice. If necessity means that
I must do certain things to succeed, then it is I who choose
not to fail. If necessity means doing this if I am not to become an object of ridicule, then it is I who choose to save
my face. In other words, the necessity is that only insofar as
I recognize it as such. Bad faith is the denial of this fact.
Now it would certainly be an exaggeration to say that social
perception of the kind delineated here precludes bad faith.
It is safe, however, to say that it makes it more difficult. The
most dangerous people are the total believers. Insofar as the
comic perspective on society, the vision of society as stage

and precariousness, makes total belief very difficult, such perspective mitigates the more murderous varieties of earnestness. In other words, there is an ethical dimension to the precarious vision.

Sartre's concept of bad faith can be used to show how the social fictions operate to provide a moral alibi. There is another very important function which these fictions carry out, namely to provide a way by which the more terrifying aspects of existence can be avoided. It is this function which can be described by Heidegger's concept of *"das Man."* The German term is difficult to translate. *"Man"* is used in German like the French *"on"*; in English the closest analogue would be "one," as used in sentences like "one would never do this," "one might feel," and so forth. That is, *"das Man"* refers to a social generality which cannot be expressed in any of the proper personal pronouns. In one of his best-known arguments Heidegger argues that this generality is designed so as to evade confrontation with the reality of death.[5] In other words, the reality of death is distorted by making it an occurrence of everyday life. The way in which people commonly talk about death, or even comfort the bereaved, well illustrates this. "We all have to go," said in a tone of easy resignation—the "we all" is precisely *"Man"*—it means everybody, but really nobody, and specifically not myself. I am not "we all." By subsuming my own death under this generality I effectively evade the stark truth that I myself will die my own, very personal, very unique death. This also is bad faith. The same is true of the comforter who tries to have one who grieves transpose his sorrow onto a general plane. Heidegger himself points to what in world literature is possibly the most penetrating picture of this uneasiness and dishonesty in the face of death—Tolstoy's story about the death of Ivan Ilyich. Authentic existence, according to Heidegger, is possible only as one acquires the courage to face one's death, to "live toward death," which includes the courage to face one's fear of death.[6]

Without seeking to interpret Heidegger's philosophy, it

would seem that this concept is singularly applicable to our argument here. We would contend that the social fictions we have been discussing function as precisely this generality. We would also contend that the concept of bad faith is fully applicable to the use of this generality to avoid the terrors of our existence. Certainly this is true of the terrors of death, as Heidegger points out. The way in which death is handled in America today could serve as an excellent example of this. There is, as it were, a conspiracy between the actuary's and the mortician's ways of looking at death, as a result of which the truth of death disappears. However, it is not only this one terror which can be avoided in this way. The same is true of any experience of ecstasy, using that term in its original meaning of *ekstasis*—standing outside oneself. There are various situations in life in which it may suddenly seem to us that we have stepped outside the everyday course of events, that we are really confronting existence. This can be an experience of terror, though it need not always be. This writer has not fully understood why Heidegger gives such a privileged status to the one ecstasy of confronting my own death. There are other ecstasies—of horror, awe, guilt, but also of sudden insight, pleasure, joy. What all ecstasies have in common is breaking through the routine, everyday, taken-for-granted course of our life. Society functions to prevent this break-through. It is especially its fictions which are designed for this purpose.

Generality shields us from the uniqueness of our existence, both the unique terror and the unique freedom of being ourselves. During World War II there occurred a tragic accident in the writer's circle of acquaintances. A little boy of about three years, the only son of his parents, fell off a roof and was killed. The family was Jewish. An elderly rabbi expressed his condolences to the father of the boy, then added: "And this at a time when we need every Jew!" It is not our concern whether the rabbi's comment was said in kindness or how the father reacted to this attempt at comfort. Our point is that we have here the kind of generalization which we feel entitled to call bad faith. For it was not "a Jew" who died—it was this one, unique, irreplaceable child. To suggest to the bereaved father that he transpose his unique anguish onto the plane of political and ethnic considerations was an act of bad faith, however well meaning it may have been. Again, as in the example given above of the Russian spy who died correctly, it is quite possible that such bad faith is merciful. That is not the point. Those who die "as soldiers," "as Communists," "as Jews" die in bad faith to the extent that this "as" becomes a fiction which vicariously dies for them. In truth it is not "a soldier" who dies, or "a Communist," or "a Jew." Only men die. Their anguish, their terror, and their courage cannot be captured in the social categories. Perhaps the deepest obscenity of society lies in the fact that it continues to try. Unlike their mammalian relatives, few men are permitted to die "off stage." To the last moment the social comedy continues all around them, and, what is more, they are expected to participate in it. "He died well." There was perhaps a time when this referred to something religious. Today it generally means that he died not only with a minimum of pain but also with a minimum of annoyance to those who had charge of his care.

One does not have to be an existentialist to perceive that existence lurks with terrors. Thrown into the world in one brief moment of consciousness, we are surrounded on all sides by mystery which includes our own destiny and the meaning of a universe not too obviously constructed for our comfort. From the first reassuring smile of the mother bending over a frightened infant, society provides us with structures in which we can live with a measure of ease and which announce to us every day that things are in order. Busying ourselves at the warm, well-lit spots of the marketplace we can forget the howling visions of the night. Existence is leaning over a bottomless abyss. Society is the Potemkin village that shelters the abyss from our fearful eyes.

It happens sometimes in the middle of the night that we wake up and cannot fall asleep again. It is in such hours that strange thoughts may come. Our own existence and identity suddenly cease to be matters of course, but highly doubtful fabrications in a world constantly threatened by nighmarish transformations. If we are what is regarded as sane, well-balanced individuals there are very definite ways of coping with such experiences. We tell ourselves very forcefully who we are. Nonsense, we tell ourselves, we have nothing to do with the faceless horrors of our dreams. There can be no question about our identity. We can promptly give name, address, profession, marital status. If necessary, we can wake up wife and children, who will laughingly confirm the identification. We can switch on the lights and walk around in our house. We call this process of recollection a coming back to reality. We would contend, however, that it is a very special reality that we come back to in this way. It is the daytime reality of society as taken for granted. And it certain is reality. But let us not too easily dismiss the nighttime from the domain of the real. Names, addresses, professions, and wives have a way of disappearing. At the latest it will be in the confrontation with death that we will be thrown back into that night-time world where identities are questioned.

Society gives us names and identities. It provides the processes by which these are appropriated and sustained. Yet we are fleeing from the truth if we think that these precarious appellations constitute all there is to our existence. Such flight is bad faith. It is one of the most common of phenomena. Again we ask, "Who are you?" And we get the answers. "I come from a leading Boston family." "I am an anarchist." "I am a Methodist bishop." "I am a recipient of the Nobel Prize." "I am John Smith." True enough. Yet all these are shorthand descriptions for the purposes of stage management. What if the stage collapses? And what if I have to leave the stage?

To live correctly means to live in accordance with one's dramatic assignment. One can, of course, appear to do so but really live one's own life behind the wings of the stage. That is simple insincerity, not bad faith. Our interest is in the sincere man, the one who honestly believes himself *to be* his role. There is the military man who avoids the perils of tenderness by being a soldier even in bed. There is the bishop who avoids doubts and anxiety by wearing his sacred robes even into his dreams. There is the political assassin who thinks of himself as an instrument of history. But there is also the businessman whose entire life becomes part of his economic enterprise or his wife whose existence derives significance only in terms of her status in the female under-world of her husband's circle. And so on. What all these instances of total identification with a role have in common is the avoidance of ecstasy. These individuals never confront the universe as men, nakedly, openly. They always hide in the costumes of the social carnival. They cannot face the world—except *as* officers, priests, political devotees, insurance salesmen, or faculty wives. That is, they cannot face the world at all. As a line from a German cabaret skit puts it, in the mouth of a subaltern government official: "When I'm on duty I'm a swine. I'm always on duty." Arthur Miller's *Death of a Salesman* gives us a contemporary picture of the final tragedy of this sort of bad faith.

Freedom is at best an approximation. None of us is free to abandon the stage—except by way of that one experience when *omnes exeunt*. But insofar as a measure of liberation is possible, it involves a measure of seeing through the fictitiousness of society. This requires ecstasy. There are different varieties of ecstasy. We would contend, however, that the experience of alternation, the perception of the fictitiousness and precariousness of society, the perception of society as stage, that these are capable of providing a very significant kind of ecstasy. We would contend again that the essential quality of this vision is comic. The precarious vision strips the general of his uniform, the bishop of his vestments, and tells the status-conscious wife of a vice-president that she is must less important than she thinks—and, therefore, freer to be happy. The precarious vision of the social world is, then, one of the most dangerous enemies of bad faith. In its perspective the excuses of bad faith dissolve into preposterousness. In their place appears once more the possibility of freedom.

PART TWO

Burden of Zion

6. Religion and the Social Fictions

RELIGION AS A SOCIAL INSTITUTION TENDS TO GIVE AN ILLUSION OF CERTAINTY TO THE DRAMATIC FICTIONS. FOR THIS REASON, RELIGION AS A SOCIAL INSTITUTION IS MORALLY DANGEROUS. RELIGION CAN BECOME THE SUPREME FICTION THAT SANCTIFIES ALL THE OTHER FICTIONS.

If one leaves aside the Marxist tradition, the two most important social-scientific approaches to religion are to be found in the works of Emile Durkheim and Max Weber.[1] Durkheim's approach not only has had a predominant influence on the French school of sociology but in many ways can be regarded as the ancestor of functionalism in Anglo-Saxon anthropology and sociology.[2] As in the discussion of social-scientific materials in Chapter 3 of this essay, it is not our intention here to make a critical or exhaustive presentation of these developments in the study of religion. Our concern is only to identify certain elements of the social-scientific understanding of religion, in order to see more clearly how religion is related to the social fictions which we discussed in the preceding chapters.

Durkheim's conception of sociological method emphasized strongly that social phenomena had to be studied as such, as phenomena *sui generis*. This means, for example, that psychological analyses will never arrive at an understanding of society. In accordance with this general approach, Durkheim was not very much interested in the psychological processes involved in religious beliefs and practices. Religion is a social phenomenon, hence it must be studied as such. And the most important social consequence of religion is that its beliefs and practices unite into what Durkheim called a "moral community" those who adhere to them. Durkheim went further than that and, in sharp distinction from other contemporary theories seeking to explain religion scientifically, maintained that society itself was both source and ultimate object of all religious devotion. Not only is religion an essentially social phenomenon, but what the religious devotee is ultimately worshiping is society itself, or rather its most awesome values. There are very few social scientists today who would defend this extreme position, and most would feel that at this point Durkheim's philosophical presuppositions tended to run ahead of his scholarly judgment.[3] However, the importance of Durkheim's study of religion lies not in this extreme position on the ultimate substance of religion but rather in the attention it drew to its actual functioning in society. Not only Durkheim himself but his disciples in the French school of sociology were greatly interested in what they called the "collective representations" of society. They stressed the fact that society could not be understood except with a grasp of the web of meanings, ideas, and values (that is, the "collective representations") which holds it members together. These "collective representations," taken together, constitute the "collective conscience" of a society—the basic moral consensus without which it would not exist.[4] In this collective conscience religion plays a crucial role. The deepest levels of the collective conscience are those which are sanctified through the religion which the society adheres to. By thus putting under its sanctions the most important elements of consensus, religion makes possible a moral community, and thus makes it possible for society to exist at all. Religion is not an accidental element of society, relating itself here and there to other social elements. Religion is essential to society, so much so that one could say that without religion in some form society could not exist.

A different way of putting this is by saying that the primary social function of religion is symbolic integration. It is this aspect of Durkheim's work which has become guiding in the functionalist approach to religion, both in British social

anthropology (with Bronislaw Malinowski as probably the
most outstanding exponent of the approach) and in American sociology (where Talcott Parsons has done most to apply
a functionalist conception to the study of religion). What
this means can be put quite simply (although, of course,
social scientists specialize in putting things in as complicated
a way as possible!). Society is viewed as a whole, a system
of assumptions, conventions, and procedures shared by a group
of human beings. The question that interests the functionalist
is how this system hangs together. Any aspect of the society
he studies, then, he will study in terms of this question.
That is, he will ask in what way this aspect helps keep the
society together. Whether the aspect being investigated is a
belief or a custom or a particular technique, this question
will always be asked. Now, quite obviously, not everything
that goes on in society is functional in this sense. Although
early functional theory tended toward this assumption, later
developments took into consideration that there are things
that happen which actually tend to disrupt society (that is,
which are disfunctional) and others which are irrelevant to
the maintenance of the system. If we return for a moment to
our picture of the stage, we can imagine that most of the
actors, most of the time, will act in such a way that the play
can go on. All the same, it happens once in a while that
individuals or groups of actors, deliberately or by accident,
do things which tend to break up the original drama. What
is more, sometimes a little boy comes in from the wings
and sits down in a corner and blows three times into a
trumpet. He does this because he feels like it. As far as the
main dramatic action is concerned his little sideshow is
irrelevant. That is, it is neither functional nor disfunctional.
It remains true that, on the stage of society, there will be a
modicum of dramatic cooperation most of the time, thus
giving validity to the basic question of the functionalist.
Religion, then, functions by integrating the actors' values
and beliefs in such a way that they are made capable of cooperation. Religion lets the actors believe that their play is

ultimately right, and, of course, as a result of this belief the play is facilitated. Or one could put the same thing by saying that religion provides the *imprimatur* for the libretto —or the *fiat spectaculum* for the whole operation.

This primary social function of religion also relates it in a very important way to the apparatus of social control. Sociologists speak of social control, a term coined by the American sociologist E. A. Ross,[5] to refer to the various techniques society develops in order to bring into line its recalcitrant members. Such techniques can be external devices, ranging from killing to social ostracism or gossip. However, as both role theory and the psychoanalytic approach have conclusively shown, the most important controls are internalized. In the process of socialization the value structure of society becomes the inner value structure of the individual conscience. Essentially the same process is meant when Mead refers to the "generalized other" as when Freud speaks of the "superego"—society no longer just confronts the child as an external reality but has become part and parcel of his inner self. No ongoing society can dispense with such a process of moral internalization. The external techniques of social control can be economically applied only if most people, having successfully internalized controls, stay in line quite naturally. To put this a little differently, a few hundred policemen are sufficient to preserve law and order in a city with many thousands of people. Why? Because most of these people will behave in a legal and orderly fashion in any case, even if they never see a policeman or think of one. But instead of the external cop they have a little, invisible cop sitting squarely in the middle of their heads. This is the metaphysical gentleman whom Freud called the "censor." This internal police force is not only more economical but far more efficient than the flesh-and-blood troopers. Without it any society is doomed, even if it uses the most brutal methods of physical repression.

The purpose of social control is to keep society going despite the occasional foibles and iniquities of its membership.

One could say that social control has three lines of defense. The first line of defense is consensus, the common taken-for-grantedness of moral *pre*scriptions and *pro*scriptions, which, if it functions well, makes social control in its proper sense unnecessary. There will be no stepping out of line and thus no need for the techniques of bringing anyone back into line. The second line of defense is the internalized social-control machinery—if one prefers, the conscience. There may here be a strong desire to step out of the collective march, but the little cop keeps banging the naughty wish back into the speechless underworld whence it came. And even if the desire sometimes wins out, there is the potent poison of repentance and guilt, often a far more powerful control than the most grisly punishments inflicted from without. Finally, there is the third line of defense when the external means of coercion have to be brought into action. This is reserved for that minority whose immorality has proved stronger than both consensus and conscience. Now religion enters vitally into each of these lines of defense. At the first line, religion coordinates the moral consensus of society, systematizes it in a certain picture of human destiny, takes up the moral imperatives one by one, and calls them blessed. At the second line, religion provides the most uncomfortable pangs that conscience can inflict, involving one fatally in guilt not only against one's neighbor (who, after all, may be presumed to be a sinner too) but also against supernatural forces, which not only possess far more sinister means of retaliation than one's neighbor but may also be so offensively righteous that one cannot even argue with their threatened thunderbolts. At the third line, religion provides the ratification of the acts of coercion performed on behalf of society. Now it is quite possible that someone reads this interpretation, thinks of all the moral notions that are dearest to his heart, and then nods happily at the thought that religion protects them so effectively. In order to avoid such reassurance it ought to be emphasized most strongly that religion offers these services to society regardless of the moral contents involved. In other words, depending upon which society we are talking about, religion will thus defend cannibalism or vegetarianism, infanticide or love of children, slavery or universal brotherhood. The functionality of religion appears to be a formal characteristic of social reality and can exist as such irrespective of the character of the moral values which it integrates.

Weber's approach to religion differs in important ways from that of Durkheim and the functionalists. While Durkheim emphasizes the objective, metapersonal character of social phenomena, Weber stresses that any social interaction depends upon the subjective meanings given to it by the individual actors. While the typical Durkheimian question about a social phenomenon is "How is this related to society as a whole?" the typical Weberian question is "What meaning does this have for the people involved?" While these two questions are not necessarily antithetical, it is obvious that they open the way to quite different perspectives. While Durkheimian analysis always carries within it the tendency toward what is called sociologism (that is, the general assumption that all human phenomena are always determined by social processes), Weberian analysis will bring out the way in which ideas, beliefs, and values help determine what direction social processes will take. In terms of the analysis of religion, Durkheimian analysis will bring out its determination by nonreligious factors, while Weberian analysis will show how religious factors can be independent determinants in certain social situations. The most famous analysis of this latter kind is Weber's study on the relationship of capitalism and Protestant ethics, which study was, among other things, Weber's most successful work in disproving the Marxist theory of religion.[6] While all of this touches upon crucial questions of the sociology of religion, it need not concern us in this essay. What is of much greater interest for us is that Weber's approach also brings into focus the relationship of religion to the social fictions, though in a way that is different from Durkheim's.

We find this focus particularly in Weber's concepts of legitimation[7] and theodicy.[8] It will be in order to look briefly at these two concepts.

The concept of legitimation has its basis in Weber's analysis of the political order. Any political order is an organization of power which has at its disposal a variety of methods by which it can coerce those who are minded to resist its commands. However, no political order persists in time unless, in addition to its power, it manages to produce some theoretical justification of this power. In other words, power wants to be legitimate. This desire for legitimation has a double source. Partly it has to do with the kind of economy already discussed above. Naked force is a highly uneconomical and ultimately inefficient method of staying in power. Even the most unscrupulous tyranny will seek to develop at least a measure of consensus among its subjects (a fact of great importance even in the sociology of totalitarianism). Since men have a desire to believe in order, this attempt will be at least partially successful, if enough time is allowed. But the desire for legitimation probably has roots within the minds of the powerful themselves. It would seem that most men want not only power but also the feeling that they have a right to it. We can see here again that collusion in fantasy between oppressor and oppressed that we had occasion to look at in the last chapter. In other words, it happens not infrequently that the propaganda of the tyrant is believed by the tyrant himself. For instance, the Marxist ideology serves as a legitimation of Communist power *vis-à-vis* the peoples of the Communist world. But it is not inconceivable that the ideology is also believed in by the Communist power elite itself. It may even happen that a politician in a Western democracy sincerely believes his own campaign oratory. There are, after all, far more sincere liars than cynical ones, if only because self-deception is psychologically easier than Machiavellianism.

It is not difficult to see how religion is related to the process of legitimation. Even in so-called secular states, or states that operate under a legal separation of state and church, the most powerful legitimations of power are the religious ones. This, of course, is most evident in acute crises of the political order, as in times of war or insurrection. As the drums roll before battle there is always a moment of silence in which the impending carnage is commended to the super-natural powers. The blessing of weapons is one of the most time-hallowed tasks of religious functionaries. But also in the routine exercise of power the availability of religious sanctions is important. Power very easily involves men in ultimate sacrifice and ultimate guilt. Therefore power requires the ideas by which men interpret their ultimate experiences, the ideas which motivate men to face death and which rationalize their guilt. It is not difficult to understand the profound proximity between throne and altar—even in states that have a republican form of government. Religion is one of the most important ingredients in theories of legitimacy.

Weber's concept of theodicy approaches the subject from a slightly different angle. As in other terms which Weber took from the vocabulary of religion, he uses the concept of theodicy in a way modified from its religious usage (where it means the problem of reconciling the idea of an omnipotent divinity with the existence of suffering or evil). Weber distinguishes between a theodicy of happiness and a theodicy of suffering. The former is the religious preoccupation of the fortunate, the latter that of their less privileged fellow men. Both theodicies are rationalizations of the social fact that some men live happily while others continue all their lives in wretchedness.

Perhaps the religion of the classical Graeco-Roman world provides one of the best examples of a theodicy of happiness. Those who lived in happiness were those favored by the gods. Not only was the shunning of the miserable an instinctive act of revulsion, but it was also a religious act. The miserable, those not favored by the gods, were religiously impure as well as socially despicable. Their wretchedness had about it a con-tagious quality and the happy had better stay away from it or they might themselves become infected with it. However, any religion which identifies divine blessing with earthly success provides this kind of theodicy. Thus the Brahmin in traditional Hindu society knows that his favored position is not just an accident of birth but is well earned as a result of good deeds in countless past reincarnations. Thus the Puritan of, say, the society of colonial New England could be self-righteously certain that his privileges were the bounty of an inscrutable providence, which sees fit to elect some men and damn others. And his latter-day secularized successor, established in a favorable position in American society, retains the same tendency to ascribe good fortune to virtue and its opposite to vice. This theodicy of happiness is, of course, closely related to the process of legitimation. Men want power, wealth, happiness, but they also want a theory which explains to them and to others that they are entitled to all these advantages. Religion frequently satisfies this need.

The theodicy of suffering performs an analogous function for those on the other side of the fence. While it is terrible to suffer it is even more terrible to suffer meaninglessly. Religion provides meaning for suffering. In this interpretation of the religion of the underdog Weber was strongly influenced by Marx on the one hand and by Nietzsche and Scheler on the other. With Marx he sees that religion, in providing a theodicy of suffering and thus relieving tensions within the social order, tends to preserve the *status quo*. This, for example, is why American slaveowners encouraged the conversion of imported Negroes to Christianity, why one of the first buildings put up in Southern mill villages was the church, and why the present authorities in South Africa encourage the activities of certain evangelists among the native population. With Nietzsche and Scheler, Weber perceived how in certain cases religion provides a focus for the pent-up resentments and hatreds of subjected groups, providing a rationalization for one's own impotence. Thus Christianity became for the slaveowner a means of social repression, but for the slave it was a means of psychological repression of his own instincts of rebellion. While society spits upon the slave, religion assists in the process by suggesting that he is despicable (thus legitimating the oppression) and at the same time providing an outlet for the slave's aggressions through a promise of supernatural bliss (thus fortifying the oppression against insurrectionary dangers). Where Weber differed from Marx and Nietzsche is in his refusal to regard these as universal functions of religion. There are important cases in which religion operates in society in a different way. One might think, for example, of the role of the Quakers in the underground railroads preceding the Civil War or the long nights of *voudun* drumming preceding the Haitian revolution. We are not concerned here with developing an exhaustive sociological theory of religion. It is important for us to bring out those functions of religion tending toward the maintenance of the social system, happily agreeing that there are exceptions and other possibilities.

However, even with these reservations the writer is convinced that the preponderant tendency of religion is to be socially functional rather than disfunctional. That is, religion will tend to provide integrating symbols rather than symbols of revolution. Religion will tend to legitimate power rather than to put it in question. Religion will tend to find rationalizations for social inequalities (both among the beneficiaries and the injured in these arrangements) rather than to seek their removal. This preponderant tendency has been well summarized by J. M. Yinger as follows:

"Insofar as it is accepted religion, by rite and symbol, gives emotional support to the fundamental values of a society; it softens the hardness of the struggle for scarce values by emphasizing values that can be achieved by all (e.g., salvation); and it lessens the tensions of those who have failed to achieve a desired level of a society's values by approved means by emphasizing supra-mundane values."[9]

Insofar as religion functions in this way, it is crucially related to the various fictions by which societies maintain themselves and thus crucially related to the problems of bad faith discussed in the last chapter. It might be added here that, whatever reservations one might make about the social role of religion in other societies, there can be no doubt that in America religion functions overwhelmingly as an integrator in the sense outlined above. We shall have occasion to take illustrations from the American scene further on, but for the moment we might just quote the apt characterization of American "civic religion" made by Will Herberg:

"Civic religion is a religion which validates culture and society, without in any sense bringing them under judgment. It lends an ultimate sanction to culture and society by assuring them that they constitute an unequivocal expression of 'spiritual ideals' and 'religious values.' Religion becomes, in effect, the cult of culture and society, in which the 'right' social order and the received cultural values are divinized by being identified with the divine purpose. Any issue of *Christian Economics*, any pronouncement of such organizations as Spiritual Mobilization, will provide sufficient evidence of how Christian faith can be used to sustain the religion of *'laissez-faire* capitalism.' Similar material from Catholic and Jewish sources comes easily to hand, from 'liberal' quarters as well as from 'conservative.' On this level at least, the new religiosity pervading America seems to be very largely the religious validation of the social patterns and cultural values associated with the American Way of Life."[10]

We can fully agree with Herberg that this description fits contemporary American religiosity in the main and also that this constitutes a betrayal of Biblical faith. We would only add that there is nothing very unusual or surprising about this state of affairs. American religion stands here in a venerable tradition dating all the way back to the sacred rattles with which Neanderthal man encouraged himself to face the dinosaurs. In any case, we would contend that the analysis of religion as the great social integrator is of very special importance in contemporary America, and not only to spoilsport sociologists.

It will now be our task to show in somewhat greater detail how this social functionality relates to the problem of bad faith that was discussed in the last chapter. It is this which interests us here. It would be quite possible to approach the problem of the social fictions from other angles. For example, there is a philosophical problem inherent in the very term of fiction. What are fictions in the first place? How are fictions to be distinguished from other forms of symbolizations? Are all fictions the same as illusions? We are not competent to discuss these questions philosophically. But we are not at the moment interested in the ontological status of social fictions. Our interest in these fictions is a strictly anthropocentric one. More specifically, we do not ask what these fictions ultimately mean, but only in what way they contribute to bad faith and human inauthenticity. It is here that the place of religion becomes clear.

We can look again at this point at the case of capital punishment, that one event in which the bad faith and the murderousness of the social fictions come together with unusual clarity. The relationship between religion and capital punishment has been perceived very clearly by the atheist critics of religion since the eighteenth century. This relationship has been stated so succinctly by Albert Camus in our own time that we shall take the occasion of quoting at some length from his essay on the death penalty:

"The verdict of capital punishment destroys the only indisputable human community there is, the community in the face of death, and such a judgment can only be legitimated by a truth or a principle that takes its place above all men, beyond the human condition. Capital punishment, in fact, throughout history has always been a religious punishment. When imposed in the name of the king, representative of God on earth, or by priests, or in the name of a society considered as a sacred body, it is not the human community that is destroyed but the functioning of the guilty man as a member of the divine community which alone can give him his life. Such a man is certainly deprived of his earthly life, yet his opportunity for reparation is preserved. The real judgment is not pronounced in this world, but in the next. Religious values, especially the belief in an eternal life, are thus the only ones on which the death penalty can be based, since according to their own logic they prevent that penalty from being final and irreparable: it is justified only insofar as it is not supreme."[11]

Perhaps, to evade the criticism that, after all, Camus was a hostile witness, we ought to also quote from a recent article by a respected Protestant churchman in this country in which precisely the same point is made, only with the opposite intention:

"We who are supposed to be Christian, make too much of physical life. Jesus said, 'And do not fear those who kill the body but cannot kill the soul; rather fear him who can destroy both soul and body in hell' (Matt. 10:28). Laxness in law tends to send both soul and body to hell. It is more than a pious remark when a judge says to the condemned criminal: 'And may God have mercy on your soul.' The sentence of death on a killer is more redemptive than the tendency to excuse his crime as no worse than grand larceny."[12]

It is not surprising, in view of this, that churchmen have been among the most valiant defenders of capital punishment throughout so-called Christian history—except for the period of the early church, when any form of killing was regarded as unthinkable for Christians, and except for the scattered witness of such groups as the Quakers. It is not even necessary to go back to the atrocities of the Inquisition to be edified by this affinity between priests and hangmen. In the long discussion in the British Parliament about the modification and abolition of capital punishment, the bishops of the Church of England stood steadfastly for the retention of the gallows.[13] In 1810 the bishops voted the death penalty for a theft of five shillings.[14] And as recently as 1948 the Bishop of Truro suggested that capital punishment should be extended rather than abolished.[15] In the great debate over abolition of the death penalty in the House of Lords in 1956, both Anglican archbishops spoke for abolition, but only after carefully dissociating themselves from the argument that capital punishment was a wrong in itself and in the hope that a modification of it will, in the words of the Archbishop of Canterbury, "refound the death penalty on its only secure and legitimate foundation as an act expressing the general will of the com-

munity for the defence of society and for the solemn vindica-
tion of the laws of God."[16]

Leaving aside for the moment the difficulties which this
traditional religious bloodthirstiness presents to adherents of
a movement founded by an executed criminal, one may ask
why this position exists and why it is so widespread among
religious people. It is here that the relationship between religion and bad faith can be seen very sharply. We have discussed
before how men put on magic cloaks for certain acts in society
for which they claim moral immunity for their persons. But
simply human conjury is not enough when it comes to some
of the most terrifying acts. Now the alibi is not just that one
does not do this personally but *qua* a particular kind of office-
holder. Now the office itself must be transfigured by supernatural spookery. The act then takes on the quality of a divine
intervention. Killing is such an act. In the same essay from
which we quoted above, Camus mentions the inscription on
the executioner's sword in Freiburg, in Switzerland: "Lord
Jesus, Thou art the Judge." The meaning of the inscription is
simple. It proclaims that the hangman is not doing the killing,
neither is the judge, nor the jury, nor the good people of the
canton watching the execution. The killer is Jesus Christ, who
is absolutely just and therefore absolutely beyond questioning. As the executioner's sword comes down on the victim's neck, we can see in the one stroke an act of religious
faith and one of bad faith inseparably linked.

It is in this fog of sanctified delusion that hangmen will
shake the hand of their victim seconds before the execution,
that priests will urge repentance on the victim to the last
moment of the atrocity, that officials presiding over all this
will afterward shake their heads and say, "I hated to do it!"—
and that there will even be people who sympathize with
them! But once more we find that the delusion (though for
different reasons) is often shared by the intended victim too.
If we may paraphrase Weber here, there is a theodicy of hanging and a theodicy of being hanged. A group of anthropologists
who made a study of a community in the Deep South some

twenty years ago have given us a bloodcurdling account of the way in which religion entered into the hanging of two Negroes.[17] The two men were sentenced to death for the murder of fellow Negroes. This is a crime for which Southern traditional jurisprudence rarely inflicted the death penalty, but preceding this trial there had been a number of Negro crimes and the general feeling in the community was that it was about time "to teach the niggers a lesson." As soon as the death sentence was pronounced everybody involved in the case was genuinely anxious that the two men "get religion." A number of preachers were employed to achieve the desired result. But only one of the two men obliged and died "reconciled." The other remained defiant to the end, making everybody feel quite uneasy and resentful against him for not playing the role expected of him. This is how the authors of the study interpret this anxiety on the part of the white authorities:

"To the whites the execution ceremony is much more than the punishment of a Negro by a group of whites. It is a ritual sanctioned by God, that is, by the most important power of the total society, whereby the complete surbordination of the individual to the society is upheld. The proper role of the victim is one of complete subordination to the caste society and to God. He must confess his crime and seek for forgiveness, not of individuals who have been harmed, but of the total society. He must accept the rightness of this supreme white power which takes his life. If he fails in this role, if he does not pray and ask forgiveness, if he does not 'get religion,' he is denying the supreme authority and is rebelling against the society. He is a 'bitter' Negro."[18]

In the case of a Negro recently executed in a Southern state for "first-degree burglary" the prisoner, apparently half-crazed by fear, reported that in the night before his execution he had a vision of Jesus and that now he was ready to go. This account was received with great satisfaction by the chaplain attending him and duly reported by the newspapers throughout the state. It made everyone feel much better.

Religion here functions as the ultimate alibi of the murderer. It is the foundation stone of his bad faith. It was religion functioning in this way which caused the original outcry of the antireligious revolt of the eighteenth century: "Destroy the infamy!" But Voltaire, who wrote these words, could still say in another place, "If God did not exist, we should have to invent Him." It was only in the nineteenth century that this antireligious revolt reached its logical consequence in Mikhail Bakunin's paraphrase of Voltaire's words, "If God *did* exist, we would have to abolish Him!" It is not an accident that this same Bakunin was tormented by the existence of capital punishment and wrote a lengthy commentary upon its religious apologists. The divinity that Bakunin wanted to abolish is that age-old supreme being presiding over countless enactments of what is rightly called the supreme penalty. There is a section in a liturgical handbook for ministers of the Lutheran Church of Sweden printed in the nineteenth century which contains instructions for proper prayers and exhortations at hangings. This handbook includes a rubric which points out that although it may happen occasionally that an innocent man is hanged, the minister should point out to all concerned that no man is innocent before God and that all men deserve death for their sinfulness, so that, presumably, the injustice of this particular execution is of a relative nature. It may also be assumed that such pious observations made everyone feel much better—perhaps even the prisoner about to be hanged to the accompaniment of this liturgy!

If capital punishment provides us with the most instructive insights into the way in which religion functions as an alibi, it must not be supposed by any means that it is the only such possibility. What happens in so-called Christian churches when so-called Christian countries go to war against each other might serve as well to make our point. It is not even necessary to arrest ourselves at recent examples of American politicians telling us that between the Strategic Air Command and the Almighty we had all the weapons we could possibly want, because, after all, the enemy right now is "godless materialism" so that the Almighty might be presumed to have some

bias in our favor. A more salutary lesson might be derived
from the spectacle of religious activities during World War I,
a spectacle which has been well preserved for future generations by less-than-patriotic observers on both sides—for example, Karl Kraus for the Central Powers and H. S. Mencken
for the Allies. Here both sides cried with equal piety to the
same divinity and military chaplains, field preachers and vicars-
military vied with each other in pronouncing Christian bless-
ings upon the latest instruments of mass slaughter. Since
then, at least in Europe, there has been some clerical soul-
searching on these practices. There is, as yet, little evidence
of this in America, except among those religious groups that
have a pacifist tradition. In a study made in 1952 of American
military chaplains by a sociologist it was found that "45 per
cent of the respondents believed that the killing of an enemy
soldier was a righteous act and the remainder called it a
justifiable act"; furthermore, "none felt that the individual
soldier had any moral responsibility in the matter except to
serve his country—a duty which in time of war takes precedence over all other."[19] It is not surprising, after hearing this,
that the military forces continue to give commissions to
chaplains and regard their work as quite important for the
fighting morale of the troops. Here again, of course, religion is
used to provide a moral alibi for whatever acts are performed
under military orders and thus to reinforce the bad faith of
the one who commits the acts. Somewhat less dramatic
examples could be given of the same function being performed
by full-time religionists in the service of penal and coercive
institutions, or in industry, or in the employ of politicians
engaged in self-styled crusades. But perhaps this particular
point has been made now.

Religion, however, not only contributes to bad faith by
providing moral alibis. In many situations it also assists the
systematized delusions by which entire social groups succeed
in hiding from themselves the true nature of their situation.
This, again, is a facet of religion that is peculiarly significant in contemporary American society. A brilliant analysis of

this process has recently been made by Arthur Vidich and Joseph Bensman in their study of a small community in upstate New York.[20] The study presents us, on the one hand, with a picture of rural America rapidly disintegrating under the impact of contemporary economic, technological, and political forces, and on the other hand, with a picture of the people of this fading rural society tenaciously clinging to their old images of themselves. There are various institutions in the community which reinforce these images (which the authors call the "public ideology"). Among them the churches are of crucial importance. They continue to proclaim the old virtues of rustic life and, implicitly or explicitly, affirm that these virtues are still operative in the present. Within the religious assemblages one can, then, act (and presumably feel) as if the dynamics of the modern age had left untouched the small town with its simple, neighborly, democratic ways. In other words, the churches play a key role in the elaborate social-psychological process by which unpleasant realities are suppressed.

What Vidich and Bensman found in the small rural community can also be found in the new suburbs.[21] Here too we find at work a powerful "public ideology," with a strong family resemblance to that of the rural community, differing from it in that its function is not to preserve an old image but to create a new one in the teeth of reality. The reality of the suburbs is that of what sociologists call a *Gesellschaft*-type society—that is, a society in which people have transitory, superficial relations with each other, in which people cannot cast down deeper roots, in which most kinds of belonging (other than those within the immediate family) are very precarious. The ideology of the suburb refers itself to what sociologists call a *Gemeinschaft*-type society—that is, a society in which people belong to each other profoundly and with the totality of their persons, in which life is rooted in community, in which human relations are not fragmented or transient. It is interesting to observe how the ideology of the suburb resembles that of the small town. The image which both hold up is that of an earlier, more bucolic, and presumably better America. The small town pretends that this image is true and was always true of itself. The suburb pretends to create this fiction *ex nihilo*. Now, in the suburb too the churches function as a powerful reinforcement of this ideology. Very often the ideology is quite synthetic, the sophisticated product of the sales propaganda of the real-estate and development promoters. With the idyllic names of their projects (constant reiterations and recombinations of such rusticity-pregnant words like "forest," "woods," "brook," "meadow," and so forth) goes the picture of the friendly rural church, a monument of New Englandish cleanness and healthy propriety, where neighbors meet and where harmless gossip mixes with wholesome fun and where children can grow up to be upstanding citizens. Sometimes, as we know, the developers actually build the church (or churches). Religion is an important part of the fantasy being promoted. The reality of suburbia, of course, can be perceived only when we follow its inhabitants as they take off on their daily commuter trains. Then we see suburbia not against the background of agricultural beatitude but as the frantic escape from the murderous competition, the noise, nerves, ulcers, and cutthroat relationships of the big city. Religion in suburbia does not provide its clientele with the means to confront the reality in which they spend their crucial waking hours. Rather it provides an easy ratification of the various escape routes that converge in the suburban way of life. Religion is one of the allegedly recreational leisure-time activities, but it also gives positive sanction to all the others. The minister of the suburban church plays an important role here. He lives like all the others, shares their aspirations and tastes and most of their opinions, but in addition he is a certified man of virtue. He thus becomes the exemplary suburbanite, the one in whom the suburban way of life is vicariously and solemnly justified. This is a "real good" feeling when one meets him at a cocktail party.

This leads over into yet another way in which religion contributes to bad faith. In the preceding paragraphs we looked at the way in which religion reinforces certain specific delusions that men have about their social reality. But religion also reinforces in a general way, quite apart from ideological distortions, the notion that the world ones lives in is essentially and ultimately all right. For lack of a better term, we could say that religion ratifies the "okay world." Again, this is of great importance in America, though certainly not an exclusively American or even modern phenomenon. In this function, again, religion contributes to bad faith—or perhaps it would be more accurate here to use Heidegger's concept of inauthenticity. For in reality man does not live in an "okay world" at all. He rushes toward his own death on a course marked by indecipherable signs and surrounded on all sides by a darkness full of pain. He can become authentically human only if, in some way, he faces and comes to terms with this destiny. The "okay world" prevents precisely that. It thus contributes essentially to inauthenticity. To revert to a picture used before, it is a Potemkin village erected to provide the illusion of safety, sanity, and order.

It seems to the writer that this function of religion can already be observed in primitive cultures, for example in what anthropologists call "rites of passage." As the great crises of life succeed each other in the biography of the individual—birth, puberty, marriage, sickness, death—the community, through its religious ceremonialism, proclaims the assurance that all these events are taking place within a cosmos that is understood and somehow controlled by the social ritual. Malinowski has analyzed funerary ceremonialism in very similar terms—the proclamation of the continued presence and cohesiveness of the community against the potent threat of death.[22] W. Lloyd Warner, in his intensive study of Memorial Day ritual in America, has given us a very similar interpretation applicable to our own society.[23] But it is not only the facing of death which provokes this reassuring response. Any experience of potential ecstasy (*ekstasis*) constitutes a threat to the "okay world" in which the routine business of society is enacted. Consequently, when crises threaten the everyday taken-for-granted routine of the individual and there looms the ecstatic possibility of confronting directly his own existence, society provides the rituals by which he is gently led back into the "okay world." Undoubtedly this process has very deep psychological roots, perhaps all the way back to the first time a mother bent over her terrified infant and whispered, "It's all right, it's all right, there's nothing to be afraid of!" For a moment then, the shadows are denied and the nightmares chased away. When we call this process inauthenticity we certainly are not suggesting that one ought to live in nightmares. But we live, in fact, in a world whose horizons on all sides are hidden in darkness, and our own lives are rushing toward this dark horizon. We must, therefore, face up to the night if we want to face up to our existence. And in speaking depreciatingly of the "okay world" we also do not wish to suggest that there is something wrong about men's quest for order, for an intelligible cosmos or for a meaning to their fate. Order is something that men seek, passionately desire, try to construct precariously in their own lives. Order is *not* something given, self-evident, secure. The "okay world" gives the latter impression, which is not only illusionary but which effectively stops the search for order before it has even started—in the illusion of already sitting safely in an oasis men abandon the search for paths through the wilderness.

We need not concern ourselves here at any length with the question of how far the psychology of religion might support or weaken these sociological observations about the integrating function of religion and thus the religious dimension of man's flight from himself. It is, at any rate, possible that the psychologist might also view religion as fulfilling deep needs for integration in the individual just as it does in society. It should also be obvious that the establishment of such needs is a far cry from an argument in favor of religion (though the obviousness of this does not seem to have reached some psychologists with religious nostalgias). To make religion a psychological function is as little an argument for it as is the establishment of religion as a social function. There is no reason whatever to assume that reality is constructed for the satisfaction of our needs. But there is no reason why we should pursue these questions further. There is, however, one psychological phenomenon that we may look at briefly in terms of our analysis of the religious aspects of bad faith, namely the way in which religious belief systems react to any challenge to their validity.

Almost any religious system will carry within it a claim to catholicity. This does not necessarily have to imply a missionary orientation or an attitude of condemnation toward those who do not adhere to the system (these seem to be peculiarly Western characteristics). But the religious system presents itself as the one true picture of the world, embracing all other perspectives within itself. What is very interesting is what happens to the adherents of the system when this claim is challenged. The almost instinctive reaction to such challenge seems to be an even more tenacious clinging to the system. This reaction, of course, makes perfect sense when we see the religious system as a means by which the individual protects himself against ecstasy. Any attack on the system powerfully evokes the possibility that one's Potemkin village may collapse and that one may be nakedly delivered to the terrors that lurk behind it. This reaction is expressed in both preventive and therapeutic procedures within the system. Under the category of prevention would come all those intellectual operations which in church tradition have been called apologetics. Since the system claims to embrace all reality, it must interpret all reality in its own categories. Whatever exists, be it the beasts in the jungle or the demons of the netherworld, must be looked at in terms of their possible location within the system. If a place is found for them they are then permitted to be, carrying neat little labels around their necks which identify them in terms of the system. If no place can be found for them they must be relegated to the outer darknesses of nonbeing. This relegation, though, is an intellectual task. That is, reasons must be found why "what *may* not be, *can* not be." But if one wants to pronounce sentence of annihilation upon beasts and demons, one also has to liquidate the theories of those who proclaim their existence. That is, the system must develop its own demonology and its own bestiary of heretics. This grappling with rival interpretations of the world is the apologetic enterprise. Every idea must be made captive and brought within the confines of the system, bound hand and foot. Catholic apologetics probably provides the model case for this sort of intellectual activity, but it is by no means the only one. Other religious systems may not possess the intellectual tools by which the great Catholic apologians have performed their task. But the aspiration is there *in nucleo*, even among quite crude sects. If the challenging idea cannot be absorbed intellectually, it can at any rate be ignored. A characteristic trait here is the inability to grasp the fact that someone may be familiar with the system but still not be a believer. The world is divided into the initiated and the ignorant—it is unthinkable, because profoundly threatening, that anyone could be in neither category. When the writer some years ago was actively engaged in the study of sectarianism he had this experience several times. The adherents of a sect, upon finding out that the writer had some knowledge of its history and tenets, immediately assumed that he was a believer. When he identified himself as a nonbeliever, it was as if the previous information about his knowledge of sectarian lore had been wiped out from their memory. They now began to tell him the simplest, most commonly known facts about the sect in question. While this mechanism cannot be called apologetics, it is carried by the same defensive reaction. One may also add here (and refer back at this point to the first two chapters of this essay) that the secularized religions of our time engage in the same practices. Thus Communism or psychoanalysis will have at its disposal a formidable apologetic apparatus by which alien ideas can be melted down and then reshaped in one's own forms.

Under the categories of both prevention and therapy would come the intellectual part of those activities called the care of souls in Catholic pastoral theology. Here the concern is not to bring in outside ideas but to prevent those inside from slipping out. This involves a variety of techniques for dealing with uncertainties and qualms on the part of believers. The confessional, the participation in ritual, ascetic, and devotional activities, the involvement in practical activity carried on under the banner of the system—all these are geared to overcoming what psychoanalysts call "resistance." Whatever happens, the believer must be prevented from what we have called "alternating"—that is, prevented from an ecstasy or conversion which will transport him outside the system, even for a moment of intellectual inspection. It might be added here that the apologetic and missionary enterprise also has a therapeutic value in this sense. Every converted idea or every individual convert is a confirmation that the system is right— and that one's questions about it were unjustified. It need not be our task here to go in further detail into the ways by which anxiety and guilt can be manipulated to achieve this goal.

Both apologetics and the care of souls involve an organization of doubt. The appearance of doubt in an individual believer carries with it the possibility that he may step outside the sacred circle and thus be lost to the faith. The persistence of doubt outside the system constitutes a total threat to all within it. In both cases the defensive reaction involves the organization of doubt in categories that have a place within the system. Needless to say, this is an operation of bad faith from beginning to end. It is the chorus of the blind insisting that all men pluck out their eyes. It is the intellectual systematization of inauthenticity.

Before concluding this discussion we might point out once more that those who maintain that religion is a vital function of society, or even its basis, do have substantial support in the evidence. But woe to them if they regard this insight as a recommendation! Religion is needed in society because men need bad faith. The paradigm of the social function of religion is the sword of the executioner at Freiburg. While he would not like to pursue this matter further at the moment, the

writer strongly suspects that a similarly disenchanting picture
will emerge if one holds that religion is vital in terms of
psychological functions. The writer would also suspect that,
provided that this is true at all, it is true because of the same
human need for bad faith. In any case, as far as our perspective
on society is concerned, we may now have established a certain
place for religion within it. It is not one likely to give comfort
to those looking for reassurance for their religious beliefs. And
it sharpens further our problem of relating social perception
and Christian faith.

7. Religious Exercises

In this chapter we would use the imagination along the lines suggested in Chapter 2 of this essay. Especially we would here clarify further the relationship of religion and bad faith. Perhaps it should be emphasized that to do so under the aspect of comedy or satire is very far from not taking seriously the perspectives that open themselves up to our view. On the contrary. In the sharp illumination of the comic we can see more clearly what the possibilities of seriousness are. The documents of the following pages are all, of course, purely products of the writer's fantasy. Our first document presents us with the sardonic view that an outside observer, here an astute Italian prelate, might have of certain features of American Protestantism. In this particular case it would not be difficult to turn his own guns on the good monsignor and start debunking the debunker. However, since the writer of this essay is himself a Protestant, he is much more interested in his own Augean stables and quite willing to leave the other task to a Catholic critic. Our second document illustrates what may happen when the know-how of the mass-communications industry is enlisted in the service of religious production. Any reader who feels that here satirical distortion has gone too far should cast a glance into the literature concerned with religious promotion, fund-raising, and ecclesiastical management. The postscript of this chapter hopefully speaks for itself.

(*i*) MEMORANDUM TO ROME

(The following pages are part of the report of Msgr. Lodovico Racciati to certain ecclesiastical authorities in Rome. Msgr. Racciati spent several years in this country. His principal mission was the comprehensive theological and sociological study of the Protestant scene. Perhaps we should add that Msgr. Racciati, scion of an old Roman family, is a witty, urbane, and darkly handsome gentleman in his middle forties. He was especially popular among various Protestant women's organizations and lectured a few times to such groups on "Why American Men Like Italian Women." This mildly risqué address was also broadcast on the radio.)

"One of the basic problems of the religious professional in American Protestantism comes from the simple fact that he has no religious certainty himself but must exhibit such certainty if he is to be effective with laymen. This problem affects a very large segment, possibly the great majority, of the ministers and religious workers. There are, of course, some who are sincerely deluded about their inner convictions and quite naturally adopt a posture of complete assurance *vis-à-vis* the laity. We must also admit the possibility that a few, by the mysterious favor of Providence, have been allowed one genuine portion of that supernatural illumination which normally is found only within the True Church. For most of these men, however, the problem is acute and painful. Their mission demands that they appear to the world as staunch champions of absolute conviction. But, alas, when they look into their hearts they find no such conviction. They have no option as to their course. They must *pretend* to be certain. Most of them, undoubtedly, pretend to themselves as much as to the others. Only a very small group will be practicing a conscious Machiavellianism. However, this moral difference does not interest us at the moment. What is important for us to understand is the intellectual and social posturing which results from this dilemma. We shall look first at some of the more sophisticated intellectual techniques to cope with the difficulty, then at some of the cruder tricks of stage management that some may feel the necessity to fall back upon.

"The general recipe, so to speak, is to arouse and sustain in the layman a feeling that he is groping around in the dark vale of uncertainty while the religious professional is basking in the calm light of certitude. This accomplishment is much less difficult than may seem at first sight. The vast majority of laymen in the respectable Protestant churches are so vague about religion in general and their own reasons for religious involvement in particular that an arousing of this feeling of religious uncertainty is actually no more than a simple pointing to the truth. Since the religious professional knows, at the very least, a little more about whatever sacred lore his sect has to offer, his role as expert and then as guide in matters of salvation is easily established. An interesting illustration of this is the statement often made by laymen in my hearing—'I would like to find out more about my faith.' If made to a minister such a statement easily provides an opening to suggest some new adult study group or other project that will add to the frantic activity he desires among his flock. Logically, of course, the statement is self-contradictory. Either one possesses a faith, then one will know what it is. Or one is interested in finding out about a faith, in which case, *ipso facto*, one does not possess it oneself. The resolution of the contradiction is purely sociological—the layman who asks this question came into the church with little if any religious motives; he now wants some religious teaching, either because he needs an intellectual rationalization of his church membership or in some cases because he has genuine religious frustrations. In this milieu of total confusion the religious professional can easily assume a stance of what the English writer Stephen Potter has called 'one-upmanship.'

"Among the broad central group of Protestants, who are untouched by the so-called theological revival (neo-orthodoxy), there is the general assumption (which we Catholics might well understand as a natural insight of reason) that religious certainty must be the result of an inner experience of conviction. The religious professional, who has had no such experience, still faces the expectation that he ought to have had one. This forces him into pretending to have, indeed, had such experience. It is possible to give this impression without lying outright. For example, it is possible to speak at length in a sermon on the wonderful benefits of religious experience. There will come a point when the audience will think that the preacher is reminiscing about his *own* experience. In the cruder sects of the lower classes this authentication of superior religious status is established almost exclusively by the *savoir-faire* of the minister or preacher in handling the highly emotional ritual of the worship service. If he has mastered certain forms of diction and gesture (sometimes this can be a performance of savage paroxysms), his status is unlikely to be questioned on other grounds. His colleague in more sophisticated churches will have to employ subtler techniques. A minister of my acquaintance has a way of blinking his eyelids very slowly and rhythmically when he speaks of these alleged religious experiences. When he stops blinking the impression obtained is of one coming back from faraway realms of the spirit. A more difficult situation occurs when a layman may ask point-blank, 'But have you yourself actually had such experiences?' Various evasive tactics are still possible then. The minister may engage his questioner in an epistemological argument about the meaning of 'experience' or he may subtly give him to understand that the question touches on unutterable domains of the forbidden. In any case, if he decides to simply say 'yes' he can have the assurance that the questioner will have a very hard time pressing him any further. Religious experiences are supposed to be beyond ordinary communication. Even the slightest attempt to put these into words will be implicitly doing the layman a favor. He will usually appreciate the effort.

"In other words, the religious professional in this milieu will have little difficulty maintaining his status on the hint that, in however modest a measure, he is having or has had privileged dealings with supernatural agencies, dealings upon which he cannot enlarge *per definitionem*. One aspect of this which interests me greatly as a student of anthropology is the common acceptance of eccentricities in the behavior of ministers, eccentricities which might even enhance their prestige among laymen who would never countenance them in their lawyer or physician. A minister admitted to me after several bottles of (incidentally atrocious) beer that he had practiced a long time before acquiring a perfectly frightening facial tic. This tic becomes particularly pronounced when he is exercising his professional duties in the pulpit or at ritual functions. This minister attributed his high prestige in both parish and community at least in part to this little gambit. It is not without scientific interest to compare this with such phenomena as sacred epilepsy among savage peoples, or with other abnormal manifestations which have been regarded as signs of divine or demoniacal possession in various periods of religious history. It is also interesting that this expectation of abnormality may extend to the minister's opinions. He may hold radical or eccentric ideas about certain subjects, such as racial equality or pacifism, which would lead to severe condemnation if held by laymen. This has an important psychological function. Since not everybody can have epileptic fits or invite Negroes to dinner, the religious professional does these things vicariously for his laymen, who are then dispensed from such difficult undertakings.

"The concept of religious experience, because of its association with Schleiermacher and the liberal tradition, is quite gauche in circles affected by so-called neo-orthodoxy. It is interesting to observe in what way the stance of the religious professional changes under these circumstances. While religious experience is generally rejected in these circles as a validation of one's religious position, with faith taking its place, this does not seem to make impossible a stance of superior insight into the mysteries. Logically one might regard this as a paradoxical result. If a man takes a position not because of knowledge but only because of faith, one might assume that he will be more humble than another who claims mystical conviction. But such is not the case in this group. On the contrary, their stance is much more assured than that of their liberal colleagues. It is of interest to investigate this phenomenon a little more closely.

"If faith is defined at all in this group, it is defined in terms derived (often vulgarized) from Kierkegaard, that is as a daring existential 'leap.' If then the neo-orthodox minister is asked 'But do you really *know*?' he may answer, 'No, I don't know—I *believe*.' This believing can then be described in rather heroic terms as risk, daring, adventure—in a word, as a great decision. One then takes an appropriate stance of devils-may-come braggadocio. This position has an obvious advantage as against the claim to superior religious experience. The religious professional can freely admit that he does not *know*, can entertain uncertainties and doubts, but he still comes out in a place of superiority. The logical difficulty inherent in this operation is commonly avoided by taking the position that nobody can understand the perspective of faith who has not himself 'leaped' into it (which is not too different from the position that only one who has had religious experience can understand what is involved). Despite this rather cavalier manner of avoiding the onus of one's choice, it may happen that an unconvinced questioner, having had it explained to him that faith is a decision, may continue to ask, 'Yes, but *why* did you make this decision?' There is a common line of defense here that we ought to look at.

"The way this line works is to make it appear that faith (of course in the interpretation of it offered by the religious professional) is the only alternative to despair. To support this position frequent if amateurish use will be made of terminology derived from psychoanalysis and existentialism. Both these ideologies are supposed to offer a gloomy, unappetizing picture of human nature, an antithesis to the optimistic notions still widely current in American society (this antithesis adds snob appeal to the argumentation —one's sophisticated pessimism is contrasted with the crude euphoria of the masses). The sum of these ideas is that human life is described as a cesspool of corruption, anxiety, and guilt, a dismal rat hole—except for that one opening into the sunshine which is the decision to have faith. While this line can have a measure of success among more educated groups, among the naturally jovial people who constitute the majority of the population, it may often meet with determined resistance. To overcome such resistance the practitioners of this line may resort to psychological techniques not too far removed from those of their more primitive colleagues in the gospel-tent school of evangelism. There is always something that people will feel guilty or anxious about. With some probing this weak spot can be found. Even when such probing is not possible, many people will eventually succumb when confronted with the firm implication that there is something vile about their innermost being, especially when simultaneously they are shown a guaranteed method of getting rid of this vileness.

"One technique of inducing in the layman a sense of inferiority and obligation is what may be called the method of historical gratitude. It is used by liberals and neo-orthodox with equal frequency, especially when other lines of a more religious nature fail. The method involves the demonstration that religion is necessarily involved in all the highest values that the layman holds and that, therefore, he ought to be involved religiously in the way that the religious professional wants him to. The method will pick out some moral values adhered to by the layman, say respect for persons, or belief in human equality, or even democracy, and then to assert that these values rest on a religious basis. Religion can then be presented as the fundamental and necessary basis of the American way of life and of the whole of Western civilization. The superiority of the religious professional is established on a pseudointellectual basis, in that he has this profound insight into the meaning of history which the layman lacks. If this method is used with some cunning, the layman can be made to feel like a perfect ingrate *vis-à-vis* every preacher from Habakkuk to Reinhold Niebuhr.

"Another technique for achieving the same goal is to make the layman feel an outsider socially rather than religiously or intellectually. This technique is based on the sociological fact that religion is still closely associated with respectability in America. It can then be maintained that those who are *inside*, the sane, sensible people who take a sound, balanced view of life, have a positive relationship with religion (of which, again, the religious professional makes himself appear as the authorized spokesman). This can easily induce in the layman that feeling of inferiority that comes from being classed among irresponsible juveniles. Even worse, it might be implied that an irreligious position (in the sense of not accepting the guidance of the religious professional) is un-American and puts the layman in the company of Communists, bohemians, and other unspeakable renegades. It may be seen that this technique works best with young people just beginning their married life or, even better, first experiencing the responsibilities of parenthood.

"I have briefly sketched some of the principal intellectual postures that religious professionals in this milieu will use to establish their own superiority before the laity. To this I would now add some of the cruder tricks by which this end is sought. There are considerable differences in this among different denominations. I cannot give an exhaustive account of all the techniques used and a few will have to serve as examples.

"One technique, mainly used by Episcopalians, is to overawe the layman with a cultural tradition, which is then identified with the religious position being promoted. To a Catholic observer, especially one from Europe, this spectacle can offer considerable entertainment. Catholic missionaries in Protestant (especially Anglo-Saxon) countries have, of course, commented on the attraction Catholicism has for people who identify it with the splendors of a civilization much older than theirs. Coupled with the Puritan instinct to feel guilty about what one is oneself, this attraction can give rise to the illusion that in walking into an Irish chapel in the slums of Indianapolis one is in fact stepping into the antechamber of the Sistine Chapel. I need not concern myself at the moment with the moral issues this complex may raise for Catholic missiology. I only wish to point out that a similar complex is involved in a certain Episcopal line.

"For well-known historical reasons anything English has always had high prestige among Americans. The Episcopalians are the principal group that can capitalize on this advantage (feeble attempts in the same direction are sometimes made by Congregationalists in New England). What is more, the Episcopal Church has enjoyed a particularly close affinity with the American upper classes. This denomination thus has the advantage of being able to cater not only to the widespread Anglophilia of Americans but also to the urgent desire of social climbers to identify with the elite. This double advantage is utilized well by Episcopal churches throughout the land. The layman who enters one of these quasi-Tudor sanctuaries finds himself confronted by a quasi-Oxonian minister, who, by deep instinct and common consent, is undoubtedly 'one-up' on him when it comes to culture.

"The personal effort that goes into this establishment of the British *raj* over the empire of American piety was powerfully brought home to me when a minister of my acquaintance, who had been a Congregationalist, joined the Episcopal Church and was in due course ordained in it. The most remarkable change occurred in the man's speech. Coming from the borough of Brooklyn, he had all his life carried the unmistakable mark of his origins on his language. After his ordination as an Episcopal minister his speech changed rapidly and he now sounds like an only slightly Americanized imitation of Rex Harrison. But his physical appearance has changed greatly too. While he was a Congregationalist he used to wear gaily striped ties, sensible business suits, and well-shined shoes. He now wears dark English tweed and long thin ties, and never shines his shoes. One touch, which I find particularly intriguing, is his habit of wearing a wrinkled seersucker suit over his clerical collar in the summer. This dramatically sets him off both against the colorless Protestants in their tropicals and the Romans sweating uncomfortably in their black garments—a subtle but impressive proclamation of an Anglican way of life! I might add that my friend, who used to be a very bashful person in any matters touching upon the erotic, now bravely sprinkles his conversation with restrained *double-entendres*, has switched from cigarettes to massive, foul-smelling pipes, and has discontinued his subscription to *The New Yorker* in favor of *Punch*. It is easily seen how such established pre-eminence in cultural matters can be put to good use in fortifying a religious position.

"Another technique of cultural terrorism, which also comes mainly from this denomination, has a somewhat better chance of being successfully adopted by non-Episcopalians. As a result of the so-called Anglo-Catholic movement, a considerable number of Episcopalian ministers have acquired some knowledge of Eastern Orthodoxy. This sometimes rather tenuous expertise can be used to captivate some laymen whose tastes run to more exotic spiritual fare than can be provided by the English line. I myself attended an incredible exhibition of this technique in an Episcopal church in Missouri (I should confess honestly that it was only *part* of the exhibition I attended), where the minister certified himself as an accomplished mystagogue in the eyes of his parish by staging an eight-hour Ethiopian mass. The choir, which had practiced for the event for months, entered into the act in shifts and people came from miles away to see the show. This, of course, is an extreme example of this approach. But even little liturgical gimmicks or obscure patristic references can have some effect in this era of ecumenicity and world-wide tourism. Naturally the method can backfire too. I read in the newspapers about an overenthusiastic Baptist minister in New Jersey whose experimentalism in what he called the "creative structuring of worship" cost him his job. He had the young people of his parish perform a Tibetan ritual dance at a meeting of the ladies' aid society, with himself offering a running commentary. The ladies not only failed to appreciate the spiritual message of the ceremony, but regarded the whole thing as an open invitation to concupiscence. The young minister in question now operates as a Jungian psychotherapist in New York City.

"American Lutherans have sometimes tried to use the Continent about the way Episcopalians use England. This will involve such tricks as referring to incomprehensible European theologians, using multisyllabic terms in German or even Swedish, and generally exhaling a sort of healthy no-nonsense beer-hall religiosity which says, 'Who are *you* to disagree with the University of Erlangen?' Unfortunately the suspicion against things Germanic produced in America by two world wars makes this approach rather difficult except among people of central-European ethnic origins. Lutherans, incidentally, are fond of adopting an unusually belligerent stance in matters of faith, no doubt trying to emulate the picture they have in their minds of their founder defiantly facing the Diet of Worms. If accompanied by a penetrating stare and a painfully crushing handshake, a feeling of squirming inadequacy can be produced in more timid types of people. Methodists often use the precise opposite of this stance. They exhibit an air of mild, meek nonaggressiveness, with an almost shy look and a generally submissive tone of voice. It is *they* who may actually appear to wince in even the gentlest handshake. This trick works best against naturally robust individuals, who may be quickly reduced to a state of apologetic bewilderment.

"Each denomination will have to face up to these problems within the limitations of its heritage. The basic difficulty, as I have suggested before, is the same for all of them—the need to impress the layman with rather scarce equipment for doing so. It goes without saying that this need is rooted in the religious and professional self-conception of the men in question. However, we should not fail to also take into consideration the economic factor in the situation. The Protestant minister finds himself in a situation of acute sectarian competition and strong pressures from all sides bidding him to 'succeed.' His livelihood, in the case of most Protestant denominations, depends almost entirely upon the good will of the laity in his congregation. A change of occupation is no longer as easy in America as it was some decades ago, especially for a man getting on in years. What with the unusual fertility exhibited by ministerial marriages in the Protestant world, it should not surprise us that the economics of the matter sometimes make for quite desperate measures to remain on top in this contest between professional virtuosity and the shifting popular tastes in religious consumption."

(ii) MEMORANDUM FROM MADISON AVENUE

(The following is taken from a brochure sent out by Ballou, Weatherbee, Inc., a public-relations firm in New York City, advertising its new market-research process of RELIGIOSCOPE. The brochure was sent to top officers in various denominational headquarters and interdenominational organizations.)

"Ballou, Weatherbee has always believed in TOTAL public relations. A firm that employs Ballou, Weatherbee can rest assured that the TOTAL process of bringing its image before the public eye will be professionally handled by our communication specialists from beginning to end. Ballou, Weatherbee not only serves its client through expert representation with the mass media, but also has its own research department providing the client with scientific insight into the situation he faces. Ballou, Weatherbee is proud of its research department, which contains among other specialists no less than eleven Ph.D.'s in the social sciences and psychology, and which is known throughout the country as a pioneer in the latest psychodynamic methods of market research. The TOTAL approach in public relations, which has made Ballou, Weatherbee famous, is now well established in the secular market (among our clients are to be found Amalgamated Energy Corporation, Chipper-EEE Breakfast Foods, International Deodorants of Brussels, The Permanent Office of the Mau-Mau Movement at the United Nations, and many others). It is with a feeling of great satisfaction that we now recommend our approach to top religious executives for revolutionary use in the spiritual market.

"Forward-looking religious executives, responsibly conscious of the multimillion investment entrusted to their care, have for years used the techniques of market research in planning their nation-wide operations. Few boards of church extension or evangelism would today hazard the establishment of a branch in a new area without first having the results of an impartial survey at their disposal. Such surveys, of course, have become standard procedure not only in the planning of denominational agencies but in the negotiation of comity agreements on an interdenominational level. In recent years, especially as a result of rising construction costs and the rapidly shifting demographic picture, the most astute religious executives have begun to apply much more sophisticated concepts of the survey process. They realize that when planning to build a new, say, Methodist church in an expanding suburban development, much more needs to be known than the number of Methodists within reach of the projected church. Thus the services of city planners, real-estate consultants, and population experts have been increasingly drawn into the strategic considerations of religious management. Before a new church is built it is thus possible to know the relationship of its area to the planned or predicted development of the entire region around it, the movements of population, and real-estate values, and so to arrive at an intelligent estimate on the advisability of this investment from a business point of view. While all this is but another example of the up-to-date flexibility and foresight of American religious executives, and certainly a development to be wholeheartedly welcomed, it still involves a concept of market research that must be called old-fashioned by the standards of the secular market. To be precise, it involves the concept that prevailed before the rise of psychodynamic methods of research.

"Certainly it is superfluous to point out that religion touches upon very profound levels of personality. It is only logical, then, to point out that it follows that religious market research must somehow touch upon these deeper psychological levels if it is to be relevant to the planning decisions. It has been found that even in the selection of breakfast cereals deep psychological forces are at work motivating the choice of one product as against another. Ballou, Weatherbee has probably undertaken the most comprehensive study in this area and our statements on this subject have the authority of scientific fact. If this is true of such apparently superficial decisions as those involving the purchase of breakfast cereals, how much more is it true of the decisions that involve the religious behavior of people! It is high time that this understanding be applied to religious research. Writers on religion of many theological persuasions have said over and over again that man has profound religious needs. And professional religionists have asserted over and over again that the purpose of their calling is the satisfaction of these religious needs. We take the liberty of adding that research can help determine what exactly these religious needs are. In this way it will greatly assist the mission of satisfying these needs. Our motto 'THROUGH DEPTH-RESEARCH TO DEPTH-IMPACT,' already amply validated in the secular domain, receives its most profound challenge in the service of organized religion. With all modesty Ballou, Weatherbee would like to offer its approach as a contribution of the mass-communications industry to the religious revival in America—and thus to the spiritual strength of our country.

"RELIGIOSCOPE, a research process developed and used exclusively by Ballou, Weatherbee, provides the religious executive with scientifically tested information on the religious needs, both conscious and subconscious, of his target audience. RELIGIOSCOPE is to be used in conjunction with a conventional community survey, a service which is included in the RELIGIOSCOPE operation. Also included is the service of an evaluation team, which not only provides a comprehensive interpretation of the findings but gives detailed recommendations concerning the practical application of these findings to the planning involved. In employing this service the religious executive will thus never face the perplexing problem of relating complex research findings to a proposed course of action. The evaluation team does this chore for him. Once the research operation is concluded, and provided that an attack on this market is indicated by the findings, a different branch of the Ballou, Weatherbee organization jumps into action and assists the religious executive in utilizing all appropriate means of mass communications in achieving his program in that area. Our job is only over when your entire program has been successfully completed.

"RELIGIOSCOPE uses the latest methods of psychodynamic research to uncover the latent religious needs of people. With the use of a rigidly controlled statistical procedure to insure representativeness, respondents are selected from the population that is to constitute the target audience of the projected religious operation. Respondents are paid a *per diem* amount for agreeing to participate in the tests (the amount being regulated in accordance with the socioeconomic status of the respondents). A full day of testing is normally required to take one group of respondents through the full RELIGIOSCOPE battery. The RELIGIOSCOPE battery begins with the respondents filling out a set of questionnaires constituting the 'multivector religio-ideational inventory' (MRII), which provides a comprehensive picture of the respondents' *conscious* history and belief formulations in the religious area, as well as general information on personal background. The next step in the battery involves administration of the 'Schleim-Dickinson religious apperception test' (RAT), a projective test which begins to provide insight into the respondents' *subconscious* religious needs. The third step in the RELIGIOSCOPE battery is the 'religio-kinetic composition test' (RKCT), in which groups of respondents enact religious rituals of their own invention, thus giving further insight into both conscious and subconscious needs. The fourth step in the battery is the 'narcosynthetic religious anticipation trauma' (NSRAT), a technique developed by Dr. Waldemar Schleim of our staff and perhaps the most exciting innovation incorporated in RELIGIOSCOPE. In this test, which each respondent takes individually, a quasi-schizophrenic state is induced by the injection of a narcotic drug (of the variety popularly called 'truth serums'—which, of course, have no physical or psychological after-effects, and can be used even on children without danger). In this state it is suggested to the respondent that he is in contact with supernatural beings, in the presence of the divinity, in heaven or hell, having visions, listening to oracular voices, and so forth. This test brings to the surface the deepest religious images found in the subconscious and is so far the most refined scientific instrument for the diagnosis of the total religious *Gestalt* of a subject. With this test the battery is completed.

"While the RELIGIOSCOPE battery is designed for adults a modification of it is now being developed for use on children. This is especially important for religious executives interested in the young-family, suburban market, where activities in religious education are essential to the success of any religious operation. Slight modifications of various steps in the battery are provided for different socioeconomic and ethnic variables.

"RELIGIOSCOPE is still in its pioneering stages, but already its efficacy has been tested in a number of situations. A top-secret government agency concerned with intelligence operations behind the Iron Curtain has used RELIGIOSCOPE in its 'anti-brain-washing' training, as we are now free to disclose. One of our national Protestant denominations is using RELIGIOSCOPE on an experimental basis in four pilot projects in different regions of the country. RELIGIOSCOPE was first used with resounding success when Swami Guptu moved his operation from California to Connecticut, in order to be closer to the cultural centers of the nation. A complete RELIGIOSCOPE research was carried through in three counties in the southern part of Connecticut. As a result, invaluable advice could be given to the Swami, who has since established himself successfully in his new location. For example, while in California the Swami had satisfied very adequately the ritual needs of his clientele, RELIGIOSCOPE now made it possible for him also to satisfy the needs for personal counseling and guidance. The 'guidance cells,' staffed by specially trained psychotherapists and located in an annex of the Swami's sanctuary in Westport, were one of the direct results of this research. RELIGIOSCOPE findings were also partly instrumental in the Swami's design of the new Ceremony of the Lotus Maidens, one of the Swami's most beautiful religious creations.

"RELIGIOSCOPE is being offered on a completely nonsectarian basis to all religious groups. Ballou, Weatherbee firmly believes in the American principles of religious equality and interfaith cooperation. At the same time, we acknowledge the individual genius of each religious tradition. While our scientific techniques can be used to advantage by any religious executive, we realize that different groups will have different problems of policy. For this reason our evaluation teams work closely together with a number of theological consultants, all professors selected from prominent theological seminaries. These consultants are called in to form an advisory panel for each individual project. In addition, a number of professional religionists are permanently employed on our staff.

"The profession of public relations considers itself to carry out an elevated calling in the marketplace where ideas and creativity meet. Along with other specialties in mass communications, such as advertising and market research, public relations builds bridges of understanding. It brings together producer and consumer, idealist and public, artist and audience. Through what Edward L. Bernays has called 'the engineering of consent,' the profession helps safeguard the flow and interchange of communication essential to our democratic way of life. Ballou, Weatherbee is proud to pioneer in the application of its professional techniques to the great cause of American religion. May this pioneering mission contribute to the mobilization of America's religious forces as our country faces the world-wide threat of godless materialism!"

ADDENDUM: The following is from a newswire dispatch from Miami Beach, dated some months after the appearance of the above brochure:

"Along with Joe ('Armpits') Allonzo and three other top bosses of the international narcotices syndicate operating out of Miami Beach, the F.B.I. arrested Dr. Waldemar Schleim, a research psychologist in the employment of a prominent New York public-relations firm. The F.B.I. alleges that Dr. Schleim was retained by the Allonzo organization to undertake market-research studies preparatory to the establishment of new branches for the sale of narcotic drugs. Dr. Schleim, on the basis of depth-psychological research, is alleged to have advised the organization as to which psychological types are most susceptible to the narcotic habit and as to what approaches are best to be used by 'pushers' in the illegal traffic. The New York firm employing Dr. Schleim has firmly denied any knowledge of his activities in Miami Beach, where he went to supervise a survey undertaken on behalf of a Protestant denominational agency, and announced that it has immediately discontinued its employment of the arrested psychologist. Following the arrest of Dr. Schleim (known as 'Wacky Waldo' in the local underworld), the F.B.I. confiscated a large quantity of clinical and laboratory equipment found in his hotel suite for use as evidence in the case."

(iii) POSTSCRIPT FROM GREENLAND

USAF Base, Ice Cap ⚹ 67,
Greenland
25 April 1977

SUBJECT: Day of Judgment
TO: All Officers and Enlisted Men of this Command

1. Information received thru channels by this Command indicates that the cosmic phenomena now being observed in various areas of the world may be preparatory to the Day of Judgment (J-Day) often referred to by religious personnel. Liaison with the USAF Space Intelligence Command and the Baptist Prediction Bureau indicates the probability that J-Day may take place at any time after 0001 hours, 1 May 1977, with its probable center located in the Mediterranean area. However, chain effects may be felt in the area of this Command. The following SOP is issued for the guidance of all personnel, with the goal of undisturbed continuity throughout this emergency of the normal activities of this Command.

2. All personnel of this Command, including civilian employees, will participate regularly in a post-wide Metaphysical Preparedness Program (MPP). Each unit commander will designate one (1) MPP officer, to be assisted by two (2) MPP noncommissioned officers, the choice of suitable personnel to be in the hands of the unit commander. Unit MPP personnel, in close coordination with the chaplains, will be responsible for MPP lectures, displays, and training. The MPP officer in each unit will be directly responsible to the post chaplain's office, which may supersede all other channels of command on questions concerning MPP.

3. All personnel on this post will attend one (1) MPP training period a day. This is to take precedence over all other duties. Appropriate guidance, including training manuals, will be issued to MPP personnel thru channels. Pending arrival of MPP materials, unit MPP personnel will use training aids for Chemical Bacteriological and Radiological Warfare (CBR), as J-Day is expected to have side effects falling generally into CBR category.

4. Unit commanders will facilitate individual MPP training for all personnel. MPP posts will be set up at conveniently located spots in unit areas for individual ministrations by chaplains and their assistants.

5. The igloo of "Eskimo Elsa" and all other establishments associated with it are placed off limits to all U.S. personnel until further notice.

6. Authority: TX 6758-97Y-6554.

FOR THE COMMANDING GENERAL:
Solomon B. Goldfarb
Maj   USAF
Assistant Adjutant

OFFICIAL: Harold J. Munseworth
    Capt   USAF
    Adjutant, MPP Section

DISTRIBUTION: R-5-8

USAF Base, Ice Cap ⌘ 67,
Greenland
29 April 1977

SUBJECT: Day of Judgment (J-Day)
TO: All Officers and Enlisted Men of this Command

1. The disintegration of the moon at 0300 hours, 28 April 1977, and the sighting of the Whore of Babylon on a purple cloud at 0530 hours this morning at Cressy Point indicates beginning of J-Day operations. Following SOP will go into effect immediately.

2. Classified information received by this Command indicates that J-Day personnel, probably Angelic, may arrive at various places without prior notice and institute summary legal proceedings in connection with J-Day. If recognized, J-Day personnel will be accorded every military courtesy normally extended to official visitors from an Allied Power. They are to have full access to all files and every cooperation from unit commanders. Theological argument is to be avoided except by qualified MPP personnel.

3. Classified information just released by the Israeli Air Attaché in Washington, D.C., indicates that J-Day personnel may use the Hebrew language. The Jewish chaplain's office announces the establishment of a rapid beginners' course in that language which is open to all interested personnel. Chaplain Shapiro will also assist unit commanders in any language problems that may arise.

4. If resurrection of the dead should occur within boundaries of the post, resurrected military personnel, until further notice, will retain rank and unit as of date of demise.

5. The legal sections of all units, in cooperation with Chaplain Shapiro, will assist personnel in preparing Certificates of Non-culpability (TX 5778-90-T88, 28 April 1977). These Certificates are to be prepared in quintuplicate and distributed as directed.

6. U.S. personnel, military or civilian, will not (repeat *not*) participate in Eskimo exorcism rites.

7. The sale of intoxicating beverages at the central officers mess or any of its branches is herewith discontinued until further notice.

8. Amendments to this SOP will be issued as required.

9. Authority: TX 6758-98X-65555.

FOR THE COMMANDING GENERAL:
Solomon B. Goldfarb
Maj   USAF
(Member of B'nai-B'rith)

OFFICIAL: Harold J. Munseworth
Capt   USAF
(Member, Baptist Church)

DISTRIBUTION: R-5-8

Message over public-address system, midnight, 30 April 1977:

THIS IS THE COMMANDING GENERAL SPEAKING. I HEREWITH ORDER A RED ALARM REPEAT RED ALARM. ALL PERSONNEL IMMEDIATELY TAKE BATTLE STATIONS FOR A RED ALARM REPEAT RED ALARM. THIS IS THE COMMANDING GENERAL SPEAKING. . . .

Message over public-address system, 0001 hours, 1 May 1977:

LORD HAVE MERCY UPON US!

Silence.

8. Antireligious Critique

THE ANTIRELIGIOUS CRITIQUE SERVES TO UNMASK THE INAUTHEN-
TICITY OF THE RELIGIOUS RATIONALIZATION. ATHEISM OR AGNOS-
TICISM MAY BE STEPS INTO FREEDOM.

In the presentation of religion in the last two chapters there is
implied a moral critique. It will be advisable, however, to make
this critique explicit before we undertake to deal with the subject from the viewpoint of the Christian faith. In explicating
this critique we shall also make clearer the remarks made on
religion in the first chapter. It is not of interest here to give a
historical survey of antireligious thought and of the ways in
which our own critique relates to it. It may be enough to refer
to a substantial tradition of thinking along these lines, beginning in earnest in the eighteenth century in France and
reaching its most incisive expressions in the nineteenth century in various European countries.[1] There are different perspectives from which this critique can be undertaken. One
may mention only a few names to indicate this—Feuerbach,
Marx, Bakunin, Kierkegaard, Nietzsche. Yet nowhere is this
critique expressed more trenchantly or more profoundly than
in the work (and especially the last work) of one whose entire
life was spent in the passionate tension between faith and
unbelief. We are, of course, speaking of Dostoyevsky and of his
last novel, *The Brothers Karamazov*. There are various types of
antireligious positions found in Dostoyevsky's work.[2] The one
which is most important for our purposes is the position
expressed so shatteringly in the figure of Ivan Karamazov. For
here atheism is the outcome not of a rationalistic metaphysics
but of a moral attitude.

The morality of this type of atheism consists in the rejection of God, not because He is improbable but because He is unjust. At the center here stands not a philosophical line of reasoning but a passionate protest. The central problem is not one of epistemology but that of theodicy. The great earthquake of Lisbon was used by some of the eighteenth-century thinkers as an occasion for asking how the omnipotent and perfect God worshiped by Christians can stand by and allow such horrors to come to pass. As Voltaire put it in his poem on this catastrophe:

> "Shocked at such dire chimeras, I reject
> Monsters which fear could into gods erect.
> But how conceive a God, the source of love,
> Who on man lavished blessings from above,
> Then would the race with various plagues confound,
> Can mortals penetrate His views profound?
> Ill could not from a perfect being spring,
> Nor from another, since God's sovereign king;
> And yet, sad truth! in this our world 'tis found,
> What contradictions here my soul confound!"[3]

Yet Voltaire, even in this very poem, arrived at a fundamentally optimistic belief in providence, which he shared with other exponents of the deism of this period. It was the Marquis de Sade who may well have been the first thinker of this same period who used the contradiction of theodicy to arrive at an uncompromising atheism. In his own words—"The idea of God is the sole wrong for which I cannot forgive mankind."[4] Albert Camus has described this moral atheism very clearly in his discussion of Ivan Karamazov from which a fuller quotation may be helpful:

"'If the suffering of children,' says Ivan, 'serves to complete the sum of suffering necessary for the acquisition of truth, I affirm from now onward that truth is not worth such a price.' Ivan rejects the basic interdependence, introduced by Christianity, between suffering and truth. Ivan's most profound utterance, the one which opens the deepest chasms beneath the rebel's feet, is his *even if*: 'I would persist in my indignation even if I were wrong.' Which means that even if God existed, even if the mystery cloaked a truth, even if the starets Zosime were right, Ivan would not admit that truth should be paid for by evil, suffering, and the death of innocents. Ivan incarnates the refusal of salvation. Faith leads to immortal life. But faith presumes the acceptance of the mystery and of evil, and resignation to injustice. The man who is prevented by the suffering of children from accepting faith will certainly not accept eternal life. Under these conditions, even if eternal life existed, Ivan would refuse it. He rejects this bargain. He would accept grace only unconditionally, and that is why he makes his own conditions. Rebellion wants all or nothing. 'All the knowledge in the world is not worth a child's tears.' Ivan does not say that there is no truth. He says that if truth does exist, it can only be unacceptable. Why? Because it is unjust."[5]

Camus has given us in his own work unforgettable expressions of this same moral rejection of religion—for example in *The Plague*, where the doctor Rieux announces that he refuses to worship a God who tortures little children, or in that haunting passage in *The Fall* in which the melancholy of Jesus is explained by his responsibility for the massacre of the innocents. The problem of theodicy is here approached from the moral position which declares the bystander to be guilty— and which indicts God as the eternal bystander. Religious submission is thus seen as an assent to injustice and the rejection of this submission becomes the first step of human liberation.[6]

The problem of theodicy in its metaphysical sense is not our concern here. However, as we have seen before, this problem has its social dimension as well. If theodicy in its metaphysical sense may be the submission to an inscrutable providence, there is also the social theodicy in which men submit to evil and suffering as it is inflicted by society. The two theodicies are not unrelated. It is in the name of the metaphysical judge that the empirical executioner brings down his sword. If suffering and injustice are accepted on a cosmic scale, this acceptance will have its obvious social and political consequences. There may well be a sort of metaphysical masochism involved in both of these theodicies, but this masochism very likely has more to do with the wish for meaning than that for pleasure. The thought of living in a meaningless universe is unbearable, as is the thought of living in a society without reason or purpose. It is better to be subjected to tyranny than to chaos. Thus even the most ferocious divinity is preferable to the void of an indifferent cosmos in which not even the sentence of damnation answers our cry for order. The gods may be unjust, they may create purgatories and hells, they may torture and kill—but all of these things are better than to conceive of their absence. One then submits to the punishing divinity as the masochist submits to his torturer. By submitting to pain, instead of rebelling against it, one affirms an order beyond oneself and the faith that this order will have a place within it for one's own being. It is very much in the same way that men submit to earthly tyrannies. It is not only fear that makes them do this. It is the often frantic desire for order, for legitimacy, which may lead to the most fanciful rationalizations designed to prove that the powers that be are ultimately just and purposeful. We often find before the onset of great revolutions that these rationalizations collapse and that rebellion reaches up to the centers of power which had previously been immune. Thus it would seem that many Russians, even those most violently opposed to the social ills of the old regime, went right on believing that there were only evil intermediaries standing between the people and the good intentions of the tsar. This rationalization collapsed with the abortive revolution of 1905. There could no longer be any doubt about the fact that the tsar himself was guilty. But the myth of the good tsar is not unrelated to the other myth that makes the tsar the vicar of divine power. The religious theodicy sustains the political one. It is an instinctive grasp of this connection that explains the antireligious animus of most of the great movements of revolt following the revolution of 1789. It is the same sound instinct which makes conservatives of all descriptions appeal to the authority of religion.

What is at the bottom of this masochism (be it religious or political) is the inability to face honestly the immense precariousness of our existence. We would then follow Sartre's rather than Freud's interpretation of masochism here—that is, masochism as a mode of bad faith. In politics this means the desperate optimism that we find so often today when people discuss the possibilities of an atomic war, always based on an assumption of rationality or even morality on the part of the policy-makers on either side, an assumption which may be plausible but certainly remains precarious. We desire to have a government that governs, that is informed, that knows what its next step is going to be. Even a bad government is better than none. Thus we seek for hidden meaning in even the most patently meaningless actions of our political leaders. Sometimes this urge to attribute sense where there is none may lead to the ironic consequence that the most sophisticated intentions are suspected behind the most hopeless blunders— the reasoning being, of course, that since such blunders are inconceivable, they must hide truly remarkable designs. This psychological complex has its religious parallel and probably a religious root. At any rate for most men the universe offers no certain answer to their cry for meaning. This silence is unbearable. Rather than suffer it men fill the void with the creations of their desperate imagination. There can be little doubt that, whatever religious phenomena may not fall into this scheme of interpretation (and there certainly are some), there are wide areas of religious psychology where such a theory of projection adequately explains whatever is taking place. Since men know deeply how precarious is the being of these gods fashioned out of the clay of their own desperation, this being must be affirmed violently, absolutely, intolerantly. We have already looked at some of the psychological fortress-building that this complex evokes. Here also the precariousness of existence is driven out of consciousness by the resolute banging of the holy tam-tams. Men crouch before their idols in the narrow spaces of their various caves. As they huddle together in this way, they can temporarily forget the great silence of the stars outside the caves. This too is bad faith.

There are, of course, atheistic movements which simply substitute a pseudoreligion of their own for the religion they seek to destroy. The best example of this is the Communist movement in its self-styled "godlessness"—with its scriptures, its altars and rites, its exegetes and heresiarchs, its catechism and its eschatology. In terms of our antireligious critique, such movements fulfill all the social and psychological functions of religion in other situations of human history—a point that has been made by many critics of Communism. As Karl Jaspers put it, Marxism, like other movements of this type, derives its psychological impetus from the urge "to liberate oneself from liberty"[7]—in other words, a flight back into religious tutelage. There are religious critics of modern atheism who, following Luther's argument that man worships either God or an idol, have maintained that this process of what might be called remythologization occurs inevitably. It seems to this writer that such argument is unfair and not in accordance with the facts. It is quite possible, as many examples of Western thought in the last two centuries show, to reject religion without constructing a synthetic one to serve as a substitute. It is possible for men to live without worshiping anything. It is their own uneasiness and lack of imagination that leads religious critics to deny this possibility. Yet it is precisely this possibility that interests us here.

To reject the comforts and security of religious submission is to have the courage to admit the precariousness of existence and to face the silence of the universe. This certainly does not mean that one must resign oneself to meaninglessness or that one must give up the quest for meaning. It does mean the surrender of illusionary meanings and false reassurances. This also involves a relentless intellectual honesty which abhors bad faith and seeks always to be conscious to the fullest possible clarity. Such intellectual honesty forces the admission that there are many questions, even vital questions, of which we are ignorant. Such intellectual honesty makes impossible the postures of absolute certainty which constitute the stock-in-trade of so many of the religious. One then dares to emerge from the warm familiarity of the sacred caverns and finds the courage to look calmly at the cold constellations of the night. The antireligious critique that concerns us here is an invitation to this confrontation with silence. It is at the same time a passionate protest against the bad faith of what goes on in the caves.

The descriptions of religious professionalism which we have put into the mouth of our Monsignor Racciati in the preceding chapter fall under the category of bad faith in this sense. It should be made very clear that this category is *not* intended to cover the entire domain of religious experience. It is quite possible, within our critique, to admit the possibility of an experience which gives inner certainty about religious affirmations. However such experience is ultimately to be explained, whether it is or is not a genuine contact with metaphysical realities, such experience need not have the character of bad faith. However, it is equally clear that the great majority of people posturing as authorities on the mysteries of life actually know no more than everybody else. This is especially true of people whose professional competence demands this posture. The antireligious critique constitutes a challenge to these alleged authorities to prove their case. It refuses to be intimidated by the paraphernalia of the witch doctor. It perceives the mystagogue as a human being and asks for a humanly intelligible account of his mystifications. It refuses to forget that he has a name, a certain parentage and biography, and perhaps a weak stomach into the bargain. By thus humanizing the religious situation it need not destroy the possibility of genuine mystery. These are men whose childhood ambitions and gastrointestinal difficulties cannot change our respect. They are very few. In them, once in a long time, we may sense the human touching upon realities other than and beyond itself. The fully human understanding of these men only underlines the strangeness of what has befallen them. We may then believe or continue to doubt their message, but we shall respect them in either case. In most cases, however, this humanizing perspective directly challenges the claim to superiority being made. The debunking consequences of both social-scientific and psychological (not necessarily psychoanalytic) understanding make this abundantly clear. What seemed like iron conviction before now takes on the character of compulsive reiteration of those propositions without which one cannot afford to live. What seemed like overwhelming majesty now appears as the art of the impresario. The community of believers reveals itself as a society for mutual reassurance. Even the crudest economic and political factors are seen to be operative in realms that had been thought of as purest metaphysics. Thus it is not simple barbarism when the psychologist raises questions about the mother of the Emperor Constantine or when the sociologist, looking at the Council of Nicea, asks who paid the bus fare of the delegates. These questions radically humanize the situation and thus show it up under a new perspective, that comic perspective of which we spoke before. The clash of rival gods is seen as a comedy of very human pretensions. In facing the religious authorities our critique will ask quite simply, "Who are you?" And it will address the same question to the competing establishments.

Any person with the semblance of profound convictions is likely to appear as a tower of truth to others who do not have such certitudes. It is not an accident that the most rapidly growing religious bodies in America today are those with the most grandiose pretensions to absolute rightness. A naturally honest skeptic will tend to attribute his own honesty to others. Their conviction will then appear all the more impressive. This is the strength of a Jesuit among doubting Protestants, of a Communist among tolerantly undogmatic Westerners, of a recently psychoanalyzed person at a gathering of those whose frustrations have not been authoritatively catalogued. It might be mentioned in passing, for the benefit of uneasy skeptics, that one of the best ways of counteracting this effect is to *bring together* rival claimants to the role of oracle. There is every chance that, like two primadonnas at a party, they will neutralize each other, in one's own mind if not in social inter-action, and the normal business of life can then continue. In other words, introduce your best Jesuit to your best Commu-nist, arrange a rendezvous between Freudian and Jungian, let your fundamentalist friend be trapped by Jehovah's Witnesses. What we have called humanization may occur then with great rapidity.

The antireligious critique recalls to us that we are all human beings. We do not know where we came from or where we are going. We were children once, discovering a strange world. We played games, we cried and laughed, we wanted to be Indian chiefs and gangster bosses. We have bad dreams now, we get sick when we eat certain foods, we have impossible fantasies of sexual fulfillment, we want everybody to listen to us with great respect. And very soon we shall all be dead. When a man comes who claims to hold the keys to the inner secret of this astounding journey, we first of all recognize him as a man. We recognize that it is another man who is speak-ing, who was also a child and with whom other foods disagree and whose wife is very fat and who will die himself. We may then listen to what he has to say. But we shall know that it is a man like ourselves we are listening to. Most of those who profess religious convictions cannot stand this attitude very well. Having identified with their particular divinity, they re-gard the attitude as an act of sacrilege in itself and as proof of the metaphysical depravity of the one who maintains it. This is why so much of religious apologetics is undertaken in bad faith. The one to whom the apologia is made is defined *a priori* as outside the circle of illumination. Whatever he says, therefore, is listened to only insofar as it can later be used against him. The goal is not communication but conversion. One does not wish to understand but to conquer. Again, the reasons for this are most human ones indeed.

Although this is not an important concern of this essay, it might be stressed here that the antireligious critique would do away drastically with the various uses of psychological argu-mentation by religious apologians. This argumentation usually hinges on some conception of religious needs being present in human beings and then of religion as supplying the satisfaction of these needs. Whether these religious needs will then be reduced to some other psychological force (say, the Freudian libido in its countless avatars) or be considered as a psychological reality in its own right (say, in the Jungian theory of archetypes), it remains by definition impossible to draw any ontological conclusions from these psychological data. In simpler words, the psychologist can never go beyond saying that we have certain needs, a statement that tells us nothing whatever about the existence or nature of that which we allegedly need. On scientific grounds there may also be very serious doubts about the legitimacy of any such psychological statement. But our antireligious critique need not go into the scientific controversies on the matter and can restrict itself to the inner logic of the argumentation. It can then be assumed, for the sake of the argument, that such religious needs do indeed exist. Religion then becomes a function of our psychosomatic being in a manner analogous to sexuality. In other words, one is religious in the same way that one likes brunettes. We happen to know that brunettes exist and that some of them, at any rate, may assist in the realization of our sexual fantasies. We have no such assurance with regard to the religious beings which we are supposed to need. It is a wild speculation indeed that would assume that the world is so arranged as to satisfy our needs and to protect us from frustration. To reason thus would make the instinct for survival an argument for the impossibility of death. Such reasoning in itself calls for a psychological explanation. If the antireligious critique would venture at all into the realm of psychological argumentation, it would most likely do so with the category of bad faith. In other words, the most important psychological problem in this area concerns the psychology of self-deception.

However, our most important concern here is not with bad faith in the individual psyche but with bad faith existing in society, as a social function. Our interest in the antireligious critique is centered at this point. Within the perspective in-

dicated in the last two chapters, religion as a social function
becomes subjected to a radical moral judgment. Religion, as
we have tried to show, offers the most important alibis for
actions undertaken in bad faith. Religion sanctifies power and
sanctions violence. Religion provides the foundation for any
system of values held with ultimate seriousness by a group,
regardless of what these values are. Most important of all,
religion gives the appearance of granite to human conventions which in actuality have the precariousness of *papier-
mâché*. The antireligious critique, as it began in the eighteenth
century, is empirically entitled to its interpretation of religion
as an obstacle to human liberty. The critique is wrong in regarding this fact to be universal. There are liberating movements that sail under religious flags. Yet there can be little
doubt about the overwhelmingly conservative and inhibitory
effect of religion in most periods of history. Nor would it seem
a coincidence that the decline of organized religion in its hold
over the Western mind has contributed to the growth of
tolerance, intellectual freedom, and creativity, and to the
realization of those human rights commonly identified with
the democratic creed.

We might mention here one argument, often used by
religious apologians, which we would also feel inclined to subsume under our over-all heading of bad faith. This is the
argument that the turning away from religion must lead to
moral anarchy and that recent history demonstrates this fact.
This is ironic in view of the fact that precisely those phenomena usually adduced as evidence for this claim are the very
ones that our antireligious critique would recognize as authentic religious apparitions—for example, the rise of radical
eschatologies of both fascist and Marxist varieties. The reason
why Communism has so much appeal in many parts of the
world is exactly its religious quality. It is the same religious
quality which makes Communism intolerantly certain of its
goals and dogmatically self-righteous in its atrocities. The
greater tolerance and scrupulosity of the West are as directly
related to the Western uncertainties as to religious convic-

tions. The irony becomes profound when we reflect upon the fact that Communism despises the West for being religious, while the West detests the Communists as irreligious materialists. As to the historical dimension of this religious apologia, even a most casual glance at the long record of religious cutthroats from the Hebrew Judges to the Dancing Dervishes will show up the spuriousness of this argumentation.

But the point at which such bad faith becomes positive indecency is when the assertion is made that without religion (preferably the religion of the person making the assertion) men become anarchists without morality or restraints. This position can first of all be seen in its clear light by looking at it in the sociological perspective of Chapter 6. In this perspective, of course, it has a certain validity. That is, it is quite true that religion supports the moral values of a society and gives moral equilibrium to its individual members. Thus a young person liberating himself from the restraints of, say, a narrow fundamentalist background will have to think through what the moral imperatives are which previously he had taken for granted. If this is anarchy, so is every step into freedom. The same problem, of course, is faced by a young Communist who begins to doubt *his* religious background and, as happens to such of this type as can escape to the West, is now facing the task of rebuilding his life without the shackles of the Marxist ideology. But the person who says that without religion there can be no morality is only convicting himself in making this statement. For what he is really saying is that *to himself* morality must have the quality of magically guaranteed givenness. In other words, he is proclaiming his own lack of freedom, his own incapacity to seek a moral order in a world where nothing is guaranteed and very little is given. By contrast, the antireligious critique will point to those who have no such delusions and who yet try to meet the ethical demands of their existence as responsible human beings. It will further suggest to the religious apologians that the argument between faith and unbelief will have to be carried on on different ground.

A similar rejection applies to the argumentation, particularly popular among so-called neo-orthodox theologians, of presenting religion (again, usually their own) as the only tonic against despair. Sartre answered this argument briefly and to the point when it was used against him. He suggested to his religious critics that they ought not to confuse *their* desperation with *his*. Again, the apologian who uses this argument convicts himself. He is, in fact, saying that he cannot face life at all unless he puts on the spectacles of his particular religious coloration. He admits that religion functions for him as a narcotic does for the addict. Against this humanly distasteful position we would bring into evidence the work of, for example, Albert Camus.[8] The rejection of supernatural comfort here leads not to a nihilistic despair at all. On the contrary, it opens the way to a courageous acceptance and affirmation of life, including in this acceptance the tragic dimensions of existence, and a serious quest for answers to the pressing ethical problems.

Perhaps the essential malady of these religious arguments is the attempt to use criteria other than truth in dealing with questions of truth. Perhaps this malady is the heart of religious bad faith. Whatever religious propositions we take, we confront thereby a burning question of truth. "God exists" —yes or no? Is the statement true or is it not? No other criterion but that of truth respects the dignity of such a proposition. The kind of religious apologetics we have just looked at *assumes* the truth of the proposition before it even sets out and then tries to substantiate the assumption by arguments that have nothing to do with the truth—such as the usefulness of the proposition to the maintenance of law and order, or the apologian's need for the proposition in terms of its moral inspiration or despair-preventing efficacy, or perhaps even the hoary antiquity of the proposition and the relative novelty of its denial. In many cases the criterion of happiness is substituted for that of truth. "God exists"—"Will I be happier if this is true? Or will society? If yes, then the proposition must be affirmed." To this line of reasoning the anti-religious critique will retort that truth and happiness have nothing to do with each other, that there are very *un*happy truths, and that this kind of hedonistic pragmatism is unworthy of those claiming the existence of a God whose attributes include perfect truth. On the contrary, intellectual honesty demands that we pay special attention to those truths that contradict our aspirations toward happiness. We shall all die. This is certainly true. And it is the most unhappy of truths.

This antireligious critique has been quite important in Europe as part of the intellectual defense against Communism. One could mention here not only Camus but critics of Communism such as Koestler, Malraux, or Jules Monnerot. Against the religious fanaticism of the Communists is placed the moderation and the restraint of the uncommitted mind that is open to the world in freedom.[9] But this critique, for different reasons, is very important in the American situation. Still moving on the crest of the postwar "religious revival," practically unchallenged on its home territory except for the silent indifference of the recalcitrant nonjoiners, the American "civic religion" continues to live in the delusion that the society could not exist without it and that the present marriage of convenience will be an eternal union. Not only is this delusion rarely challenged in America (where, if this is possible, there are even fewer atheists than Communists), but all the authoritative voices proclaim religion as the necessary foundation of the American way of life and next only to the H-bomb as America's most powerful weapon of defense. The temptations of bad faith in such a situation may be well-nigh irresistible, especially for those who have a vested interest in the religious boom. Where religion is safely embedded in political establishment and social respectability, the antireligious critique offers the unexpected possibility of an honest look at reality. Its debunking thus becomes a moral imperative. At this point we find a strange and instructive affinity between the antireligious critique and the prophetic mission of the Christian faith. It will be our task in the last part of this essay to look at this affinity in greater detail and to draw from it certain consequences for Christian existence in society.

PART THREE
Exodus

9. Christian Faith and the Critique of Religion

THE CHRISTIAN FAITH IS NOT RELIGION IN THE SENSE OF OUR ANALYSIS. THE CHRISTIAN FAITH IS CLOSER TO THE ANTIRELIGIOUS CRITIQUE THAN TO RELIGION. IN FACT, THE CHRISTIAN FAITH PROVIDES A RADICAL ANTIRELIGIOUS CRITIQUE OF ITS OWN.

There are certain kinds of insight which had best remain private. If our argument had to stop at the point it reached in the last chapter, there might be good grounds for subsuming it under this advice. It may be true, indeed, that the debunking of fictions is a step toward freedom. At the same time, there is good reason to be pessimistic about men's capacities for and inclinations toward such a goal. Also, he who tears down Potemkin villages is morally obligated to linger on as the inhabitants gaze down into the precipice that had previously been hidden from their eyes. Unless the debunker has the inner substance not only to observe but to be prepared to speak helpfully in this situation there is something morally distasteful about the debunking enterprise. Applying these considerations to the present essay, we would regard the analysis (including the amount of polemic and satire that was felt to be necessary for its accomplishment) as the prelude to an act of affirmation. In this case the basis for the affirmation is given in the Christian faith.

Yet it may be advisable to add one other word of clarification. It is a common practice of preachers to jolt their audience out of their restful dozing by some peculiarly violent line of argumentation, but all this is followed by an emotionally soothing sequel which exempts all present company from the indictment and perhaps even admits later that it put certain things a little strongly in order to make a point. The writer of this essay would emphatically disavow such an intention. What has been said so far is to be taken in the sense in which it was said and no other. In other words, the content of these last chapters is not intended to provide a withdrawal from the argument but rather to carry the argument further.

In this and the following chapter we would look backward on the course of the argument, beginning with the problem given to Christian faith by the antireligious critique. We would then look at the relationship of Christian faith to the bad faith made possible by the fictitiousness of society, and then ask some very broad questions about the significance for this faith of the precarious vision of social existence. In these considerations what is said, as will be clear, is said from the position of Christian faith. It will be clarified later in what sense this position is held as against the varieties of bad faith discussed before.

The crucial point of the relationship between Christian faith and the antireligious critique is to be found in a theological proposition. The proposition states that the revelation of God in Jesus Christ (which is the object of Christian faith) is something very different from religion (which is the object of the antireligious critique. The consequence of this proposition is that, far from being affected by this critique, the Christian faith has important affinities with it. Needless to say, this is not an original proposition. The most comprehensive statement of the proposition in contemporary theology is undoubtedly that of Karl Barth.[1] In the terms of the thinking behind this essay, however, the writer would rather point to two other thinkers—for the general relationship of Christian faith and religion to Dietrich Bonhoeffer,[2] for the relationship of Christianity and atheism to Simone Weil[3] —with full cognizance of the fact, it ought to be added quickly, that these two authors are strongly contradictory in many aspects of their thought. It is certainly suggestive that these two names are frequently given in both Europe and

America when people speak of truly contemporary witnesses to the faith—that of the young German theologian executed by the Nazis a few weeks before the end of World War II and that of the strange Jewish expatriate from France who died in 1943 in her English exile. It would be difficult in this century to find two other thinkers with that combination of merciless intellectual honesty and passionate commitment to Christianity, or any that would share such clear consciousness of the realities of the modern world. Finally, it seems to this writer that no consideration of religion as it exists in society can by-pass the disturbing shadow of Kierkegaard's attack on the Danish church of his time.[4] It should be required reading especially for those who speak glibly of the "rediscovery of the church" in our own time.

It goes without saying that the question of Christianity and religion involves massive theological problems. It is not the task of this essay to solve these problems. We would rather see how the above-mentioned proposition relates to the socio-logical and moral perspective that has emerged in our argu-ment so far. We would look at the proposition not as part of a process of theological system-building but as providing sharp illumination to our own problem, which has a socio-logical rather than a theological point of origin. In other words, we want to ask some relatively simple questions: Society being a structure of fictions, what is Christian existence in society? Religion being closely related to the bad faith of the social fictions, what is the relationship of Christian faith and religion? In what way is the Christian faith, then, rel-evant to being a fully conscious and morally responsible participant in the social drama?

Christian faith means to believe the proclamation of God's revelation in Jesus Christ. Its point of origin and its only lasting point of reference is in the person of Jesus Christ. Of course we know very well what immense streams of religious thought and life have come from this point, pro-viding power for the erection of magnificent interpretations of the world, of mighty institutions, and (almost as if in

passing) of an entire civilization. But Christian faith remains
bound to this one point where it confronts the person of
Jesus Christ asking the timeless question, "Who do you say
that I am?" Christian faith before Easter and after it is
contained in the answer (indeed, *is* the answer) that Peter
gave to the question at Caesarea Philippi—"You are the
Christ, the Son of the living God." And after Easter it becomes what may well have been the first Christian confession
of faith in the religious underworlds of the Roman Empire
—"Jesus Christ has risen from the dead." Beyond all the
relativities of history, both question and answer retain the
same significance. Are we abandoned in the boundless ocean
of being or is there a God coming toward us out of the envelop-
ing mystery? Do we confront a God who is pure majesty or a
God who enters into the travail of creation? Can we address
this God? Dare we hope? Christian faith is the affirmation
that God has decisively entered into our destiny, has broken
into history and begun within it the redemption of man from
all bondage, but especially from the bondage of guilt and
death. Christian faith affirms that this divine invasion has a
name, place, and date. The name is that of Jesus, the place
and date are given by the span of His life on earth. The
Christian faith further affirms that the God who is beyond
the spiral nebulae has taken upon Himself the shape and the
fate of one biped species of mammals on an insignificant
planet in the immensity of the galaxies—an affirmation that
either is rank madness or finds its simple explanation in the
assertion that this God loves His creation, that His essence is
that love, and that only for the sake of such love did He call
the cosmos out of nothingness. In Jesus Christ we receive
one brief glimpse of this divine mystery, but the mystery has
such magnitude of splendor that this one glimpse is all we
need to light our path for the remainder of our days. We
can now address God because we find that He has already
addressed us. And we can dare to hope. Christian faith, then,
is the affirmation that death is not the last word about human
existence, that there is a human destiny beyond tragedy, that

our encounter with Jesus Christ has a sequel beyond the grave. In the light of this encounter we look differently at ourselves and the world around us. Both we and the world appear under the double aspect of sin and grace, magnificence and degradation, sentence of death and promise of glory. Such is the proclamation and the faith which affirms it. Whether we can participate in this affirmation or not, we must come to terms with the stupendousness of the claim.

This proclamation comes to us from the outside. It does not well up from some inner depths of religious experience. It does not concern so-called spiritual realities within us. It concerns the person of Jesus Christ and certain specific events concerning Him, all events which confront us from the outside. In other words, the Christian faith is not a spiritual concern. But something more drastic is involved in the relationship between Christian faith and religion. The religious enterprise of human history, not only in its crasser forms but above all in its exhibitions of greatness and profundity, constitutes man's attempt to reach out into the universe and grasp the divine. The proclamation of God's revelation in Jesus Christ pronounces a radical judgment over this attempt. It declares the entire enterprise to be bankrupt. Whether this means that there is no point of contact between revelation and religion, or whether such contact is possible, is not our concern here (this question, of course, is still a very live theological issue, as expressed in the controversy on the matter between Karl Barth and Emil Brunner). What is important for our argument is that God's coming into the world in Christ prejudges any attempt of ours to come to Him. It is here, at this one point of Jesus Christ, that God has allowed Himself to be found. The religious enterprise continues to search for Him elsewhere. What the proclamation of Jesus Christ demands is faith. The religious enterprise circumvents this demand and seeks to meet God on other grounds. In other words, religion is lack of faith. And the Christian proclamation passes judgment on religion *as* lack of faith.[5]

That the encounter with the Biblical God, be it in the New Testament or the Old, involves judgment of the world is a commonplace of Protestant rhetorics today. But "world" here means all too frequently all that which is outside the religious community of the one who takes himself for the spokesman of the divine judgment. The abomination of modern secularism and all sorts of other characteristics of contemporary society is then taken to be a religious judgment on an antireligious world. Against this conception it is very important to emphasize that God's judgment first and foremost applies to religion, much more so and long before it also applies to those not concerned with religious matters at all. In other words, God's first quarrel is with Israel. If this were clearly understood there would be much less of the futile and often reactionary condemnation of the modern world that seems to be a favorite pastime of many religious spokesmen.

It seems that this antireligious character of God's dealings with men is a consistent theme in the Biblical tradition. Or to put this in different words, the ancient Hebrew knife of circumcision continues to cut away at man's religious roots. In many ways the Old Testament (and not only the prophetic movement in it) is a story of God's denial of man's religious needs. There can be little doubt that the non-Hebrew religions of the ancient Mediterranean world satisfied these needs quite well, certainly infinitely better than the inexpedient harangues that men like Amos or Isaiah had to offer. In these other religions man was safely held in the recurring cycles of nature and its divine forces. Through his body and blood he was linked securely to the life-giving earth. Religion provided for him a cosmos in which both men and gods were at home. It is just this religious security which the terrible Hebrew God is bent on undermining. And so the Hebrews were denied the comforts of the old orgies, of the mystic participation in the rhythms of the fields and the hills, of the pantheon filling the universe with divine beings.

It was a sharp knife indeed that cut them off from the life-giving mysteries of the past. And it was a truly terrifying God that drove them into the wilderness to listen to strange words under a strange mountain. The fleshpots of Egypt were far more than material goods. Much more importantly there were the spiritual fleshpots, all the comforts of the gods of the Nile. The memory of these fleshpots stayed with Israel, even after the encounter at Sinai and the conquest of Canaan, as a persisting, sometimes irresistible temptation.[6]

It was not the world that Israel left, not the world in the profane or secular sense, but the religious world, the world of the gods. It was not so much profane wickedness as religious idolatry that offered the most serious threat to Israel's covenant with God. Under the aspect of this God, all religious efforts are ultimately the building of idols. The characteristic feature of an idol is its manufacture by human hands—and minds. The roots of religion are within man. But the God of Israel is not to be found within man or anywhere within the natural order of the cosmos. He is the creator of both man and cosmos, His worship the opposite of idolatry. The psalmist expresses this opposition of creator and idol when he says, "For all the gods of the peoples are idols; but the Lord made the heavens" (Ps. 96:5). It is not at all a fanciful interpretation if we subsume under this same judgment of idolatry the many efforts by which man has sought, by his own activity, to satisfy his religious cravings. The peoples have more idols, and more religions, than there are pebbles of sand—"*but* the Lord made the heavens." In this "but" lies the judgment over the religious enterprise in all its forms.

In trying to understand the relationship of Christian faith and religion we thus do well to look backward in history. We may recall that great divorce which the Hebrew God established between Israel and the luxurious religious world surrounding it. We recall that it was not only kings but priests that the prophets thundered against—and priests of Yahweh as well as priests of Baal. And, above all, we recall that it was a religious crime for which Jesus of Nazareth was condemned by a religious assembly—the secular power played second fiddle in this enterprise. Finally, as Protestants we might do well to recall that the witness of the Reformation was directed not against the world but against the church. The old fleshpots continue to lure and the history of Christianity is one of religious restorations. Yet whenever the Christian faith breaks forth once more from this Babylonian captivity of religious forms, it threatens those religious forms. We then find such passionate witness as that of Kierkegaard against the religious institutions of his day: "The official worship of God (with the claim of being the Christianity of the New Testament) is, Christianly, a counterfeit, a forgery."[7]

As Frederick Neumann once put it in a lecture on Ecclesiastes, we encounter God in the Bible as Him who resists us. The claim of the Christian (and, indeed, of the entire Biblical) proclamation is a claim to truth. This truth is outside myself. It is a hard element of reality, against which my wishes or needs come up as against rock. It is truth over against all my religious aspirations. If I affirm this claim in faith, then it is for its truth that I affirm it—not because of its psychological or social utility. To worship God as anything less than truth must be to offend Him most seriously. Either the Christian faith is true or it is nothing at all that merits our attention.

We may now return to the preliminary remarks on religion which we made in Chapter I.[8] Religion may be defined here quite simply as providing ideas that transcend the individual and are capable of giving ultimate meaning to his life. If the antireligious critique brings out the spuriousness involved in the religious enterprise, the Christian critique of religon brings upon the enterprise an even more radical judgment. This is well expressed in Barth's essay on Ludwig Feuerbach in which the significance of the latter's *Essence of Christianity* (a work which provided the cornerstone of Marxist atheism) for Christian theology is affirmed. In this essay Barth maintains that only the confrontation with the living God of the Christian faith makes it possible to challenge Feuerbach's anthropocentric interpretation of religion:

"One had better look out if one picks up the only weapon that will take care of Feuerbach. No one may strike him with it unless he has himself been hit by it. This weapon is no mere argument which one exploits in apologetics, it should rather be a ground on which one can stand, and with fear and trembling allow to speak for itself. Whether or not we stand on this ground will be tested by our answer to this question: are we capable of admitting to Feuerbach that he is entirely right in his interpretation of religion insofar as it relates not only to religion as an experience of evil and mortal man, but also to the 'high,' the 'ponderable,' and even the 'Christian' religion of this man? Are we willing to admit that even in our relation to God, we are and remain liars, and that we can lay claim to His truth, His certainty, His salvation as *grace* and *only* as grace?"[9]

In other words, from the ground of Christian faith Barth finds himself assenting to Feuerbach's interpretation of religion as a human projection. In this agreement we find the crucial relationship of Christian faith and the antireligious critique.

It is now important for us to look at the implications of such a Christian critique of religion in terms of the problems raised in the second part of this essay. One of the most serious indictments of religion by its critics lies in the way in which religion is used to give an illusion of security in a very insecure world, an operation that we have felt entitled to call one of bad faith. It may thus be in order to take up this charge first of all. It was one that vitally concerned Bonhoeffer in his thoughts toward the end of his life. Bonhoeffer was struck by the capacity of modern man to get along quite well without the *deus ex machina* of religious interpretation. It is this capacity which finds expression in Bonhoeffer's concept of the "world come of age." As fewer and fewer areas of life are felt to be in need of the religious hypothesis, religion is relegated to the faraway borderline situations of human experience. This is how Bonhoeffer characterized the hopeless character of this development:

"Religious people speak of God when human perception is (often just from laziness) at an end, or human resources fail: it is really always the *Deus ex machina* they call to their aid, either for the so-called solving of insoluble problems or as support in human failure—always, that is to say, helping out human weakness or on the borders of human existence. Of necessity, that can only go on until men can, by their own strength, push those borders a little further, so that God becomes superfluous as a *Deus ex machina*."[10]

Against this relegation of God to those realms of mystery where men feel the need for an emotionally supportive hypothesis, Bonhoeffer maintains that the Christian faith speaks of God not on the borders but in the middle of life. This is another way of saying that the Christian faith is not a "religious concern." It does not set out to produce "spiritual" life, does not meet "spiritual" needs or aspirations. In Christ, God became incarnate *in the world*, the real world, not some phantasmagora of the spirit. Both incarnation and resurrection took place in that same real world. The risen Christ is Lord of all the world, not just of a certain mystical sector of it. That is, either the Christian faith is relevant to all of life or it is not relevant at all.

With even greater sharpness Bonhoeffer rejected the position that religion (the Christian religion or any other) be offered as a medicine to combat despair, an activity of many theologians that he described aptly as "rummaging in garbage cans." This involves a kind of psychological blackmail by which the "world come of age" is to be pressured back into religious tutelage. Bonhoeffer describes the activity of these latter-day evangelists in contemptuous terms:

"Wherever there is health, strength, security, simplicity, they spy luscious fruit to gnaw at or to lay their pernicious eggs in. They make it their object first of all to drive men to inward despair, and then it is all theirs. That is secularized methodism. And whom does it touch? A small number of intellectuals, of degenerates, of people who regard themselves as the most important thing in the world and hence like looking after themselves. The ordinary man who spends his everyday life at work, and with his family, and of course with all kinds of hobbies and other interests too, is not affected. He has neither time nor inclination for thinking about his intellectual despair and regarding his modest share of happiness as a trial, a trouble or a disaster."[11]

Bonhoeffer was greatly concerned with the inability of religious spokesmen to be relevant to the problems of the working classes, but we would suggest that his remarks are relevant beyond this particular social milieu. There is an increasing number of other people who refuse to patronize the "religious drugstore," as Bonhoeffer once called it (not to apply the nastier term of "religious comfort station" which he uses elsewhere). One is reminded here of Camus' passionate rejection of religion as a betrayal of the ordinary happiness of ordinary men. Bonhoeffer saw correctly that there is a fundamental indecency in trying to obtain religious commitment via the detour of despair. It so happens that some men don't despair so easily. To them such religion has nothing to say, except perhaps to revile them for their failure to kneel down in the muck.

While these observations are most pertinent in terms of the psychological functions of religion (and the bad faith involved in so-called religious needs), we would maintain a very similar relationship of the Christian faith to the social functions of religion. We have discussed the important way in which religion validates and sanctifies social roles. We would suggest, quite analogous to the statements by Barth and Bonhoeffer quoted above, that Christian faith, when it is true to itself (that is, when it remains on the ground of confrontation with Jesus Christ), cannot fulfill this function. On the contrary, Christian faith puts in question the assumptions, the self-righteousness, and with these the bad faith of the social carnival. The pretensions of the masquerade collapse in the encounter with the God of truth. Men stand before God as men and as nothing but men. The protective armor of their many roles melts away in that instant of judgment. Kings and beggars, judges and thieves, archbishops and revolutionaries share in the same judgment—and are offered the same grace. We may find here, as it were, a sociological dimension of Jesus' saying that we must become like children. It is a child that says, "The emperor is naked!" The perspective of the Christian faith, in very much the same way, denies the emperor his robes—and addresses him as a naked man.

Religion functions in society as a basis of morality, of law and order, of respectability, of a sound and sober way of life. Especially in America today this one sentence constitutes the total creed of many self-consciously "churched" people, and not a few of their so-called religious leaders. This is why considerations such as the above are of particular importance for the contemporary American situation. For the consequence of this understanding of the Christian faith is, of course, that the latter cannot be any of these things. What is more, when it is believed to be that, it not only threatens to become bad faith but (what is infinitely worse) takes on the character of blasphemy. For God is truth and wants to be worshiped in truth.

Christian faith cannot be the basis of morality. Different societies have different and contradictory systems of morals. Religion supports all of them, as it functions in these different societies. Its social function is subjected to the general relativity of values, beliefs, ideas of men. The love of God, as it reveals itself in Jesus Christ, is not a new or superior system of morality. Before the cross of Jesus Christ *all* systems of morality are relativized and judged. The Christian life is not obedience to a new law, but a living out of God's love in faith, which makes it possible to freely seek moral solutions to the ever-new problems that face us. The Christian faith does not glorify lawlessness or immorality. Yet, between the sinner and the Pharisee, it was the sinner whose company

Jesus sought. Whenever Christianity is presented as the basis
of morality, in the sense of society, God's free grace is rejected
in favor of a law made by men.

Christian faith cannot be the basis for law and order. Again,
this does not mean that Christianity is some sort of revolutionary doctrine which seeks the overthrow of existing social
structures. But, as with morality, any system of law and order
is relativized, judged, and thus declared to be less than ultimate
before the cross of Christ. Nor is it unimportant that
this same cross was erected in history by the forces of law
and order. God came into the world not as power and majesty
but in lowliness, humility, and suffering. In the passion of
Christ the contempt and oppression of all the victims of
social order is thrust upon the shoulders of the incarnate God.
From that moment on all violence against men becomes
violence against Him. Behind the face of every victim waits
the spat-upon face of Calvary. There is no social order without
violence. There can, therefore, be no social order which is
ratified in the sign of the cross. Any talk of Christian
societies, Christian states, Christian economies (or, for that
matter, of Christian revolutions and Christian futures) is
a betrayal of that cross. Christians, like other men, are caught
in the ambiguities and relativities of the human condition.
Like other man, they are compelled to seek moral paths
through the turbulent jungle of human affairs. They have
not been given the luxury of a supernaturally guaranteed
thruway.

Christian faith cannot be the basis of respectability. In
different societies there are different criteria by which status
and prestige are determined. There are many (including
ours) in which religion is part of the equipment required to
furnish a socially acceptable habitat. Such a situation puts
the atheist and even the avowed agnostic not only outside the
pale of the religious community but also outside the confines of the world of respectability. Thus in our society the
man in the gray flannel suit who commutes between his urban
pursuit of money and his suburban haven of happiness is

typical not only of respectability but also of our "churched"
population. Religion, in its role as guardian of respectability,
connives at greed, restless competition, and public irrespon-
sibility on the one hand, while on the other it reserves its
special favors for the cult of heterosexual bliss. Those who
reject suburban tastes and middle-class conceptions of work,
let alone those who challenge that one wife and 3.2 children
residing in a mortgaged split-level ranch house constitute
the apotheosis of sexual and emotional fulfillment, are not
only enemies of respectability but almost by definition enemies
of religion. Thus the so-called Christian churches of America's
great suburbia have nothing to say to the juvenile delinquent
of the inner city, nothing to the ethnic minorities that fail
or refuse to conform to the expectations of middle-class social
workers, nothing to the homosexual, and little to the divorced
person, nothing to any kind of social or political or even
intellectual rebel. Not only does religion become a middle-
class leisure-time activity, but its contents are marked by a
family cult in the private domain and a deadly conservatism
in the public one.[12] Again, this religious complex is revealed
as a denial of Christian faith when placed in confrontation
with the figure of Jesus Christ. It was not a coincidence that,
when God became man, He did so among the despised, the
rejected, those living on the sorrowful peripheries of society.
Prostitutes, criminals, political traitors, racial outcasts, va-
grants, and men of uncertain address or occupation—in a word,
the permanent inhabitants of social-work case reports and
police blotters—these were His customary companions. It
would be surprising indeed if His presence were now to be
found primarily among the respected and respectable, the
happy and healthy (not forgetting those who proudly exhibit
their "mental health"), all those whom everybody would consider good prospects for credit cards and for church membership. A reader of the New Testament would more likely look
for Him in a different section of town. Nor would it be
difficult to find that section. It is the one normally left un-

touched when church extension boards make surveys to scare up new candidates for church membership.

Christian faith cannot be the basis of a sound and sober way of life. Such a way of life always demands that the metaphysical questions of human existence be sealed up and bottled away. Not only must one give no thought to mystery, death, anguish, and guilt, but there must be none of the ecstasies that tear one away from the serious pursuit of socially acceptable goals. Religion that fills the churches every Sunday morning with organization men on a short leave from their desks (one is tempted to say that they "have just stepped out for a moment"), accompanied by their domestic entourage, is certainly consonant with this form of bad faith. As we have tried to show, religion even ratifies this bad faith. But the Christian faith can only serve as an irritant in this tranquil (and tranquilized) idyll. Far from reassuring men in their sound and sober arrangements, it tears them out of their security, puts them and all that is theirs under judgment, throws them up against all the metaphysical questions that can be asked and thence into the luminous night of God's desert, a night stabbed with terror but also with pangs of joy. Religion, as the guarantor of soundness and soberness, functions to prevent ecstasies. The Christian faith propels men into the most shattering ecstasy conceivable. Religion sanctifies the ground upon which men live their social roles. The Christian faith makes men look on as the ground trembles before God's presence. In other words, religion is an excellent investment for a fuller, more satisfying life. The Christian faith is not. We shall have occasion in the next chapter to ask further what this singular social inconvenience of the Christian faith means for the bad faith in which men exist in society. For the moment we shall arrest ourselves a little longer at the question of its relationship with the anti-religious critique.

One of the main emphases of Bonhoeffer's later thought was the assertion that the Christian life was secular, that the Christian was not a *homo religiosus* but a man simply being a man, that Christ was to be found in the world and not in some religious enclaves within it. It was along the same lines that Bonhoeffer felt that the Christian faith ought to welcome the fact that this world has "come of age," has emerged from religious tutelage, and is able to stand on its own feet without the support of a *deus ex machina*. It goes without saying that Bonhoeffer was going directly against the prevailing tendency in religious thought. While most spokesmen of the churches habitually deplore the secularization of Western civilization and, in one way or another, look back nostalgically on the time when (supposedly) Christendom was a reality, Bonhoeffer bids Christians to welcome secularization as an expression of the maturity and liberty of modern man. He also perceives (correctly, it seems to this writer) that secularization has its historical roots in the Biblical tradition itself. By denuding the cosmos of its divinity and placing God totally beyond its confines, the Biblical tradition prepared the way for the process we now call secularization. As Max Weber has shown convincingly, Protestantism played a key role in this modern development. It was Protestantism even more than Renaissance humanism which inaugurated the great process which Weber called "disenchantment." As Weber put it:

"That great historic process in the development of religions, the elimination of magic from the world which had begun with the old Hebrew prophets and, in conjunction with Hellenistic scientific thought, had repudiated all magical means to salvation as superstition and sin, came here to its logical conclusion."[13]

Weber's main interest, as is well known, is the relationship of this Protestant (and especially Calvinist) "disenchantment" and the process of the "rationalization" of life that made modern capitalism possible. However, Weber's concept has implications not only for economic behavior but for the entire cultural development of the post-Reformation world. It is, for example, very difficult to imagine the startling rise of modern science and technology without the great

Protestant "disenchantment" of which Weber spoke. As the sky is emptied of angels it is opened to the calculations and manipulations of the scientist. Nor is this a matter of pure conjecture. Very much in the Weberian tradition on this question, Robert Merton, for example, has given us illuminating insights into the role of Puritanism in the early development of modern science in England.[14] That some of the effects of its own cultural role were never *intended* by Protestantism is but one of the perpetual ironies of history. Just as Calvin would have been horrified by what Weber called the "spirit of capitalism," so the early Puritan scientists in the Royal Society would have been aghast at the "scientism" of their successors. It remains true that for Protestants to damn the secularization process has in it some of the qualities of a dark-haired father blaming his daughter for not being a blonde.

But there are more important reasons for desisting from the damnation of the "world come of age" than a sense of historical authorship on the part of Protestantism. Bonhoeffer has expressed this in his call for a "secular," a "religionless" Christianity. The God of the Christian faith wants man's freedom. It is only thus that the miracle of the incarnation can be understood. An old Jewish myth speaks of the creation of the world as an act of contraction (*tsimtsum*) on the part of God. It was necessary for God to take back into Himself some of His infinity so that there should be room for the world to appear. Simone Weil has (probably unknowingly) given expression to this Jewish idea of *tsimtsum*, but related it to the Christian concept of God's *kenosis* (humiliation, self-emptying) in Jesus Christ:

"On God's part creation is not an act of self-expansion but of restraint and renunciation. God and all his creatures are less than God alone. God accepted this diminution. He emptied a part of his being from himself. He had already emptied himself in this act of his divinity; that is why Saint John says that the Lamb had been slain from the beginning of the world. God permitted the existence of things distinct from himself and worth infinitely

less than himself. By this creative act he denied himself, as Christ
has told us to deny ourselves. God denied himself for our sakes
in order to give us the possibility of denying ourselves for him.
This response, this echo, which it is in our power to refuse, is the
only possible justification for the folly of love of the creative
act."[15]

We would suggest that man's "coming of age," his possible
liberation from the kind of religion which depends on illusion
and bad faith for its psychological motor forces, is part of the
same renunciation of God. It is God withdrawing, deliberately
not using His infinite powers to coerce man's infinitesimal
weakness, inviting man to respond freely and willingly to God's
address. In other words, Christian faith cannot gain from
man's bondage but must always welcome his liberations.

These considerations give us a striking perspective on the
antireligious critique, and beyond that on the phenomenon of
modern atheism. Suddenly it seems that atheism is closer,
in essential ways, to the Christian faith than that is to the
religious enterprise against which atheism rebels. Simone Weil
stated this idea succinctly and brilliantly in the following
passage:

"Religion, in so far as it is a source of consolation, is a hindrance
to true faith: in this sense atheism is a purification. I have to
be atheistic with the part of myself which is not made for God.
Among those men in whom the supernatural part has not been
awakened, the atheists are right and the believers wrong."[16]

It can be said, then, that atheism constitutes a negative
witness to the reality of God. It keeps pointing to this and
that in the world, and in men's minds, and keeps repeating
that God is absent. This, in itself, is an act of freedom which
comes close to the category of faith. As Karl Kraus, the
Austrian writer, put it, ". . . the true believers are those who
miss the divine."[17] But the witness goes more deeply. The
Christian faith proclaims a God who is utterly transcendent,
who is not part of the cosmos but confronts it as creator and
redeemer. In other words the Christian faith emphatically

speaks of an absent God, who cannot be found and cannot be used in any way—except as He consents to be found
and offers Himself to be used for man's redemption. Insofar as atheism underlines the absence of God, it is a
negative witness to His transcendence and sovereignty. It
is even possible that atheism, in smashing the many factories
of idols, can serve as a *praeparatio evangelica*—a path-maker
for the Gospel. We would suggest further that the antireligious critique, in its psychological and sociological debunking of religion (we may add to this the historical and
philosophical debunking jobs which have similar consequences), is capable of serving as a kind of underside of
the prophetic mission of the Christian faith. Finally, we
would suggest to the Christian theologian that he may find
friends where he sought enemies, and enemies where he
went looking for friends.

Christian faith calls in this way for an exodus from the
worlds of illusion and bad faith. It is an exodus out of the
Egypt of deceptive social safety, but also out of the Zion
of deceptive religious security. Of the two types of bondage
the second is more dangerous to man's relationship with God,
because, in addition to all other illusions, it adds the illusion
that he already rests in such a relationship. It is depressing,
but hardly surprising, that this kind of self-satisfied religious
satiation can be found also among those who interpret their
faith in heroic terms of daring and adventure. As both
Dietrich Bonhoeffer and Simone Weil saw very clearly, the
consciousness of abiding safely in the bosom of the church
(which Simone Weil called the "patriotism of the church"—
and Bonhoeffer scathingly called "cheap grace") is one of
the most serious obstacles to an honest confrontation with
the Christian faith. Again we would suggest that the obstacle
lies in the way of an invitation to bad faith. The church proclaims, possesses a certain faith. This faith is addressed to each
individual, in his unique existence before God. He cannot hold
this faith except as the unique individual he is. As a substitute
to this painful acquisition of faith, the individual can instead

identify with the church, the social collectivity which (in sociological terms explained in the first part of this essay) holds the faith as an ideology. His real act of decision, then, is not toward the faith but toward the church that claims to possess it. By identifying with the church he deludes himself into thinking that he has made a decision of faith. Actually he has only joined a club and accepted its bylaws. The bad faith of this operation is reinforced by theologians and apologians who bid us find out "what was really meant"—in the canonical writings, the church fathers, and whatever other sources the church regards as authorities. It is assumed that, having found out "what was really meant," all that is now required is an intellectual assent and thereby one has arrived at a state of faith. This, of course, is a delusion too. One may find out to one's full satisfaction what the New Testament means and agree wholeheartedly that the church (or one of the churches) adequately represents this meaning. This realization, however, does not get one a single step further toward the affirmation that this meaning is the truth, let alone the decision to base one's own life on it. The church is the primary locale of this great social fallacy.

This is why there are acute dangers involved for an honest confrontation with the Christian faith in the so-called "rediscovery of the church" of recent Protestant history. A new emphasis on the church has been, rightly or wrongly, one of the contributions of the theological revival of the last few decades. This essay is not concerned with going into these theological issues or even speculating on the implications of some of our perspectives here for a doctrine of the church. However, in a purely sociological sense, the new emphasis on the church encourages many people to "leap" (or, if one prefers, to "alternate") into the church in lieu of "leaping" into an affirmation of personal faith. It is also possible, of course, that there is a counsel of despair involved in this movement. The world has appeared as a singularly uncomfortable and inhospitable place for those who would seek ways of morally relevant action in it. The retreat into a

religious ghetto, nicely furnished with all the liturgical trap-
pings (after all, the "rediscovery of the church" has been
logically accompanied by a liturgical revival), is a more
comfortable course. One may add in passing that such a ghetto
is also more conducive to satisfying one's avowed or un-
avowed "needs" for mystical titillations. The new ecclesiology
can serve as a rationalization of this retreat. The churches,
appalled and baffled by the overwhelming social, economic,
and political problems of the postwar world, can then with a
better conscience spend their time with "spiritual" concerns.
Against this boom of "religious interests," not only in our
churches but throughout our society, one cannot repeat often
enough William Temple's incisive comment that it is a
great mistake to think that God is primarily interested in
religion—or Dietrich Bonhoeffer's to the effect that only he
who shouts out for the Jews has the right to sing Gregorian
chants.

If one agrees with the position that the Christian faith
concerns existence in the world, and not a religious existence
lived in withdrawal from the world, then very serious questions must be raised about the traditional postures of, let us
say, certified Christians. Hendrik Kraemer once commented
on the lamentable fact that Christians could normally be
recognized by the sickbed odor they exuded and spread around
them. One should add quickly that this aroma of otherworldliness is still much more palatable in the case of the honest
pietist or fundamentalist than in the case of back-slapping,
guffaw-swapping, "one of the boys"-style ecclesiastics of a
more recent model. This otherworldliness penetrates religious
activities and gives them their peculiar character of bizarre
unreality, even (and perhaps especially) when the attempt
is made to give them an everyday, matter-of-fact character.
Incidentally, the same aura of otherworldly unpleasure and
unfunniness hangs over church bazaars and get-togethers of
Communist clubs. The seriousness of the *agape* meal looms
as an opressive shadow over the profane conviviality of the
back-yard barbecue. This otherworldliness will not surprise us if

we understand the sociopsychological function of religion as an escape from the world and a mystification of worldly reality.

Christian faith places one into the world and particularly into those places of the world that call for loving responsibility. It would seem to follow from such a "secular" understanding of the Christian life that the Christian, more than other men, must be totally open toward the world and all its possibilities. The Christian faith cannot provide the intellectual appointments with which to furnish a sacred cave, a religious meaning system within which one can hide from ambiguity. On the contrary, the Christian faith explodes these dens of seclusion and sends their former inhabitants out into the open fields of the world. In this way a real dialogue between faith and unbelief becomes possible. If this dialogue is to be carried on in good faith, it means a deliberate surrender of those religious pretensions which Dostoyevsky's Grand Inquisitor summed up in his phrase "miracle, mystery and authority." The Christian is not one possessed by irresistible forces from the beyond. He is a human being and remains one. It is as a human being that he enters into conversation with others.

In recent Protestant theology much use has been made of the term "kerygma," which is the New Testament term for the proclamation of the Gospel. Such proclamation, presumably, is made with authority, with the claim to a dignity going beyond the human nature of the proclaimer. The paradigm of such proclamation for this writer is the customary little ritual preceding the sermon in Lutheran churches. The liturgy is over and the preacher has mounted the pulpit. He raises his hands and the congregation rises. He then brings greetings to them "from God our Father and our Lord Jesus Christ." The congregation then sits down and listens. What is being said, it is assumed, is not just the labored effort at communication of the Lutheran pastor in question, but a message coming with the same authority

that pronounced the greetings. Again, this essay cannot go
into a theological discussion of what the New Testament
calls *exousia* (apostolic authority). But it is possible to ask,
even while accepting the traditional Protestant posture of the
kerygma, whether an acceptance of the "world come of age"
may not also involve what can be called a nonkerygmatic
posture—that is, a stance on the part of the Christian which
deliberately and meticulously surrenders any claim to authority.

It would seem that only in such a posture is genuine dialogue
possible. One cannot converse honestly unless one puts all
one's cards on the table. A claim to religious authority,
carried into a dialogue however polite, is a club held under
the table. A claim to authority always projects the point
at which coercion will replace communication—*"Believe* or
shut up"—or even *"Believe* or be damned." Real dialogue
implies that partners enter into conversation as equals, that
they take each other's position as profoundly serious, and
that, in principle, they are willing to change their own
positions as a result of the dialogue. If, despite this careful
surrender of any human superiority, there remains authority
in what is attempted to communicate in the dialogue, then
this authority is not that of the speaker but of that which
passes through his words. It would seem that the possibility of
such a nonkerygmatic posture is implied in the incarnation.
God, who has all possible and conceivable authority, divests
Himself of all authority in His *kenosis.* Jesus Christ, the incarnate God, refrains at all times from using the powerful instruments of "miracle, mystery and authority" to convince
men—and finds the temptation of Satan in the suggestion that
these instruments be used. Would it not be strange if the
followers of this Jesus Christ could not risk subjecting their
faith to the openness of human communication, would have to
protect it constantly by the armor plate of religious suzerainty?
God wants the free assent of men. God wants human freedom. These, it would seem, are necessary affirmations of

the Christian understanding of God's dealings with humanity, and at the same time warrants for the total openness of the Christian toward the world. In this openness lies the decisive Christian answer to the antireligious critique.[18]

10. Christian Faith and Bad Faith

THE CHRISTIAN FAITH RADICALLY DEBUNKS THE SOCIAL FICTIONS.
THE CHRISTIAN FAITH IS THUS RELATED TO SOCIAL PERCEPTION.
CHRISTIAN ETHICS IS IRRELEVANT UNLESS IT SEES THROUGH THE
FICTITIOUSNESS OF SOCIAL STRUCTURE.

In the last chapter various statements were made from a
Christian platform, as it were. Anyone who has followed
the argument of this essay so far may well ask how the
writer manages to get up on this platform without having
to apply to himself that category of bad faith which has
previously been used in these pages with some generosity. It
must already be evident from the previous chapter that the
writer would maintain emphatically that Christian faith need
not be, and in its essence *is* not, bad faith, as that category
has been elucidated above. Any amplification of this position
will, of necessity, take on a somewhat personal character.
Since this essay is in no way the writer's *apologia pro vita sua*,
this is not an endearing prospect. However, the integrity of
the argument demands a measure of amplification at this
point. The writer, therefore, asks for indulgence if at this
one point in the essay some fairly personal statements are
made.

In the theological milieux of American Protestantism with
which the author is familiar (and which do not include the
grim fortresses of what remains of fundamentalism) there
are patent advantages to sailing under the banners of either
neo-orthodoxy or liberalism. In the first case, one is "in with"
the bright young men (using the adjective "young" in about
the sense that politicians would in referring to candidates for

public office); in the latter case, one can find social refuge
with some of the older gentlemen, which often has unexpected intellectual charms of its own (such as, for example,
the delicate pleasure of dabbling in heresy). If one has
difficulty locating oneself under either banner, at least by and
large, one may find oneself (to mix metaphors bravely) in
the situation of the man who lands on the floor in a game
of musical chairs. The writer must confess that this is exactly
where he habitually finds himself in the game of theological
encampment. This observation requires some explanation.
Perhaps the easiest way of explaining this would be to say
that the liberals pose a theological problem, the neo-orthodox
a psychological one. Or in different words, the difficulty with
the liberals lies in what they say, with the neo-orthodox in
how they say it. When it comes to the liberal conception of
Christianity, the writer is compelled to say what the lady
said to the palaeontologist at the cocktail party—"This is very
interesting, if you're interested in it." Not finding that his
natural reason predisposes him either toward religious hypoth-
eses or to the "ethics of Jesus," and not convinced at all that a
religious rationale is needed for such goals as world peace or
racial equality, the writer has few interests which would make
possible any sort of identification with liberal Christianity.
Insofar as Christianity is relevant, its relevance lies in the
very unnatural and unreasonable message with which the
neo-orthodox concern themselves. However, while the writer's
theological predilections thus propel him toward the neo-
orthodox camp, he faces a grave psychological problem as
soon as he enters *that* territory. The problem can be described
very simply. Yes, indeed, what is being talked of here is of the
greatest interest—but how do these people work up the air
of total conviction with which they do the talking? The
liberals, at any rate, have the courtesy to make clear at frequent intervals that they are talking out of the limitations
of their human location. The neo-orthodox have the discon-
certing habit of posturing as the listed subscribers to a private
line to headquarters. The kerygma is thrown down with

bravado from a pulpit suspended in midair between heaven and earth. This writer has great difficulty not only with the astounding indifference in some of these quarters as to what happens to the kerygma when it hits the ground, so to speak. He also is severely perplexed by the feat which allows people to climb into this lofty position. It may be allowed to point here once more to Monsignor Racciati's discussion in Chapter 7 of the less-than-convincing rationalizations normally given for this acrobatic achievement.

As the good monsignor points out, there may well be people who have had a mystical or even miraculous experience of metaphysical reality, an experience of such conviction that thereafter doubt is possible only as an intellectual exercise (say, like that of a philosopher playing with solipsism). Unfortunately the writer has not been thus privileged. He suspects strongly that he shares this underprivileged condition with the overwhelming majority of people. His suspicion even extends to those, be they monsignors or other fully accredited experts in religious communication, who claim such privilege. But even if he is willing to grant to these their authentic virtuosity in these matters, this does not assist him or others in his boat to muddle through within their amateur status. This has a very simple semantic consequence in terms of the use of words like "faith" and "believe." If one is in this underprivileged position and uses language honestly, then one may be fully aware of and intellectually agree with the more sophisticated theological uses of these words (as, for instance, Luther's identification of faith with trust, confidence—*fides*=*fiducia*), but ultimately one will have to use the words in their quite ordinary, common-usage sense. That is, when one says "I believe" rather than "I know" one is expressing a view of which one is not completely certain. That this view is much more than a mere opinion or theoretical hypothesis, that it is the result of passionate commitment and may lead to the most far-reaching existential consequences, is beside the point here. If one says "I believe," in this sense, one faces the fact that one is essentially in the same boat as the unbeliever—that is, one has essentially the same position *vis-à-vis* the kerygma that he has. The message of redemption in Jesus Christ comes to believer and unbeliever alike from the outside, refraining from coercion, asking an act of faith. Speaking theologically, this means that the Christian remains a sinner (that is, one separated from God) also intellectually. Speaking humanly, it means that what is called for is a decision made on less than overpowering evidence.

This has the further consequence that one who believes in this sense cannot escape the question of unbelief (or, for that matter, his own question) as to why he makes this decision. Not even a radical Calvinist doctrine of election absolves him from this necessity, for it is he who decides to assent to this doctrine. As we have seen, it is in the rationalization of such decisions that one skirts dangerously close to bad faith. Thus the writer finds himself unable to see Christian faith as the only alternative to despair. As Bonhoeffer has pointed out very clearly, this simply is not true. Indeed, the choice to take refuge in a religious system rather than face courageously the uncertainty of the human condition can itself be called an act of despair. Nor can the writer find much to recommend itself in the masochistic submission to an alien truth which is characteristic of so much religious thinking. If one takes seriously the notion that God is truth, then such a *sacrificium intellectus* is not only an offense against one's own integrity but against God.

There can be no basis for Christian faith except in the encounter with the figure of Jesus Christ, as it becomes manifest in the testimony of the Bible and the living proclamation in the church. Faith is the decision to stake one's existence on this figure. This is not a negative choice, because of any number of alternatives, because one cannot face finitude, meaninglessness, guilt, or death. It is a free and positive choice, not *away* from the realities of the human condition but *toward* this figure in whom the human condition is transfigured. To be human means to live with inconclusive information on the ultimate meaning of things. To have faith in Christ means to say that, if there is any meaning at all, it is here that one must find it. Perhaps, in the dialogue between faith and unbelief, one can go one small step further. One can add that in making the decision of Christian faith one chooses to believe that the ultimate truth about man is joy rather than courage. Another way of putting this is to say that the comic aspect of man's existence is more significant than that of tragedy (a point which we shall develop a little further in the following chapter). Unbelief will point out that in the world we are surrounded by signals that do not interpret themselves (a point that has been very much developed in Sartre's philosophy). There are signals of joy and signals of sorrow. It is our choice if we give more weight to the ones rather than to the others. This is true. But this also means that there is no rational priority to either choice. Christian faith follows the signposts of joy, considers them as the tokens of God's presence and as marking the path of human destiny toward its fulfillment.

The Christian confession that "Jesus Christ has risen from the dead!" is a shout of joy. Perhaps it is not only a Protestant but a generally Western characteristic that the attention of the faith has shifted from the jubilation of Easter to the somberness of Good Friday. Yet the Christian message is not primarily that "Jesus Christ has been crucified." That, in itself, would hardly have provided the basis for a proclamation. The proclamation announces the cross, but under the aspect of its having been overcome in the victory of the Resurrection. Perhaps Protestants can learn something here from the Eastern church—a thought that obtrudes itself upon anyone who has ever witnessed a Greek or Russian Easter service. The innermost secret of the Christian faith is not darkness but blazing light, not conviction of sin but an exultation that embraces not only all men but the whole infinite expanse of being. In the words of a Russian Easter hymn:

"For meet is it that the heavens should rejoice, and that the earth should be glad, and that the whole world, both visible and invisible, should keep the Feast. For Christ is risen, the everlasting joy!"[1]

If these remarks delineate the position of Christian faith, as the writer would understand it, as against the possibilities of bad faith of a religious nature, it may now be in order to relate this Christian faith to the varieties of bad faith that involve the social perception and self-perception of men. These considerations may also serve to introduce the ethical significance of Christian faith in dealing with these social problems.

We would venture to say that the perspective on society developed in the first part of this essay, while it does not lead directly to a Christian ethic of society, supplies important prolegomena to such an ethic. There is a wealth of theological writing in the field of "social ethics," some of it dealing in a profound and challenging way with the moral problems faced by men in their social relationships. However, there is one thread that runs through many of these which is most likely to lead to a distorted view of social reality, and that is the understanding of social roles and institutions as given in very much the same way as natural phenomena are given. Thus ethicists will speak of "the family," "the state," or "the economy" as if these were hewn out of granite, while actually, as we have tried to indicate, they are manufactured out of the most precarious of fictions, assumptions, and "as if" agreements. This is most true, of course, when social institutions are conceived of as actually given in natural law, as in Catholic social doctrine, but also when they (or their ideal prototypes) are thought of as "orders of creation," as in Emil Brunner's ethics.[2] There follows the almost irresistible tendency to speculate ethically not about men but about social roles. One then looks not at the moral problems of human beings engaged in government or warfare or agriculture, but one theorizes about the ethics of "the statesman," "the soldier," or "the peasant." There is then only one step to the bad faith which provides moral alibis in the name of mythological entities such as "the state," "the law," "the system of free enterprise," and so forth. Of course the ethicist like the sociologist, or, for that matter, the man in the street will speak of institutions in these abstract terms, and furthermore such abstraction is a necessity of analytic thinking. The danger, as we have tried to show, begins when these abstractions are taken to exist as moral realities which supersede the moral imperatives of real human beings. We would suggest that the perspective on society developed in the first part of this essay may be helpful in avoiding this danger.

The confrontation with the living God of the Christian faith strips men of their alibis and disguises. The aprons of fig leaves spun with the lies of institutional ideologies cannot cover man's nakedness as God seeks him out in his hiding places. In this, indeed, all men are the children of Adam, who said, "I heard the sound of thee in the garden, and I was afraid, because I was naked; and I hid myself" (Gen. 3:10). Or, in the words of the Epistle to the Hebrews: "And before him no creature is hidden, but all are open and laid bare to the eyes of him with whom we have to do" (Heb. 4:13). The God "with whom we have to do" has not recognized the sovereignty of our card-house institutions or the extraterritoriality of the moral hiding places which men have concocted among themselves. He steps into the palace of the king and the judge's chambers, ignoring the royal mantle and the judicial robes, and addresses the naked man underneath the costume as He addressed Adam: "But the Lord God called to the man, and said to him, 'Where are you?'" (Gen. 3:9). And as kings and judges renounce their human brotherhood with their victims, pointing to the immunity of their office, God will address them in words no different from those addressed to Cain: "What have you done? The voice of your brother's blood is crying to me from the ground" (Gen. 4:10).

Every literate man knows that certain positions in society entail responsibilities, privileges, and immunities. There are many books written about this, such as textbooks of ethics, codes of law, constitutions, and statutes. We would suggest that God, regrettably, has not read any of them. We would further suggest that this proposition of the illiteracy of God follows of necessity from the realization of God's truth as against the bad faith of social subterfuge.

To illustrate this proposition we might turn briefly once more to the case of capital punishment. We have looked before in some detail at the fabric of social fictions which provides moral alibis for all the individuals participating in this killing and which actually pretends that no individual did any killing at all. In a well-ordered modern state there are ample possibilities of documentation for this claim to personal immunity. The judge can point to the statute books, the governor to the constitution of the state, the warden to the prison regulations, and so forth. Any literate man can easily verify the authenticity of the claims. It is most unfortunate that God is illiterate. He has read neither statute books nor the constitution of the state, nor the prison regulations. Also, judges, governors, and wardens can point out to anyone that they have been duly appointed or elected to their respective offices; they have impressive documents to show that will verify this to any man who would question their jurisdiction or proper authority in the matter. It is again most regrettable that God is illiterate. The appointment of Judge Smith has been registered in all appropriate offices, published in the daily press, and entered in various official handbooks. God, alas, was not informed about the appointment. He continues to look upon Smith as a human being and judges him as human beings are judged in the divine presence. Since God is not only truth but also mercy, it is not beyond imagining that Smith's delusions about his own status may be a mitigating circumstance in the judgment. But God would not be God if He recognized these delusions as the truth.

This denuding character of the encounter between God and

man is understandable in terms of the Christian doctrine of
creation. God created the heavens and the earth. And then
He created man. He did not create society. That latter
achievement belongs entirely to man's own ingenuity. But
God looks upon man and continues to address man as His
creature. In other words, God addresses man as man and as
nothing else. Even a human father will often find it hard to
resist a smile when his son, whom he watched as a yelping
infant on the day of his birth, steps up to him as a vice-
president of the corporation or *aide-de camp* to the commanding general. But human fathers, themselves part of the social
drama, may eventually be taken in. God is above the social
drama and is never taken in. Man enters into the world naked,
without a name, without social roles, without involvement
in the great institutions. For the remainder of his life he
impresses upon others and upon himself the importance of
his name, social roles and institutional positions. God remains unimpressed. In the words of Job: "Naked I came
from my mother's womb, and naked shall I return" (Job
1:21). It would seem that no Christian understanding of
society can dispense with this awareness of man's persisting
nakedness beneath his social masquerades.

Perhaps the most terrifying aspect of the confrontation with
God's address is not the judgment over man's sin but the
profound challenge to his most cherished identifications.
One dreams that one finds oneself on the street naked. One
wakes up, shakes off the nightmare and the embarrassment,
and repeats to oneself with pleasure one's repertoire of
title roles: "I am Mr. James Sutherland Smith"—"I am the
husband of Mrs. Alice Jennison Smith"—"I am vice-president
of the Epitomy Manufacturing Corporation"—"I am a registered Republican," and so forth. Into this reassuring recital
comes God's address—and returns one in an instant to
nakedness. "And the foundations of the thresholds shook
at the voice of him who called" (Is. 6:4). Not least the
narrow thresholds which hold in our self-conceptions and
our self-esteem!

But God's challenge is not only to the consciously contrived identifications of social one-upmanship. The challenge extends to the deepest, most taken-for-granted conceptions as to who and what one is. In the American racial situation it is easily said by Northern preachers of racial equality that God is "color-blind." This, of course, is quite true, in quite the sense intended by those who say it. But to grasp the weight of what is said one must realize the depths of self-identification involved in a Southerner saying to himself and to others, "I am white." Lillian Smith has given us a haunting description of this process of self-identification under the telling title "The White Man's Burden is his Own Childhood":

"So we learned the dance that cripples the human spirit, step by step by step, we who were white and we who were colored, day by day, hour by hour, year by year until the movements were reflexes and made for the rest of our life without thinking. Alas, for many white children, they were movements made for the rest of their lives without feeling. What white southerner of my generation ever stops to think consciously where to go or asks himself if it is right for him to go there! His muscles know where he can go and take him to the front of the streetcar, to the front of the bus, to the big school, to the hospital, to the library, to hotel and restaurant and picture show, into the best that his town has to offer its citizens. These ceremonials in honor of white supremacy, performed from babyhood, slip from the conscious mind down deep into muscles and glands and on into that region where mature ideals rarely find entrance, and become as difficult to tear out as are a child's beliefs about God and his secret dreams about himself."[3]

The proclamation that God is "no respecter of persons," that He does not know the difference between "white" and "black," that the racial system of the South is a moral evil—this proclamation is not just a statement of inconvenient ethical injunctions but a shattering blow to the very roots of self-esteem. The Southerner whom Lillian Smith describes in the above passage may lose all he has, worldly goods and social position, perhaps even his sanity, but in the deepest recesses of his self there will be something that will say, "I am white." God's reply to this final self-affirmation is quite simple: *"No—you are not white—you are a human being."* In this confrontation the bad faith of the racial posture is sharply revealed. For "to be white," as any student of Southern society knows, is not a biologically objective fact of the pigmentation of the skin but rather a socially concocted myth. In a biological sense a man "is" this or that color. That, presumably, is a fact of nature. But in the socially relevant sense a man "is white" by the fiat of the myth. Enough has been written about the racial fantasies involved in this myth (as illustrated best by the case of very light-skinned "Negroes") to dispense with further elaboration. The crucial point is that "to be white" is not a biological fact but a social fiction. The system of oppression that appeals to this fiction is a system of bad faith. Both fiction and bad faith will not hold up in the confrontation with the God of truth. It goes without saying that the same argument applies to other racial, national, or ethnic identifications. Here too we have to deal with the illiterate God. Everyone knows very well that we have no choice in certain situations but to act "as white Southerners," "as Americans," "as Europeans," "as Jews," and so on. After all, this is what the social libretto says—here is our name and next to it it says in clear writing "a Jew," "a German," or whatever the play has cast us as. Again it is a great pity that this libretto has not come to God's attention. He thus remains inconsiderately uninterested in our description in the *dramatis personae.* Indeed, it is in the etymologically literal sense of the word (*persona=* dramatic mask) that God is "no respecter of persons."

It is in this society-shattering sense that we may understand Paul's declaration that in Christ "There is neither Jew nor Greek, there is neither slave nor free" (Gal. 3:28). And we are certainly justified if we regard this declaration as being of significance beyond the confines of the Christian community itself. The church, the community that confesses Christ, is to be in the world as a promise of the new human order that lies in the eschatological future. Christ is Lord over the world as well as over the church. The nonrecognition of ethnic and social identifications within the church foreshadows their nonrecognition in the world under the Lordship of the triumphant Christ. It gives one deep pause to read on in this same statement of Paul's and find it continues with the assertion that in Christ "there is neither male nor female." We would venture to suggest (at the risk of engaging in very daring exegesis) that there is much more involved in this final assertion than a call for equality between the sexes. We would suggest that, as God challenges all our social identifications, He also challenges our sexual identification. God refuses to recognize our protestations and moral deductions to the effect that "we are Jews," "we are Greeks," "we are whites," "we are American citizens." He challenges no less our self-identifications as men and as women, our pretensions of virility and femininity. The divine answer to the statement "I am a man" is, once more, "No—*you are not a man—you are a human being.*"

We would argue here somewhat analogously to the way in which we approached the relationship of fact and fiction in the racial situation. There are, of course, objective biological facts involved in human sexuality. Yet even a cursory glance at the wealth of anthropological literature on sexuality in different cultures will immediately show us that the complex of values, emotions, and moral ideals implied in the statement "I am a man" is not biologically given but socially learned. In other words, there are sexual roles just as there are other roles in society. Once more, the total identification of oneself with the sexual role is an act of bad faith. Any amount of delving into psychiatric literature about human sexuality will show us, even among the least "maladjusted," the tremendous precariousness of sexual identification. It would, for example, be of great interest to have Rorschach data available on the judges, jurors, and prosecuting attorneys who in Anglo-Saxon countries continue to this day to throw homosexuals in jail for years, and this frequently for acts engaged in discreetly and voluntarily by adults. The persecution of homosexuals is so vicious for very much the same reasons that racial persecution is. While the persecutor in the latter case uses his victim in bad faith to bolster his spurious self-identification as a member of a superior race, the persecutor in the former case forces upon and hence out of his victim the confirmation of his own usually shaky self-identification as a "normal" male. One beats the Negro to feel white. One spits upon the homosexual to feel virile.

It is not our concern here to enlarge upon the question of a Christian ethic of sexuality, of the moral problems of homosexuality, or of the question as to the proper use of the police powers of the state in areas of private morals. We would only suggest that a truthful approach to these areas— that is, the only approach allowable in the confrontation of our existence with God—will make us wary of speaking very glibly about what is "natural," "normal," or "given" in the sexual roles of men and women. It is remarkable how Christian thought in these areas succeeds in going ahead happily as if the wealth of anthropological research on these matters in the last century, at least, had never happened. We might quote as an example not one of the worst cases but one of the best—the report on homosexuality of a committee set up a few years ago by the Church of England (a report, let it be added hastily, which is remarkable for its sensible and enlightened approach to this question):

"Right reason thus points to the ineluctable conclusion that the use of the sexual organs, being governed by the nature of sex itself and by the recognized purposes of coitus, is proper only in the context of a personal relation which is both heterosexual and specifically marital. Considered, then, in terms of objective morality, it is evident that homosexual acts are contrary to the will of God for human sexuality, and are therefore sinful *per se*."[4]

We would suggest, as a helpful exercise, an examination in the light of the perspective on society developed in the first part of this essay of the phrases "recognized purposes," "specifically marital," and "objective morality"! The American reader, who has strong nerves and the will to carry problems to their "ineluctable conclusion" might amplify the exercise by reading, in succession, a good anthropological treatise on human sexuality,[5] the first Kinsey report, and some of the laws on sexual offenses now on the statute books of American states.[6]

A simple definition of a humanist ethic might be one which orients its conceptions and imperatives toward men rather than institutions. Thus, a humanist ethic, such as is generally accepted in Western democracies, would hold that political institutions exist for the welfare of men. Recent history has given us ample opportunity to observe the consequences of a contrary ethic that maintains that men exist for the welfare of the state. It is one of the ironies of history (and one of the consequences of the Babylonian captivity of the Christian faith in religious forms) that Christian ethical thought has frequently found itself in the antihumanist camp. We would suggest, from our understanding of society and of the Christian faith, that a Christian ethic will always be humanist in the sense just given. God is concerned with men. He addresses men. He addresses institutions only in the sense that men, in their real life in society, exist in institutional involvements. Thus different words must be addressed to the king and to the peasant. But both are addressed *as men*.

But Christian faith is relevant for social perception not only in such extreme cases as capital punishment or racial oppression (although the debunking, unmasking character of the Christian faith becomes very clear in the way it challenges the pretensions involved in such human situations). We would once more point to Bonhoeffer's assertion that Christ is Lord not only over the so-called "boundary situations" of human existence, but also Lord over the central areas of life (the "middle of the village," as Bonhoeffer called it). For, as we have seen, men come up against the problem of bad faith not only when they are jurors in sodomy cases or participants in other forms of legal lynching. Bad faith looms as a constant possibility over everyday life and its most ordinary pursuits. We might return here once more to the case of occupational or professional ideologies.

A good illustration of this might be the self-image of the advertising man in America, as it appears in his professional publications and gatherings, as well as in his speaking about himself personally.[7] This self-image presents the adman as a rather gay, reckless figure, in some ways a professional fun-maker, descended in apostolic succession from the storytellers and town criers of olden times. He practices an art by which he gives color and amusement to people who might otherwise live very drab lives. Like all artists he has a measure of poetic license with the truth and mainly plays on the emotions rather than the intellect. In our own society this fun-maker also carries on a worthwhile, even crucial economic mission. His activities help move the goods, on which movement depends our prosperity. Advertising and abundance go together. The advertiser serves the public by showing it the way to a new, abundant life. Also, he serves as a bridge of communication between manufacturer and consumer. The adman represents the exuberance, the enterprise, and the confidence of our society.

It will be apparent to most non-admen that this self-image has a very shaky relationship with reality. The economic assumptions of the ideology are, at any rate, not beyond all reasonable doubt (that is, the notions about the economic beneficence of advertising). But its noneconomic aspects are shaky enough too. One may point out the discrepancy between the image of the fun-maker and the image of the communications expert. What is more, the apostolic succession of the first image is spurious. We are dealing here with the most synthetic of fun-making—based on careful market research, with a steady eye on the sales statistics and another eye peeking over the shoulder of the psychoanalyst for technical hints, the whole operation calculated for profit from beginning to end. Beyond that, the gay and reckless figure of the adman is

not much in evidence when one has once looked a little more
deeply into the world of Madison Avenue. This is a world of
much anxiety and frustration, taking its grim toll of nerves,
dreams, and ulcers. Finally, the license which the adman takes
with the truth and with men's emotions is rarely poetic. It is
the art of the sharp salesman, not that of the poet, which is
in demand here.

Why is such an image adopted? This is not a very difficult
question to answer. Men never like to face unpleasant aspects
of their life. They invent ideologies to pretty up the picture.
Groups of men reinforce each other in the conviction that the
ideology is the truth. Advertising, as an occupation, presents
a very high degree of conflict and tension. It demands a
nervous, sharply competitive life. It involves the constant
necessity of manipulating oneself and other people. If viewed
under an ethical aspect it presents even greater doubts and
anxieties. It is normal for men to shy away from anxiety and
guilt. Occupational ideologies provide a convenient method
for doing this.

Perhaps the problem of guilt is where the Christian faith
relates most directly to this type of ideology. To ask men to
see through their own ideological befogment is to push them
into facing the moral ambiguity of their situation. The psychological tendency is, of course, to resist this attempt. Men
tend psychologically either to suppress their guilt or to analyze
it away. If the Christian faith involved only the proclamation
of God's judgment, it would only reinforce this tendency (as,
indeed, it has where it was mainly understood in this way—
compare the Freudian paradise of the "Puritan mind"!). But
the Christian faith primarily proclaims God's grace. The victory of Christ over sin and death involves the possibility that
men may face their own guilt in a new way. Christian faith
holds that man is justified by grace in the real world, as a real
human being—that is, as a sinner. This belief makes it possible
for man to face himself and to dispense with the narcotic of
ideology. This can be a very liberating experience, not only
emotionally but in the way in which it may now become

possible to seek avenues of responsible action in one's situation. With this new freedom there is at least a chance of modi-
fying some of the morally questionable features of the situation. As long as the situation is shrouded in ideology, there is
not even a chance. Thus Christian faith is relevant not only to
social consciousness but also to the (sometimes slim) possibility of social action. It is important to stress, however, that
liberation begins in the realm of consciousness. Truly liberating action in society is dependent on this first liberation.

A few years ago a group of American military chaplains met
in western Germany with a group of German churchmen to
discuss problems of the military chaplaincy. This was the
period when the new west-German army was just being organized and the problems were very timely. One of the
American chaplains delivered a lecture describing and praising
the chaplaincy in the American armed forces. He spent much
time on the so-called "character guidance program," emphasized the close relationships among religion, morals, and
patriotism, and finally stressed the direct contribution of the
chaplain's work to military morale. The Germans were somewhat taken aback by this interpretation, which for them had
rather disturbing similarities with views associated with a
relatively recent past of German history. But there was little
discussion immediately after the lecture. Some time later a
group of the participants in this meeting were sitting together.
Suddenly one of the German churchmen leaned over to the
American who had given the lecture and asked him: "How
does the function of the chaplain in the American army differ
from that of the *politruk* in the Soviet army?" The import of
the question did not immediately register with the American,
because the question had to be translated and there had to be
an explanation of the Russian term (*politruks* are Communist
political officers attached to all units of the Soviet army, their
task being the political guidance and morale of the troops).
When the meaning of the question became clear to the American and his colleagues there was a long, painful silence. Then
the Americans began to ask questions—not belligerently but in

a mood of embarrassment and urgent curiosity. It was quite clear that the one question asked by the German churchman had suddenly opened up a completely new perspective on their situation to these chaplains. It would, of course, have been easy for them to defend themselves against the question within the categories of their professional ideology. That they did not do this, that they really listened to the question and tried to meet it, was not in small measure due to the Christian context in which both questioner and questioned faced each other. It is in this kind of encounter that the Christian faith can become liberating in the social perception and consciousness of men.

There is something radically "subversive" about this liberation. And, one might add, the Roman authorities showed great wisdom and political acumen in feeding the Christians to the lions (by the time the practice ended, of course, the Christians had become sufficiently domesticated to be innocuous to society). However, it would be erroneous to view the "subversion" of the Christian faith in the way in which, for instance, a Marxist would understand the development of revolutionary consciousness. Christian faith is radical because it challenges social assumptions at their very roots. Christian faith, as we have seen, can never exercise the conservative function normally assigned to religion. On the other hand, Christian faith takes a far too realistic view of man to be revolutionary in too many situations. Christian faith rejects the ideology of the conservative, because it sees through the fictitiousness by which the *status quo* rationalizes and maintains itself. Christian faith rejects the utopianism of the revolutionary, because it will not accept the fantastic hopes for the future with which revolutionary activity justifies its own existence. It is bad faith to oppress men in the name of conservative principles. It is also bad faith to engage in atrocities on the promise of a future justice, a promise for the fulfillment of which there is little rational hope. Thus the Christian view of social reality cannot easily be enlisted in the service of "liberalism" or "conservatism." In some concrete, real situa-

tions the political decisions of the Christian may be "conservative," in other situations "liberal." The Christian perspective will militate against delusions concerning the future as well as against those concerning the present. To pursue
this further at this point would take us far beyond our immediate concerns, however, and it may be more profitable to
return once more to the main thread of our argument.

It should be clear by this point that the challenge of the
Christian faith to carefully cherished self-identifications is
frequently a very shocking, disagreeable business. The natural
inclinations of man lead him to take society for granted, to
identify himself fully with the social roles assigned to him,
and to develop ideologies which will organize and dispose of
any doubts that might possibly arise. There is an instructive
affinity between Christian faith and the analytic enterprise of
the social sciences in that both serve to disturb this happy
state of affairs. The Christian faith, in its prophetic mission,
confronts man with a truth of such force that the precarious
pretensions of his social existence disintegrate before it. The
debunking effect of social-scientific analysis is far from contradictory to this prophetic mission. Indeed, it might be called
its profane auxiliary. The smashing of idols, with whatever
hammers, is the underside of prophecy.

But there is another aspect, perhaps one that might be
called more positive, in the affinity between Christian and
sociological "subversion." This aspect we have already touched
upon in our discussion of role theory. It has to do with the
extreme precariousness of human identity, not just of certain
specific social identifications but of identity in any sense of
the word. If we follow the insights of modern social psychology into the character of identity, we get a picture that
makes it very difficult indeed to speak of "human nature" in
any very meaningful sense. Human identity appears as a result
of a socialization process in which it is others that "name"
one—"name" in the fullest sense of the word. It is others, by
their recognition, who bestow upon the child his sexual identity, his identities of race, nationality, and class, and the total

complex of beliefs, categories, and values that goes with these several identities. "Human nature" (as soon as we get beyond strictly zoological facts) is a social product, one that is socially relative depending upon the accidents of birth and biography. But identity is not only produced socially. It is also sustained socially. Self-esteem, self-respect, and even the profounder levels of self-image depend upon the continuing recognition of their validity by other human beings. If this recognition is drastically withdrawn, it normally takes little time before the whole precarious edifice collapses into a whining misery of infantile terror. We are what we are by the recognition of others. Since all such recognition is, by its innate nature, highly precarious, so is whatever it is that we are. There is no more distressing realization of the contingency of our being than to understand that we are dependent for our very identity upon other human beings—creatures, that is, who may forget or change their minds, and creatures who will surely die.

This is not the place to speculate philosophically as to whether it would not be quite possible to get along without a metaphysical concept of the self. Nor is the writer qualified for such a philosophical task. It might be said, however, that a social-scientific slant on the question would certainly not induce one to tend toward the notion of the self as some kind of solid, stable entity persisting in time. If one looks at the bewildering repertoire of roles and "social selves" (William James) that any individual has, and then asks, "But who is he *really?*" there is no empirically satisfactory way of answering the question. The social psychologist (or, for that matter, the sociologist) will probably have to rule out the question and satisfy himself with the description of the repertoire as it develops in the individual's different social relationships. A psychologist might give an answer to the question in terms of something that could be called the individual's "nature," but unfortunately the likelihood is that, in doing so, the individual becomes either a zoological or a mythical entity which he himself has great difficulty recognizing once he is out of the social situation in which the psychologist makes the interpretation. An existentialist might possibly answer, "Ask him!" and add that an individual is that which he chooses himself to be. Which, if understood within a social frame of reference, is perhaps the best answer that could be given, unless one operates with a concept of "soul" that has no relationship to the empirical self. But, as Sartre has pointed out, this means that there is no such thing as "human nature." Or rather, there is not—unless one posits God. It would seem that this Sartrian insight is significant for our argument here.

The reason why it is so difficult to answer the question "Who is he really?" is that there are no convincing criteria for deciding which recognition is definitive. After all, the individual in question is recognized by some as a virtuous man and by others as a crook, by some as sincere and by others as cynical, by some as endowed with a sense of humor and by others as a deadly bore. Even if there is a measure of consensus about him among his associates (as there usually is— or society could not go on), this is also an accident of the individual's situation. Remove him from the group that thought him virtuous and put him in some other context and very soon he may act the role of snarling villain. What is more, his own recognitions of himself are vague and contradictory. His picture of himself varies with the situations in which he finds himself. And if one psychologist calls him type A and another type B, there is no way of deciding which one is to be our authority.

Scholastic theology defined God as the only noncontingent being. And an Arabic proverb defines man as the one who forgets. God is the one who remembers. God calls man out of nothingness and gives him a name and remembers him for ever. Beyond the contingencies and precariousness of his identity, *man is he whom God addresses*. His being (his "nature," if one prefers) lies in that fact of God's address. His identity is that as which God addresses him. This is what Luther meant in his saying that man exists as long as God speaks to him, be it speaking in anger or in mercy. Or to put this in the terms used above, God's recognition is the definitive one. Only in this perspective can we answer the question as to who we are. Let it be added here most emphatically that we are not presenting this at all as an argument for the existence of God. Such argumentation would once more be producing a *deus ex machina* in just the sense criticized by Bonhoeffer. What we are saying again, however, is that there is here too a certain affinity between the contingency of man's being, as understood by the Christian faith, and the precariousness of man's identity, as understood by the social-scientific enterprise.

There are important consequences to this perspective in terms of the social mission of the Christian church, that community in which the risen Lord is witnessed to in the world. Quite apart from what the church may or may not do in the way of social action, the church, if it is faithful to its mission, can play a vital role in society and its clash of ideologies. *The church is the place of truth.* When we say this, of course, we are fully aware that this is pretty much the opposite of what the empirical church normally is (*vide* Chapter 6 of this essay). But the church can be the place of truth when it stands on the ground of Jesus Christ and no other—that is, when it liberates itself from its social and psychological functionality. The church can then be not only the proclaiming church but the listening church, providing those rare opportunities in society where men can look truthfully at themselves and their roles. This too is an essential feature of the non-kerygmatic posture we discussed before. We would suggest that one of the most urgent tasks of the church in our present situation is the providing of such places of truth (be it in the local congregation or in other locales), places where men can think through in freedom the moral and human dilemmas of their social roles. The work of the European laymen's institutes since World War II has been a serious effort to realize this shape of the *Ecclesia audiens*.[8] The demands of the American situation are not essentially different.[9]

Even within the church there is often the idea that theological thought and understanding of society are strictly segregated activities of the Christian mind. Both theologians and sociologists spend much time erecting methodological fences which keep out the uninitiated (and, incidentally, imprison the initiates). We would suggest that the intellectual tasks of gaining an understanding of the Christian faith in depth and of gaining a broad perspective on society are related. We may conclude this chapter with the motto of the Zoé Brotherhood, a movement for the laity in the Church of Greece—"Conquest in the Wideness through Victory in the Depth."[10] And we may add to this a brief passage from a prayer of Eusebius Matthopoulos, the founder of Zoé:

"We pray Thee to give us a living faith, a sure hope and an active love.
We pray Thee, O Lord our God, to keep us ever free from the spirit of self-deceit and pride and from the spirit of fanaticism.
We pray Thee to give us a correct knowledge of ourself."[11]

11. Christian Faith and the Social Comedy

THE CHRISTIAN FAITH, BECAUSE IT VIEWS THE WORLD UNDER THE ASPECT OF REDEMPTION, REVEALS SOCIETY UNDER THE ASPECT OF COMEDY. THE CHRISTIAN FAITH RELATES TO MEN STRIPPED OF THEIR SOCIAL ROLES. CHRISTIAN ETHICS HUMANIZES THE SOCIAL COMEDY AND FREES MEN FROM THE BONDAGE OF DEADLY EARNEST-NESS.

In the course of this essay the term "comic perspective" has crept up before. Indeed, it was pointed out that the perception developed in the first part of the essay was essentially one of society as a comedy—notwithstanding the all too apparent intrusions of tragedy into the comic action. It may now be possible to draw some of the implications of this comic character of society in terms of the Christian faith.

The essence of the comic is discrepancy. This is well expressed in what are probably the most famous theories concerning the comic among recent thinkers, that is the theories of Freud[1] and Bergson.[2] In Freud's theory the discrepancy is between the exorbitant demands of the superego as against the world of the libido underlying it. Freud places strong emphasis on what he himself calls the "unmasking" character of wit. In Bergson's theory the discrepancy is between the living organism and the mechanical world. One is moved to laughter when something living acts like a machine. This laughter reveals the distinctive, unique quality of life as against all other phenomena in the world. This essay is not the place to discuss fully these theories or other interpretations of the comic.[3] It seems to this writer that Freud's theory, indeed, tells us much about the psychology of laughter but little about the phenomenon of the comic itself. Bergson's theory, on the other

hand, does penetrate into the phenomenon itself, but its identification of the comic discrepancy with that between the
biological and the mechanical would seem to be too broad. It
hardly seems possible for a plant to be comic. As to animals,
they appear as comic in the degree to which it is possible to
look at them in anthropomorphic terms. In other words, this
writer would suggest that the comic is a specifically and exclusively *human* phenomenon. He would suggest further that
the essence of the comic discrepancy is not that between life
and matter but between spirit and world, as that latter discrepancy is revealed in the human condition. Man exists as a
conscious being in an unconscious and apparently uncon-
scionable world. It is in this basically human discrepancy
that the clue to the comic is to be sought.

However, whether this interpretation may seem fanciful or
not, or whatever one's conception of the comic may be, there
can be little doubt about the sharp light which the comic
perspective throws on crucial aspects of the human condition.
We might quote Bergson at this point:

"A situation is invariably comic when it belongs simultaneously
to two altogether independent series of events and is capable
of being interpreted in two entirely different meanings at the
same time."[4]

Bergson is speaking here of the comic in general, but the
words he uses to describe the comic situation are deeply appropriate not only to the phenomenon we have called "alternation" but to the human condition in general. The aspect of
spirit and the aspect of world, as interpretations of human
situations, always constitute "independent series of events."
When the worldly aspect is suddenly perceived as coexisting
with the spiritual one, there takes place the "unmasking" of
which Freud speaks. Thus we find out that the philosopher
has haemorrhoids. Or we laugh because he turns out to be
an anxious miser or an inveterate seducer. The comic source
here is this discrepancy between spirit and all that which is not.
No doubt this is why sexuality has been a source of comedy

from immemorial times. It reveals most sharply the discrepancy between spiritual aspiration and bodily bondage, as Montaigne has commented upon. Sexuality then "unmasks" the pretensions of the spirit, as Freud has illustrated comically enough in his theory of everyday slips of the tongue, mistakes, and misnomers. And the comic in death, also an age-old theme, has the same source. Death, like sex, is the ultimate debunking of spirit by body. The pretensions of intelligence and will are "unmasked" in the facts proclaimed by a body oblivious of spirit. In the same way, the social drama takes on the character of a comic farce when looked at under the aspects of sex and death. Men engage in grandiose undertakings on the stage of society, involving the most complicated acts of deception, manipulation, and violence. But during all this time their libido keeps churning away within them, wanting one thing and one thing only, a thing ridiculously irrelevant to the empire-building being undertaken by the man to whom this libido belongs. And eventually everybody involved in the plot dies. Under the aspects of sex and death it is difficult to take social ambitions very seriously.

The declaration that the social drama is a comedy may well raise eyebrows and elicit the comment that one can only say this by being inhumanly blind to the tragic aspects of social existence. We would not accept this objection. The tragic and the comic perspectives are not mutually incompatible. The same human condition which provides materials for tragedy also and at the same time produces the stuff of which comedy is made. And to see the comic even in the midst of events that powerfully rouse our "tragic sense of life" (Unamuno) does not at all imply some sort of callousness toward human suffering. One may recall here a remark made somewhere by David Rousset, a Frenchman who has written about Nazi concentration camps as a former inmate. Rousset remarked that one of the new insights of his imprisonment was the realization that the comic is an objective element of reality, persisting and capable of being recognized no matter how wretched one may be subjectively. In other words, the comic has a status in reality beyond the observer's psychology. It is not just an element of certain types of human consciousness, but an essential ingredient of the human condition as such. Thus the Nazis were, indeed, the monsters of a nightmarish horror show, but at the same time they were inexorably ridiculous, appearing as figures of a surrealistic farce (Rousset uses the term *"ubuesque"* to describe this aspect, after Alfred Jarry's surrealistic play *King Ubu*). One might add that the art of Charlie Chaplin (and not only in *The Great Dictator*) is based on the same principle—as, indeed, is any comedy with a deep compassion for the vicissitudes of human existence.

Both tragedy and comedy place the social drama into the perspective of human finitude. Both a tragic and a comic mood allow us to perceive the failure of pretensions, ambitions, and aspirations before the hard facts of man's finite situation. The tragic hero finds his will and his virtue dashing against the walls of fate. The world, perhaps even his own body as a part of this world, defeats him. The comic hero enacts before us the same destiny, but in a different key, as it were. Both tragedy and comedy proclaim to us that pride is foolish, remind us of our humanity and hence of our imprisonment. But in tragedy what is put in question is man. In comedy not only is man questioned and not taken at face value, but there is also a question about the imprisonment. One can put this differently as well. Tragedy accepts the walls of the prison and perceives the human situation in terms of this acceptance. Comedy gives the impression that the walls too are not as grim as they look. Tragedy is perception of the human situation only under the aspect of immanence. Comedy is a signal, an intimation, of transcendence. It is here that its Christian significance is to be found.

The transcending direction of comedy is probably best expressed in the art of the clown. The clown is the living defiance of the laws of nature and the laws of man. He defies gravity and the resistance of matter. He waves his wand and the walls of our prison collapse. He walks into the presence of

kings and laughs in their face. Not only are the social limitations of our existence thus denied, but finitude as such,
finitude as the mode of human existence in the world, is
transcended in the magic of the comic moment. We laugh and
for one moment the walls are really gone. The comic catharsis
is thus a very different one from the tragic one. Tragic catharsis makes us look upon the greatness man is capable of even
within his finitude and thus prepares us to accept the human
condition. Comic catharsis presents us with a fleeting image
of man transcending his finitude and, if only for a brief moment, gives us the exhilarating idea that perhaps it will be
man after all who will be the victor in his struggle with a
universe bent on crushing him. In other words, tragedy gives
us a sense of human courage, comedy a sense of wild, irrational
hope. As Enid Welsford has pointed out in her discussion of
the clown as a figure in Western literature, it depends on our
general conception of human destiny how we shall look at the
clown. If death is the last fact about man, then the art of the
clown is a pathetic piece of emotional relief, a passing moment
of benign illusion, doomed to the tragic finale of all things
human. If, on the other hand, the universe is not a mindless
machine destroying all within it, if death should turn out to
be not the ultimate reality of the human phenomenon, then
the clown's magic takes on a strange new dignity. The comic
transformation now may suddenly appear as a promise of a
reality yet to come. If we are now to put this in Christian
terms, we obtain a somewhat startling perspective on the
relative importance of tragedy and comedy. This bears looking
into a little further.

A Christian understanding of human existence would reverse the common belief that tragedy is more profound than
comedy. On the contrary, this Christian understanding would
say it is comedy that gives us the more significant insights
into the human condition. Tragedy can never go beyond
immanence (this, incidentally, is why a Christian tragedy is
a contradiction in terms). Comedy can. More than that, in a
way strangely parallel to that of the Christian faith, comedy

overcomes the tragic perspective. From the Christian point of view one can say that comedy, unlike tragedy, bears within it a great secret. This secret is the promise of redemption. For redemption promises in eternity what comedy gives us in its few moments of precarious liberation—the collapse of the walls of our imprisonment. It would not be surprising if, to the blessed, redemption appears after the terrors of the world as a form of comic relief. But there can be no doubt about one thing. There will be no tragedy in heaven—by definition, as it were. But man will remain funny for ever. If nothing else there will be material for endless comedies in his relations with the angels! The tragic thus shows us man in time, but the comic may well give us an intimation of what man is and always will be, even in eternity.

But our concern in this essay is not with heaven, so it is probably high time that we return to our theme, which is not the angelic but the social comedy. We would now suggest that such a Christian understanding of the comic has direct applicability to the perception of society. One can, obviously, conceive of society as essentially a tragic drama. Society then is seen as part of that inane world which bears down upon us and which will inevitably succeed in destroying us. But if society is conceived of as a comic drama, our social perception partakes of the secret referred to above. That is, in all our debunking of the cardboard structures of the social world there is a faint hint of redemption.

This sense of comedy may be illustrated by the difference between a Christian and a revolutionary challenge to the pretensions of the *status quo*. The revolutionary is almost always a thoroughly humorless type. He sees people as part of structures, either those he wishes to tear down or those he hopes to erect. Those who defend the *status quo* appear to him as fools or scoundrels. Revolution is an earnest undertaking. The revolutionary takes it and himself too with very great seriousness. There is little room for any comic perspective. The Christian challenge to the *status quo* begins by not taking it as seriously as it takes itself. It refuses to see individual human beings as incarnations of social symbols and principles. As we have tried to show before, the Christian challenge to society lies above all in its radical humanizing of all social problems. This process of humanization carries with it a comic perspective. It "unmasks" human pretensions very much in the sense meant by Freud in his discussion of wit. Finally, because it lives in confrontation with God, this Christian challenge cannot take itself ultimately seriously either. Only God is ultimately to be taken seriously. Everything human remains less than serious by comparison. Needless to say, this does not mean that the Christian challenge to injustice or cruelty will be less than serious in the sense of detached amusement, comfortable readiness to forgive everything, or lazy lack of commitment. Yet it will be less than serious in the sense that it will know that its own actions are caught in the comic ambiguities of all human endeavor and also in that it will never lose sight of the pathetic humanity that also is a quality of one's worst enemy.

Thus at the bottom of any debunking job undertaken in a Christian spirit is not a nihilistic guffaw but a redeeming smile. The "unmasking" of society is undertaken on behalf of an affirmation of man. This is done without the frantic hopes of the revolutionary utopian and without the misanthropic cynicism of the uncommitted observer. Debunking which is really the underside of Christian prophecy may sometimes be very sharp indeed, but it is not likely to become real bitterness. There is always an awareness that this particular colossus staring us in the face at the moment, like all the colossi of this world, is swallowed up in Christ's victory and will be swept away when this victory is consummated. Nothing human is ultimately dangerous, not even the most determined stupidity. Thus nothing human can ultimately keep us from the liberation of laughter.

The Christian faith bids us love our enemies. We would suggest that an essential part of this humanly unthinkable undertaking is to view these enemies under the aspect of the comic. In other words, the humanizing perspective of the

Christian faith takes the enemy less seriously than he takes himself, addresses him as a human being instead of as the representative of awesome social forces, and thus may unexpectedly open the way for simple human communication. The following passage from a report on Christians in the Communist zone of Germany, published in a Swiss newspaper, illustrates this possibility:

"And then we experienced that here and there a few of us began to talk to half and full Marxists with love. With love—that means undiplomatically, in all frankness and freedom, yet not self-righteously or moralistically. And almost everywhere where that happened, we saw that the evil spirits stole away and the sea became still. In the place of their dialectically grounded desire to liquidate us (for the moment only rhetorically) came human respect, then the assurance that they wouldn't do us any harm because we were 'good honest people' whom one protects and defends. Then, here and there, something quite different occurred. Suddenly the mask which looks so deceivingly like the real face fell, and revealed a helpless man who sinks under his load of sin and guilt, and who clings to the Christian who has treated him with a bit of love, who hasn't lied to him like the others."[5]

It goes without saying that this attitude will not always lead to these results in the situation of facing Communist functionaries. But its very possibility is a direct outcome of the humanizing quality of the Christian challenge developed above, a quality which includes in a very profound way the comic perspective on the social drama. As little men put on their terrifying masks and headgears and war rattles, and march into the arena with solemn chants, there is always some old lady who smiles at them, not unkindly, and suggests that the boys go play elsewhere where they cannot hurt anybody. We know all too well that even unimpressed grandmothers can be killed in the great war games of society. But there is also a possibility that men may discover their own humanity. This possibility is the important nexus between the comic perspective and Christian ethics.

To be ultimately serious about society means *ipso facto* to

be caught within it. Thus even the revolutionary, who seeks to
overthrow society and build a new one on the ruins of the old,
is ultimately serious about his social involvements. Only a
conception of man which transcends society can take social
involvements with a grain of salt—or with tongue in cheek.
Certainly the Christian faith is not the only such conception.
But in the Christian understanding of man and of the nature
of redemption lies an unusually fertile opportunity of gaining
distance from the social problems pressing on one at the
moment. Thus the refusal of taking society as ultimately serious (which means refusing to take it at the face value it usually puts on itself) not only is an experience of personal
liberation but also has relevance to the effort to grasp society
intellectually. To return to the general argument of this essay,
we would now say that, insofar as the Christian faith contains
within it a specific type of comic perspective and a specific interpretation of comedy, to that extent too does the Christian
faith contribute to a clear perception of society. It is a commonplace observation, but still an important one, that a measure of distance allows one to see more clearly. The Christian
faith, when it is true to itself and really is "in the world but
not of it," provides distance from society and thus creates opportunities for perception. Thus the Christian faith relates to
the enterprise of the social sciences not only because of its
radical challenge to social delusions and alibis. In a more
benign way, as it were, it relates to the "sociological imagination" (Mills) by way of the comic perspective on the social
carnival. The Christian sees man as having a destiny over and
beyond society, man straddling two worlds, those two worlds
that Simone Weil called those of gravity and grace. In thus
transcending society, the Christian faith at the same time
makes it possible to see society more clearly.

Dietrich Bonhoeffer made the important distinction between "ultimate" and "penultimate" concerns in his *Ethics*.
The entire domain of social and political action, however
serious its involvements may often be, will always be "penultimate" in the Christian economy. Thus the Christian will

engage himself in action passionately, but he will not allow his commitment to blind him to the comic aspects of his situation. He will deal with men without forgetting that they were children not so long ago. He will protest against injustice, but he will not absolutize this protest or make it the basis of his existence. He will build for the future, but he will do so in full awareness of the precariousness of all human construction on the quicksands of history. Above all, he will remember that the central message of the Christian faith is not a call to struggle but a call to joy.

We quite miss the point if we only laugh at Don Quixote because he rides against windmills. The point is that, in the magic of the Quixotic universe, the windmills really cease to be windmills and are metamorphosed into a promise of glory. Of course, we know that "in this aeon," as the New Testament puts it, the ride of Don Quixote ends in a sad return to what we take for granted as reality. But the Christian faith means looking toward the aeon that is to come. The magic moment of comedy foreshadows this aeon, when redemption becomes the one overpowering reality of the universe. Christian faith, just because it strives for clear perception, cannot look at Don Quixote through the eyes of Sancho Panza. The windmills of the Quixotic attack are the battlements of the New Jerusalem, as yet dimly seen on the horizon. But it is toward this horizon that the human caravan is moving. Don Quixote rides toward the dawn of Easter morning.

12. "You Are the Man"

AN EXEGETICAL POSTSCRIPT

"And the Lord sent Nathan to David. He came to him, and said to him, 'There were two men in a certain city, the one rich and the other poor. The rich man had very many flocks and herds; but the poor man had nothing but one little ewe lamb, which he had bought. And he brought it up, and it grew up with him and with his children; it used to eat of his morsel, and drink from his cup, and lie in his bosom, and it was like a daughter to him. Now there came a traveler to the rich man, and he was unwilling to take one of his own flock or herd to prepare for the wayfarer who had come to him, but he took the poor man's lamb, and prepared it for the man who had come to him.' Then David's anger was greatly kindled against the man; and he said to Nathan, 'As the Lord lives, the man who has done this deserves to die; and he shall restore the lamb fourfold, because he did this thing, and because he had no pity.' Nathan said to David, 'You are the man.'"

(II Sam. 12:1–7—RSV)

There is no intention here of ending this essay with a sermon. The writer has no authority to preach and every reason to remain in a nonkerygmatic posture. Having come to the end of the argument, however, it is very desirable to illustrate at least by one specific example how this argument relates itself directly to the Biblical witness. The above passage from the Old Testament is taken as a very dramatic illustration of what we would like to suggest here.

The passage we have quoted directly ought to be read in the larger context of this Biblical narrative. Most people (if only thanks to Hollywood!) will recognize this larger context as the story of David's adultery with Bathsheba and the subsequent murder of Uriah, Bathsheba's husband. Those not familiar with the story ought to begin reading it at the beginning and then read on beyond the incident of David's encounter with Nathan (II Sam. 11 to II Sam. 12:25), otherwise our considerations here will make little sense. But it might be in order to at least summarize the entire story and relate it to the incident in the quotation.

In the context of the Biblical narrative it might be imagined that the episode occurred not too long after David had established himself as king in Jerusalem. His days of guerrilla warfare in the hills were over and he could settle down to being a comfortable if not exactly magnificent potentate. The partisan chief now safely established in power, perhaps getting a little flabby around the middle, preferring to reminisce about past heroics than to engage in new ones in the present—the picture is a familiar one and not without its comic aspect. We may find traces of irony right at the beginning of the story, which opens, "In the spring of the year, the time when kings go forth to battle." There were, indeed, battles going on. David's troops, under the command of Joab (a partisan type of truly Macedonian ferocity), had crossed the Jordan and were besieging Rabbah (what is now Amman), the Ammonite city. However, this bellicose season finds David enjoying a lazy Mediterranean siesta on the roof of his palace in Jerusalem—"It happened, late one afternoon, when David arose from his couch and was walking upon the roof of the king's house"—an ideal setting for erotic reconnaissance. And indeed—"he saw from the roof a woman bathing"—after which the, again, hot-bloodedly Mediterranean course of events could well be described in the Spanish proverb *"Hay que ser hombre"* (of which a fairly castrated Anglo-Saxon translation might be "Boys will be boys"—except that David was certainly no boy and very much what the Spanish would call *hombre!*).

Bathsheba came to join the royal couch, in the best tradition of sloe-eyed oriental docility, and promptly became pregnant. Since her husband, Uriah the Hittite (that is, a foreigner residing among the Hebrews—a fact which, in terms of Near Eastern concepts of hospitality, made David's adultery even

more serious) was out fighting with Joab's troops, she had
every reason for anxiety—there seemed no way of attributing
paternity to Uriah, and the Hebrew penalty for an adulterous
woman was death. The following part of the story is pure
burlesque. David brings Uriah back from the front on a three-
day pass, doing everything but tuck him into bed with Bathsheba, but Uriah remains steadfast in his adherence to the
tabu against sexual intercourse during times of war. The
annoying martinet eats and drinks at the king's table to his
heart's delight, even becomes drunk in the most soldierly
fashion—but he "did not go down to his house."

It is certainly possible that to this point David's actions
were motivated by the desire to settle the matter discreetly
and without harming anyone. There is no evidence of any
great feeling for Bathsheba on the part of David, but we might
even imagine that he strongly wished to protect her as well as
himself against the consequences of the rendezvous. It is also
not difficult to imagine David's rising annoyance at Uriah's
offensive virtuousness. When the Hittite returned to the front
without having so much as looked in the direction of his nuptial bliss, David the sensible man of the world became David
the king—in the full bloodthirsty meaning that this title had in
those days. He sends word to Joab to assign Uriah to the
most dangerous place in the battle line and to make sure that
he is killed there by the enemy. The plot succeeds and the
inconvenient husband lies dead before the walls of Rabbah.
When Joab informs David of what happened, the latter sends
a comforting message—"Do not let this matter trouble you,
for the sword devours now one and now another"—or, to use
contemporary GI language, "This is the way the ball bounces."
Upon hearing the same news, Bathsheba dutifully mourns for
her husband (probably for the prescribed period of seven
days) and then moves without further ado into the royal
harem. As far as the mores of the period were concerned,
the whole matter had been settled in a very satisfactory and
even humane manner (after all, David could have killed

Uriah right away—he had shown admirable scruples all through the affair!).

It was a general characteristic of Yahweh that He did not let well enough alone, as any other sensible god would do, but sent His thoroughly unpleasant emissaries to harass people who were neither better nor worse than anyone else, and who were simply trying to do their best in difficult circumstances. Just as the whole episode had been safely settled, with Bathsheba respectably incorporated in David's seraglio and a son just having been born to the couple, Nathan makes his appearance with the nasty story quoted at the opening of this chapter. The fact that David did not suspect Nathan's intention earlier in the interview might be an indication of how far from his mind the whole affair was by now. On the other hand, David being also the highest judge of the land, it might well be that Nathan frequently came to him with such stories. We know the rest of the story. David the judicial authority becomes David the one who is judged. After Nathan's scorching indictment David acknowledges his sin and repents. Nathan announces God's forgiveness to him—but not without David having to bear some of the consequences of his act. The child born to Bathsheba dies. And Nathan's curse that "the sword shall never depart from your house" becomes sadly fulfilled in the fate of David's sons Amnon, Absalom, and Adonijah.

The whole story debunks David's royal stature in a double way. The first debunking is the indirect one of irony. The second debunking is the very direct one of judgment. Both make the king David disappear and the man David take his place.

There is high comedy in the bedroom farce with which the story opens. We would suggest once more that this is the comedy inherent in human sexuality and coming to the fore most drastically when there are very grandiose pretensions. Immediately before the beginning of the Bathsheba story the Biblical writer gives another glowing account of David's victories and the glory coming from them on the people of

Israel. There is a profound discrepancy between David the heroic king and empire-builder—and David the Peeping Tom and seducer. And this discrepancy sharply humanizes the situation. The effect of this can certainly be seen if one simply reads the story in a modern mood, as it were. But the effect becomes much more telling if one tries to put oneself back mentally into an age when kings were gods and when royal historians vied with each other to remove from the subjects of their writing every vestige of human weakness. The Old Testament repeatedly astonishes us by the audacity of its writers in describing the great heroes of their own people. And even if in our story the writer does not dare to express his own disapproval of David (who, by the time the account was written down in its present form, must have been more sacrosanct to every Hebrew grade-school pupil than George Washington would be to an American one today), he cannot refrain from writing objectively about his hero's deed, "But the thing that David had done displeased the Lord." One has to see this sentence against a background of magnificent epics and panegyrics to great kings of the ancient Mediterranean world to grasp its import fully.

David's royal pretensions are debunked comically before they are debunked in judgment. We see David, the erstwhile wholesale collector of Philistine foreskins, in a full-scale portrait of a not-so-young lecher leering over the battlements of his castle. We see him inquiring about the object of his voluptuous peeping like any Don Juan of the bazaars. We then see him, the great king, cast into fits of anxiety by the woman's laconic message "I am with child." We see him reduced to organizing the buffoonish banquet for Uriah, an underling in his army and a foreigner to boot—the king of Israel trying to play pimp to one of his servants on behalf of the latter's own wife. And all this degrading game of hanky-panky turns out to have been in vain as Uriah, the steadfast and (we may assume) superstitious soldier, returns to the front, his wartime economy of chastity as intact as when he came. We don't know very much about the Hebrews' sense of humor, but it is perhaps not too much to say that he who will not listen to the quiet voice of irony will find himself deafened by the thunderous address of judgment. The irony, which in our story is but subtly implied, gives way to the direct, explicit account of judgment. The bedroom farce becomes a tale of murder and of the cursing of generations.

The brief story is, of course, full of deceptions, most of them perpetrated by David. But more important, from our point of view, are the deceptions which David perpetrates on himself and which afford him alibis for his actions. We would suggest that there are, at the least, three layers of such deception in the story. The first one chronologically is probably the deception of sensible realism (as David might have called it to himself). This might well begin with the self-satisfied assertion that, after all, it is not David's fault that he has come into the world with such lustful loins (or, to put it in modern terms, Casanova did not *order* his libido) or that beautiful Hebrew women insist on taking baths in locations where he is forced to observe them. And, the thing having happened, every sensible man could only try to cover up his tracks as discreetly as possible. It may also be assumed that David told himself, quite sincerely, that he had to do all these things in order to protect Bathsheba, or perhaps even to preserve the *bon ton* of the court. The effect of these thoughts is that what was a moral issue now becomes one of social engineering. Regrettably, David failed absurdly as a social engineer. As social engineers are wont to do when this happens, he found that the next realistic step involved murder.

The second deception is that of the logic of war. David the seducer becomes David the military leader. He gives orders to Joab to let Uriah be killed in battle. It is worth noting that he does not order Joab to kill Uriah directly. From everything we know about Joab there is little reason to think that such an order would have dismayed the latter in any way. We may assume safely that this fiction was concocted for the benefit of David himself rather than that of Joab. The fiction, of course, was that David did not kill Uriah—the Ammonites did. We have here, in capsule form, the essence of bad faith as we have discussed it throughout this essay. Although we do not know this from the Biblical account, it is quite possible that David had prepared some additional rationalizations as to why Uriah had to be placed in a particularly exposed position of the battle line. Perhaps he even convinced himself that the Hittite's loyalty to the Hebrew cause was in question and that he might even be an Ammonite agent. Be this as it may, we are once more on safe ground if we assume that David's message of encouragement to Joab after the murder of Uriah was, again, designed to comfort David himself. Joab had probably forgotten the whole episode as soon as it was over. *He* needed no encouragement. *David* did. And the way David comforted himself is the way military leaders have comforted themselves since times immemorial for the blood which they themselves have shed—"the sword devours now one and now another"—"*C'est la guerre*"—and ultimately this means, of course, "Don't blame me—blame the war!" Within this deception of the logic of war David actually has two alibis for the murder. He can say that the Ammonites killed Uriah. He can also say that the war killed him. What is important is that David did not kill him.

The third deception, which is not explicitly stated but which we can also assume, is that of David's royal prerogatives. It would be most surprising, in that age and in that part of the world, if somewhere along this chain of events David had not drawn himself up before his conscience and said bravely, "I am the king." And who dares blame the king? Is it not sacrilege in itself to apply to the king the standards one applies to other men? David was probably too pious a follower of Yahweh to include in this alibi some notion of his own divinity. But, comparing his own conduct with that of neighboring colleagues in kingship, he might well have comforted himself with the thought that his own interpretation of royal prerogatives was straight bedouin democracy compared with theirs. After all, compared with the sacred incest, the human sacrifices, the forced labor of hordes of slaves surely this whole

story about Bathsheba and her tiresome husband was but a
peccadillo for one who could call himself king! What is more,
anyone knowing anything about politics must realize that he
had no choice, once the confounded man insisted on staying
away from that woman's bed. The kingdom not only was
surrounded by enemies from without but was shaky enough
from within as well. The slightest sign of weakness in Jerusalem might create an excuse for the quarrelsome Hebrew
tribes to go their own ways as before. No, it is clear that David
had no choice. To be king sometimes means the duty to do
unpleasant things. The murder of Uriah was not just the removal of a sexual rival (and perhaps not that at all—it is quite
possible that, after one bite into the forbidden fruit, David
would have been all too happy to leave the lady to her rightful
spouse!), the sordid conclusion of an adulterous escapade. No,
the interests of the kingdom demanded Uriah's liquidation.
His death was a necessity of *raison d'état*. Indeed, it would be
grossly misleading to say that David caused the man to be
killed. The king, Yahweh's anointed shepherd over Israel,
had given an order. Uriah's death was but a sacrificial offering
before this dread sovereignty. Posterity would understand.

As God's judgment confronts David in the person of Nathan, these layers of deception and excuse are cut through with
one terrible stroke. David is not standing now before his mirror
or before that other mirror that kings have in the devotion of
men like Joab. He is standing before truth itself. And the truth
is quite simple, after all the rationalizations—"You have smit-
ten Uriah the Hittite with the sword, and have taken his wife
to be your wife, and have slain him with the sword of the
Ammonites." The truth always appears simple after one
emerges from the welter of rationalizations. There is no discussion now of David's noble motives in seeking to protect
Bathsheba and being humane about the whole thing. There
is no talk of war and its hazards. The Ammonites, indeed, are
mentioned—but only to make perfectly clear that the Ammonite sword that killed Uriah was morally held by the hand
of David. And there is very strong mention of David's king-

ship—but as an additional condemnation, not an excuse: "I anointed you king over Israel, and I delivered you out of the hand of Saul. . . . Why have you despised the word of the Lord, to do what is evil in his sight?"

It is hardly necessary to stress the irony of Nathan's approach, the story told to the highest judge of Israel and inducing that same judge to condemn himself as one who "deserves to die" (the Hebrew phrase is even more deadly—the offending man is called by David a "son of death"). We would only stress the double weight of Nathan's climactic words to David—"You are the man." We cannot know how Nathan pronounced this terrible sentence, but there are two emphases that are possible. "*You* are the man"—not the Ammonites, not Joab, not the imaginary scoundrel of Nathan's story—"*You*, David—*you*, the murderer." But also another emphasis is possible: "You are the *man*"—not the king, not Yahweh's anointed, not the great victor over Israel's enemies, but, "You, David—a man like any other and worse than any other—a man like the cheap, cruel, repulsive character whom you have just condemned yourself—in fact, a man who is a 'son of death.'"

In reading this story it is important, of course, not to project into it the moral ideas and outrages of our own time. The story is found in a part of the Old Testament where each page drips with blood. We cannot imagine that David's conscience reacted to violence and bloodshed in the way a conscience would whose conception of God's will has been shaped by the New Testament as well as the Old. Perhaps it is especially important not to inject into the story the outrages of a Puritan sexual ethic. It is well to keep in mind that nowhere in this whole story is there the slightest hint of anything we might call "love" today and that the background of the story is not some sort of cozily bourgeois monogamy but an Oriental harem with many wives, concubines, and slaves, the most brutal exploitation of which was kept in bounds not so much by what we would today call ethics but by ferocious and horrifying tabus. All the more remarkable is what emerges

clearly as the essence of David's sin. For what was the deepest
sin in Nathan's story, the sin of the rich man who took away
the poor man's lamb for his own feast? David himself characterized the sin, which was also his own—"he had no pity."

David's sin is pitilessness. It is the sacrifice of what is dearest
in another's life for the routine needs of one's own existence.
Bathsheba's virtue and safety are sacrificed to David's momen-
tary lust, just as the poor man's lamb is sacrificed for the
miserly ostentatiousness of his rich oppressor. And Uriah's life
is sacrificed for the temporary exigencies of royal prestige and
raison d'état. What is life or death to one man becomes a
matter of convenience or inconvenience to another. And so
the life of Caryl Chessman was spared for the convenience of
President Eisenhower's trip to South America. When there
was no more danger of the President being even slightly in-
convenienced by Chessman's death, the way was open for the
gas chamber. With all the relativities of time and history, the
way is not so long from the walls of Rabbah to those of San
Quentin. And the voice of God's judgment remains the same
now as then.

The story does not end with Nathan's condemnation of
David. David acknowledges the odious identification with the
rich man in Nathan's story. David repents and he is forgiven.
Dietrich Bonhoeffer once referred to David as a shadow of
Christ in the Old Testament. The story of David's sin is not
only one of judgment but also one of grace. What concerns us
most, however, is the relationship of both judgment and
grace to the process of David's perception of himself. The
encounter with God brushes aside all the pet illusions with
which men hide themselves from their own conscience. Nothing but the truth is good enough then. As men confront God's
address they also perceive themselves in a new—that is, a more
truthful—way.

We would venture to argue one more time that in this
"You are the man" of our story lies the essence of that Chris-
tian humanism of which we have spoken before. And this
Christian humanism involves not only moral imperatives but

also perception. It means to see men as men and to address them as such. It means to ground all moral imperatives in men and not in institutionalized fictions. It means to see through the deceptions of social structure, through the web of bad faith and rationalization. There is a very great liberation in acquiring such perception, though even this liberation pales compared with that which comes from God's eternal recognition of ourselves as men created and men redeemed —as Nathan said to David, "The Lord also has put away your sin; you shall not die."

Notes

NOTES FOR PART I

Chapter 1

1. C. Wright Mills, *The Sociological Imagination* (New York, Oxford University Press, 1960), pp. 5 f.
2. *Cf.* Alfred Schuetz, "The Stranger—An Essay in Social Psychology," *American Journal of Sociology*, XLIX (1944), pp. 499 ff.
3. Arthur Koestler, *Arrival and Departure* (New York, The Macmillan Co., 1944), pp. 177 f.

Chapter 2

1. In formulating these propositions I have relied mainly on the conceptual apparatus of role theory and reference-group theory, as commonly used in American social psychology (*vide* Chapter 3), but am also very much indebted to the teaching of Alfred Schuetz.
2. In formulating this psychoanalytic interpretation of Lutheranism I have made use of various ideas of Erich Fromm's. It may be evident from the rest of this essay that I consider this interpretation to have no validity whatever.
3. Paul Tillich, *Systematic Theology* (Chicago, University of Chicago Press, 1957), II, p. 105 (footnote). Italics mine.
4. Martin J. Heinecken, *God in the Space Age* (Philadelphia, The John C. Winston Company, 1959), p. 142.

Chapter 3

1. Desiderius Erasmus, *The Praise of Folly* (Princeton, Princeton University Press, 1941), p. 37.
2. William James, *The Principles of Psychology* (New York, Henry Holt & Co., Inc., 1893), I, p. 294.
3. A very good summary of role theory, with a bibliographical guide, may be found in Theodore R. Sarbin, "Role Theory," in Gardner Lindzey, *Handbook of Social Psychology* (Cambridge, Mass., Addison-Wesley Publishing Company, Inc., 1954), I, pp. 223 ff.

For a critical discussion *vide* L. J. Neiman and J. W. Hughes, "The Problem of the Concept of Role," *Social Forces*, 1951:30, pp. 141 ff.

4. Charles H. Cooley, *Human Nature and the Social Order* (New York, Charles Scribner's Sons, 1902), esp. cc. V–VI.

5. George H. Mead, *Mind, Self and Society* (Chicago, University of Chicago Press, 1934), esp. c. III. For an excellent critical discussion *vide* Maurice Natanson, *The Social Dynamics of George H. Mead* (Washington, Public Affairs Press, 1956).

6. A comparison of the following commonly used textbooks of social psychology, written from quite different points of view and over a period of fifteen years, may be illuminating in this connection: G. W. Allport, *Personality—A Psychological Interpretation* (New York, Henry Holt & Co., 1937); K. Young, *Social Psychology* (New York, Arthur C. Croft Publications, 1944); T. M. Newcomb, *Social Psychology* (New York, The Dryden Press, Inc., 1950); S. A. Asch, *Social Psychology* (New York, Prentice-Hall, Inc., 1952); E. L. Hartley and R. E. Hartley, *Fundamentals of Social Psychology* (New York, Alfred A. Knopf, Inc., 1952).

7. *Cf.* Natanson, *op. cit.*, pp. 3 f.

8. Possibly the most comprehensive application of role theory to the analysis of institutions may be found in Hans Gerth and C. Wright Mills, *Character and Social Structure* (New York, Harcourt, Brace & Co., 1953).

9. *Cf.* esp. Talcott Parsons, *The Social System* (Glencoe, Ill., The Free Press, 1951).

10. Ralph Linton, *The Study of Man* (New York, Appleton-Century, Inc., 1936), esp. c. VIII; *ibid.*, *The Cultural Background of Personality*, (New York, Appleton-Century, Inc., 1945).

11. Melville J. Herskovits, *Man and His Works* (New York, Alfred A. Knopf, Inc., 1952), pp. 43ff.

12. Harry Stack Sullivan, *The Interpersonal Theory of Psychiatry* (New York, W. W. Norton & Company, Inc., 1953). It may be instructive to see the similarities (terminology apart) between this and a work radically different from it in its theoretical assumptions—N. E. Miller and J. Dollard, *Social Learning and Imitation* (New Haven, Yale University Press, 1941). It appears that both a radical behaviorism and a sociologically modified psychoanalytic interpretation come up with views of socialization that can quite easily be put in Mead's concepts.

13. *Cf.* two recent brilliant essays in social psychology—Erving Goffman, *The Presentation of Self in Everyday Life* (Garden City, N.Y., Doubleday & Company, Inc., 1959); Anselm L. Strauss, *Mirrors and Masks* (Glencoe, Ill., The Free Press, 1959).

14. *Cf.* the brief (and possibly still the best) introduction into the problematic of the sociology of knowledge in Robert K. Merton, *Social Theory and Social Structure* (Glencoe, Ill., The Free Press, 1957), cc. XII and XIII; also, *ibid.*, in Georges Gurvitch (ed.), *Twentieth Century Sociology* (New York, Philosophical Library, Inc., 1945), c. XIII.

15. *Cf.* Carlo Antoni, *From History to Sociology* (Detroit, Wayne State University Press, 1959).

16. *Cf.* Hans Barth, *Wahrheit und Ideologie* (Zurich, Manesse, 1945).

17. Max Scheler, *Versuch einer Soziologie des Wissens* (Munich, Duncker & Humblot, 1924); *ibid.*, *Die Wissensformen und die Gesellschaft* (Leipzig, Neue-Geist-Verlag, 1926).

18. *Cf.* esp. Karl Mannheim, *Ideology and Utopia* (London, Routledge & Kegan Paul, 1936); *ibid.*, *Essays on the Sociology of Knowledge*, ed. Paul Kecskemeti (New York, Oxford University Press, 1952).

19. For a recent presentation of the field *cf.* W. Stark, *The Sociology of Knowledge* (Glencoe, Ill., The Free Press, 1958).

20. H. H. Hyman, "The Psychology of Status," *Archives of Psychology*, XXXVIII (1942): 15. For good presentations of the problematic of reference-group theory *cf.* M. Sherif, "The Concept of Reference Groups in Human Relations," in M. Sherif and M. O. Wilson (eds.), *Group Relations at the Crossroads* (New York, Harper & Brothers, 1953), pp. 203 ff; also, Merton, *op. cit.*, cc. VIII–IX. It is interesting that both reference-group theory and sociology of knowledge are treated in the last-named work, with apparently no feeling on the part of the author that the two subjects belong together.

21. Tamotsu Shibutani, "Reference Groups as Perspectives," *American Journal of Sociology*, LX (1955), pp. 562 ff.

22. *Ibid.*, p. 563.

23. For a very good discussion of this *cf.* Asch, *op. cit.*, pp. 450 ff.

24. *Ibid.*, pp. 451 ff.

25. *Cf.* J. A. M. Meerloo, *The Rape of the Mind* (New York, The World Publishing Co., 1956); also, William Sargant, *Battle for the Mind* (Garden City, N.Y., Doubleday & Company, Inc., 1957).

26. *Supra*, pp. 20 f.

27. *Cf.* Everett C. Hughes, *Men and Their Work* (Glencoe, Ill., The Free Press, 1958). Most of the studies of Hughes and his associates are scattered in the issues of the *American Journal of Sociology*; *cf.* an entire issue devoted to these—LVII (1952), pp. 423 ff. Also *cf.* the section entitled "The Terror and Therapy of Work," in M. R. Stein, A. J. Vidich, and D. M. White (eds.), *Identity and Anxiety* (Glencoe, Ill., The Free Press, 1960), pp. 181 ff.

One of the best studies of an occupational ideology is F. X. Sutton *e.a.*, *The American Business Creed* (Cambridge, Mass., Harvard University Press, 1956).

28. *Cf.* H. S. Becker and J. W. Carper, "The Development of Identification with an Occupation," *American Journal of Sociology*, LXI (1956), pp. 289 ff.

29. S. K. Weinberg and H. Arond, "The Occupational Culture of the Boxer," *American Journal of Sociology*, LVII (1952), p. 463.

30. Hughes, *op. cit.*, p. 117.

31. Mills, *op. cit.*, pp. 25 ff. *Cf. ibid.*, "The Professional Ideology of Social Pathologists," *American Journal of Sociology*, XLIX (1943), pp. 165 ff.

32. Gunnar Myrdal, *The Political Element in the Development of Economic Theory* (1929), discussed in Stark, *op. cit.*, pp. 55 ff.

33. Erasmus, *loc. cit.*

Chapter 4

1. *Cf.* Thorstein Veblen, "The Intellectual Pre-Eminence of Jews in Modern Europe," in Max Lerner (ed.), *The Portable Veblen* (New York, The Viking Press, Inc., 1948), pp. 467 ff; also, Georg Simmel, "The Stranger," in Kurt Wolff (ed.), *The Sociology of Georg Simmel* (Glencoe, Ill., The Free Press, 1950), pp. 402 ff.

2. Wolff, *op. cit.*, pp. 40 ff. Also, *cf.* J. Huizinga, *Homo Ludens* (paperback edition by Beacon Press).

3. Wolff, *op. cit.*, pp. 49 f. Italics mine.

4. *Cf.* Huizinga, *op. cit.*, p. 6.

5. *Gamesmanship, Lifemanship* and *One-Upmanship* (all published in the United States by Henry Holt & Co., Inc.).

6. *Essays*, III:5 (Trechmann translation, Oxford University Press, II, p. 337).

7. *Op. cit.*, pp. 208 ff.

8. On the law as a game *cf.* Huizinga, *op. cit.*, pp. 76 ff.

9. The study in question was Floyd Hunter, *Top Leadership, U.S.A.* (Chapel Hill, University of North Carolina Press, 1959).

10. This thought was once expressed to me by Noel Perrin, of Dartmouth College. He put it much better than I have here, but this was the gist of it.

Chapter 5

1. Our argument here is influenced by the discussion of nihilism in Simone de Beauvoir, *The Ethics of Ambiguity* (New York, Philosophical Library, Inc., 1948), pp. 57 ff.

2. *Cf.* Sartre, *Being and Nothingness* (New York, Philosophical Library, Inc., 1956), pp. 47 ff.

3. *Cf.* Heidegger, *Sein und Zeit,* (Tuebingen, Neomarius, 1949), pp. 126 ff.
4. *The Observer,* July 1, 1952, quoted in Arthur Koestler, *Reflections on Hanging* (New York, The Macmillan Co., 1957), pp. 3 f.
5. Heidegger, *op. cit.,* pp. 252 ff.
6. On the differences between Heidegger's and Sartre's approach to the philosophy of death *cf.* Maurice Natanson, "Death and Situation," *The American Imago,* 16:4 (Winter 1959), pp. 447 ff.

NOTES FOR PART II

Chapter 6

1. *Cf.* Emile Durkheim, *The Elementary Forms of the Religious Life* (Glencoe, Ill., The Free Press, 1947); H. H. Gerth and C. W. Mills, *From Max Weber* (New York, Oxford University Press, 1958), part III; Max Weber *Gesammelte Aufsaetze zur Religionssoziologie* (Tuebingen, J. C. B. Mohr, 1947). Of the last, most of the works have now been translated into English. The most famous of these is *The Protestant Ethic and the Spirit of Capitalism* (London, George Allen & Unwin, 1930). A good notion of the Marxist approach can be obtained from the anthology *Marx and Engels on Religion* (Moscow, Foreign Languages Publishing House, 1957).
2. *Cf.* Bronislaw Malinowski, *The Foundations of Faith and Morals* (London, Oxford University Press, 1936); *ibid., Magic Science and Religion* (Glencoe, Ill., The Free Press, 1948); William J. Goode, *Religion among the Primitives* (Glencoe, Ill., The Free Press, 1951); Talcott Parsons, *The Social System* (Glencoe, Ill., The Free Press, 1951), part VIII; Robin M. Williams, Jr., *American Society* (New York, Alfred A. Knopf, Inc., 1954), pp. 304 ff.; J. Milton Yinger, *Religion, Society and the Individual* (New York, The Macmillan Co., 1957).
3. For a critique of Durkheim's position *cf.* Malinowski, *Magic, Science and Religion,* pp. 37 ff.
4. Durkheim's French phrase could be translated as either "collective conscience" or "collective consciousness," but the latter translation is bound to be misleading. Durkheim did not hold a theory of a "group soul." The collectivity which interested him is a moral not a metaphysical fact.
5. E. A. Ross, *Social Control* (New York, The Macmillan Co., 1901).
6. *Supra,* footnote 1.
7. Gerth and Mills, *op. cit.,* pp. 78 ff., 271; also, Max Weber, *The*

Theory of Social and Economic Organization (New York, Oxford University Press, 1947), pp. 124 ff., 130 ff., 324 ff.

8. Gerth and Mills, *op. cit.*, p. 274 ff., 358 ff.

9. Yinger, *op. cit.*, p. 65.

10. Will Herberg, *Protestant–Catholic–Jew* (Garden City, N.Y., Doubleday & Company, Inc., 1955), pp. 279 f.

11. Albert Camus, "Reflections on the Guillotine," *Evergreen Review*, No. 12.

12. Jacob J. Vellenga, "Is Capital Punishment Wrong?", *Christianity Today*, October 12, 1959, p. 9.

13. Arthur Koestler, *Reflections on Hanging* (New York, The Macmillan Co., 1957), p. 169.

14. *Ibid.*, p. 166.

15. *Ibid.*, p. 41.

16. *Parliamentary Debates (Hansard)*, Vol. 198, No. 115, July 10, 1956 (London, Her Majesty's Stationery Office). It may be added that in the United States, with the exception of the so-called "peace churches," the attitude of Protestant churches toward the issue has been largely one of indifference, although some national denominations have recently passed resolutions in favor of abolition.

17. A. Davis, B. G. Gardner and M. R. Gardner, *Deep South* (Chicago, University of Chicago Press, 1941), pp. 527 ff.

18. *Ibid.*, p. 533.

19. From Waldo W. Burchard, "Role Conflicts of Military Chaplains," *American Sociological Review*, October 1954, pp. 528 ff.

20. Arthur Vidich and Joseph Bensman, *Small Town in Mass Society* (Princeton, Princeton University Press, 1958).

21. *Cf.* J. R. Seeley, R. A. Sim and E. W. Loosley, *Crestwood Heights* (New York, Basic Books, Inc., 1956); William H. Whyte, Jr., *The Organization Man* (New York, Simon and Schuster, Inc., 1956); David Riesman, "The Suburban Sadness," in William M. Dobriner (ed.), *The Suburban Community* (New York, G. P. Putnam's Sons, 1958).

22. Malinowski, *Magic, Science and Religion*, pp. 29 ff.

23. W. Lloyd Warner, *The Living and the Dead* (New Haven, Yale University Press, 1959).

Chapter 8

1. *Cf.* Albert Camus, *The Rebel* (New York, Vintage Books, Inc., 1956). For a tendentious but in part illuminating discussion *cf.* Henri de Lubac, *The Drama of Atheist Humanism* (New York, Sheed & Ward, 1950).

2. *Cf.* de Lubac, *op. cit.*, pp. 161 ff; Nicholas Berdyaev, *Dostoievky* (New York, Sheed & Ward, 1934); Romano Guardini, *L'univers religieux de Dostoîevski* (Paris, Éditions du Seuil, 1947).
3. B. R. Redman (ed.), *The Portable Voltaire* (New York, The Viking Press, Inc., 1949), p. 566.
4. Simone de Beauvoir, *The Marquis de Sade* (New York, Grove Press, 1953), p. 56.
5. Camus, *op. cit.*, p. 56.
6. The most consistent elaboration of this position in twentieth-century philosophical ethics is probably that of Nicolai Hartmann. *Cf.* his *Ethik* (1926).
7. Karl Jaspers, *Vernunft und Widervernunft in unserer Zeit* (Munich, Piper, 1950), p. 28. It is not impossible that a similarly masochistic movement underlies Dostoyevsky's submission to throne and altar during his years of imprisonment; *cf.* his biography by Avrahm Yarmolinsky—*Dostoevsky* (New York, Criterion Books, Inc., 1957).
8. *Cf.* my article "Camus, Bonhoeffer and the World Come of Age," *The Christian Century*, April 8 and 15, 1959.
9. *Cf.* Camus, *op. cit.*, pp. 294 ff.

NOTES FOR PART III

Chapter 9

1. *Cf.* esp. Karl Barth, *Die kirchliche Dogmatik* (Zollikon-Zuerich, Evangelischer Verlag, 1945), vol. I/2, pp. 304 ff.
2. *Cf.* Dietrich Bonhoeffer, *Ethics* (London, S. C. M. Press, 1955); *ibid.*, *Prisoner for God* (New York, The Macmillan Co., 1954).
3. *Cf.* Simone Weil, *Waiting for God* (New York, G. P. Putnam's Sons, 1951); *ibid.*, *Gravity and Grace* (New York, G. P. Putnam's Sons, 1952).
4. *Cf.* Walter Lowrie (ed.), *Kierkegaard's Attack Upon "Christendom"* (Princeton, Princeton University Press, 1944).
5. *Cf.* Barth, *loc. cit.*; also, Anders Nygren, *Agape and Eros* (Philadelphia, The Westminster Press, 1953).
6. *Cf.* Eric Voegelin, *Israel and Revelation* (Louisiana State University Press, 1956), esp. Part 2.
7. Lowrie, *op. cit.*, p. 59.
8. *Supra*, pp. 15 ff.
9. Ludwig Feuerbach, *The Essence of Christianity* (New York, Harper & Brothers, 1957), p. xxix. Barth's essay was printed as an introduction to this English edition.

10. Bonhoeffer, *Prisoner for God*, p. 124.
11. *Ibid.*, pp. 146 f.
12. *Cf.* my article "The Second Children's Crusade, *The Christian Century*, December 2, 1959.
13. Max Weber, *The Protestant Ethic and the Spirit of Capitalism* (London, George Allen & Unwin, 1948), p. 105.
14. Robert K. Merton, *Social Theory and Social Structure* (Glencoe, Ill., The Free Press, 1949).
15. Weil, *Waiting for God*, p. 145.
16. *Ibid.*, *Gravity and Grace*, p. 168.
17. Karl Kraus, *Widerschein der Fackel* (Munich, Koesel-Verlag, 1956), p. 425. My translation.
18. Some of these thoughts have been expressed to me by Eberhard Mueller, of the Evangelical Academy Bad Boll in Germany. The concept of dialogue (*Gespraech*) with the world employed at Bad Boll and other European laymen's institutes is one of the most interesting efforts by Christians in our time to take a non-kerygmatic posture in the communication of their faith. *Cf.* Eberhard Mueller, *Die Welt ist anders geworden* (Hamburg, Furche-Verlag, 1955); H. R. Mueller-Schwefe, *Die Stunde des Gespraechs* (Hamburg, Furche-Verlag, 1956); also, Franklin H. Littell, "On the Theology of Discussion," unpublished manuscript read at the conference of the European laymen's institutes at Bièvres, France, in the summer of 1959.

Chapter 10

1. I. F. Hapgood (ed.), *Service Book of the Holy Orthodox-Catholic Apostolic Church* (Boston, Houghton Mifflin Co., 1906), p. 227.
2. *Cf.* Emil Brunner, *The Divine Imperative* (Philadelphia, The Westminster Press, 1943).
3. Lillian Smith, *Killers of the Dream* (New York, W. W. Norton & Company, 1949), p. 91.
4. D. S. Bailey (ed.), *Sexual Offenders and Social Punishment* (London, Church Information Board, 1956), p. 75.
5. *Cf.*, for example, Bronislaw Malinowski, *The Sexual Life of Savages* (New York, Halcyon House, 1929); or, Margaret Mead, *Male and Female* (New York, Mentor Books, 1955).
6. *Cf.* Morris Ploscowe, *Sex and the Law* (New York, Prentice-Hall, Inc., 1951).
7. The following paragraphs are taken from an unpublished report of mine on two seminars on the human and ethical problems of mass communications held at the Hartford Seminary Foundation during the academic year 1959–60.

8. *Cf.* the brochure *Signs of Renewal,* a summary of these experiments published by the World Council of Churches.

9. *Cf.* my article "Evangelical Academies in America?" in *Christianity and Crisis,* March 31, 1958.

10. *Cf.* Peter Hammond, *The Waters of Marah* (London, Rockliff, 1956).

11. Seraphim Papakosta, *Eusebius Matthopoulos* (London, S.P.C.K., 1939), pp. 106 f.

Chapter 11

1. Sigmund Freud, "Wit and Its Relations to the Unconscious," in A. A. Brill (ed.), *The Basic Writings of Sigmund Freud* (New York, Modern Library, Inc., 1938).

2. Henri Bergson, "Laughter," in W. Sypher (ed.), *Comedy* (Garden City, N.Y., Doubleday & Company, Inc., 1956).

3. *Cf.* Francis Jeanson, *Signification humaine du rire* (Paris, Editions du Seuil, 1950).

4. Bergson, *loc. cit.,* p. 123.

5. Charles C. West, *Communism and the Theologians* (London, S. C. M. Press, 1958), p. 385.